TOOL KIT FOR PUBLIC–PRIVATE PARTNERSHIPS IN URBAN PRIMARY HEALTH CENTERS IN INDIA

DECEMBER 2020

ASIAN DEVELOPMENT BANK

ADB

Note:
In this publication, "$" refers to United States dollars.

On the cover: (*Top photo*) In India, provision of primary health care services using public–private partnership arrangements with nongovernment organizations is being pursued to reduce the pressure on secondary and tertiary health care facilities; (*left photo*) Nurses at Kilinochchi District General Hospital attend to a newborn infant in the maternity ward; (*right photo*) Dr. Prakash Chand Mahate, a physician at a community health center in Chandanpur, India, says improved roads have resulted in reduced maternal and infant mortality and increased immunizations (photos by Rhommell Rico and ADB).

Contents

Tables, Figures, and Boxes --- v
Acknowledgments ---vi
Purpose of the Tool Kit -- vii
Abbreviations --viii
Executive Summary ---ix

1. Public–Private Partnerships in Urban Health Care: The Context ----------------------------- 1

    A. Background 1
    B. Government Response...3
    C. Public–Private Partnerships in the National Health Policy (2017) 3
    D. What Are Public–Private Partnerships? 5
    E. Public–Private Partnerships in Urban Health Care..5

2. Public–Private Partnerships in Urban Primary Health Centers ----------------------------- 7

    A. Drivers of Public–Private Partnerships in Urban Primary Health Centers 7
    B. Factors Impacting Public–Private Partnerships in Urban Primary Health Centers 9
    C. Challenges in Public–Private Partnerships 13

3. Tool Kit--- 22

    A. Planning for Public–Private Partnerships in Urban Primary Health Centers 22
    B. Project Preparation or Preprocurement..25
    C. Procurement 30
    D. Post-procurement 30

4. Recommendations --- 35

    A. Institutional...35
    B. Project Preparation 35
    C. Costing and Budgeting 36
    D. Procurement...36
    E. Payments 36
    F. Performance 37
    G. Staff...37
    H. Other Processes to Establish and Develop Public–Private Partnerships
        in Urban Primary Health Centers 37

Appendixes --- **40**

1. Sample Budget Sheet...41
2. Sample Request for Proposal Document (Competitive Bidding)...................................43
3. Sample Request for Proposal Document (Expression of Interest Selection Process) 59
4. Sample Concession Agreement (Government-Owned Urban Primary Health Center) 73
5. Sample Concession Agreement (Rented Urban Primary Health Center)....................................96
6. Sample Concession Agreement (Bio-Medical Waste Management)................................117
7. Sample Concession Agreement (Diagnostic and Pathological Services) 134
8. Sample Concession Agreement (Appointment of Specialist Doctors)................................154
9. Sample Concession Agreement (Appointment of Training Provider) 172
10. Sample Key Performance Indicators for Urban Primary Health Centers
    under Public–Private Partnership 190

Tables, Figures, and Boxes

Tables

1 Public–Private Partnerships in Urban Primary Health Centers—Key Parameters 13
2 Challenges in Public–Private Partnerships in Urban Primary Health Centers 18
3 Information to Be Included in Requests for Proposals 26
4 Tool Kit for Public–Private Partnerships in Urban Primary Health Centers—Overview 33
5 Recommended Process to Establish and Develop Public–Private Partnerships
  in Urban Primary Health Centers 37
2a Public–Private Partnership Types Suitable for Corporate Social Responsibility Funds...........11
4a Overview of Lowest Bidder versus Expression of Interest Procurement 29
6a Roles of Governments in the PPP Process...32

Figures

1 Urban Population as Share of Total Population, India..1
2 Tool Kit for Public–Private Partnerships in Urban Primary Health Centers—
  Work Flow Overview 34

Boxes

1 Risk Allocation in Public–Private Partnerships in Urban Primary Health Centers 8
2 Corporate Social Responsibility and Public–Private Partnerships in Urban Health Care.........10
3 Other Types of Existing Public–Private Partnership Arrangements in Urban Health Care 21
4 Procurement Method: Lowest Bidder or Expression of Interest?...............................28
5 Payment Mechanism 29
6 Roles of Central, State, and Municipal Governments
  in Public–Private Partnerships in Urban Primary Health Centers 32

Acknowledgments

This *Tool Kit for Public–Private Partnerships in Urban Primary Health Centers in India* was prepared by Prashant Sharma, PPP Consultant and Ajoy Halder, Legal Consultant, under the supervision of Sonalini Khetrapal, Social Sector Specialist (Health), South Asia Human and Social Development Division (SAHS), Asian Development Bank (ADB). Sungsup Ra, Director, SAHS, provided the overall guidance for the development of this tool kit. The tool kit was peer reviewed by Anouj Mehta, Principal Infrastructure Specialist, Southeast Asia Department, ADB; and Eduardo Banzon, Principal Health Specialist, Sustainable Development and Climate Change Department, ADB.

ADB acknowledges the support of the Government of India in the development of this publication. ADB is particularly grateful to Manoj Jhalani, Former Additional Secretary and Mission Director, National Health Mission (NHM), Ministry of Health and Family Welfare (MOHFW); Vandana Gurnani, Additional Secretary and Mission Director, NHM, MOHFW; and Preeti Pant, Joint Secretary (Urban Health), MOHFW for their support and guidance. ADB also deeply appreciates the support and input of state NHM teams in Karnataka, Odisha, Rajasthan, and Uttarakhand in the development of this tool kit.

Purpose of the Tool Kit

The scope, audience, and usability of the tool kit was defined at the request of the Ministry of Health and Family Welfare (MOHFW), Government of India.

Scope of the Tool Kit

This tool kit primarily focuses on the establishment and development of urban primary health centers (UPHCs) within the National Urban Health Mission (NUHM) framework through public–private partnership (PPP) arrangements with nongovernment organizations, where such organizations partner with the government by taking on the responsibility of operating and managing all the functions of a UPHC at no cost to end users.

Who is the Tool Kit For?

This tool kit is designed to be used by health department officials at the state level, especially those involved in urban primary health care. The tool kit may also be useful for officials in MOHFW who are tasked with the development of urban primary health care, as well as the development of PPPs in public health care in general.

When Can the Tool Kit be Used?

While several states have already established PPPs in UPHCs, this has often been carried out in an ad hoc manner. Other states have not established such PPPs yet, but are actively considering this option to augment the provision of urban primary health care services. This tool kit can be used as a guideline by all states, regardless of where they are in the development and realization of their strategy, policies, and processes with respect to PPPs in UPHCs. For states that already have such a program on the ground, this tool kit may be used to streamline and improve their policies and processes. For states that are still considering this option, this tool kit may provide them with suggestions and guidelines on the development of their policies and processes.

Abbreviations

ANM	auxiliary nurse midwife
CSR	corporate social responsibility
DHO	district health officer
EOI	expression of interest
KPI	key performance indicator
M&E	monitoring and evaluation
MOHFW	Ministry of Health and Family Welfare
NGO	nongovernment organization
NHM	National Health Mission
NHP	National Health Policy (2017)
NUHM	National Urban Health Mission
OECD	Organisation for Economic Co-operation and Development
OOP	out-of-pocket
PPP	public–private partnership
RFP	request for proposal
RKS	*Rogi Kalyan Samiti* (Patient Welfare Committee)
UPHC	urban primary health center

Executive Summary

Introduction

India has witnessed rapid urbanization over the last few decades. Currently, 34% of the population (over 440 million people) live in urban areas.[a] By 2050, it is projected that India's cities will have added 416 million urban dwellers.[b] This rapid urbanization has significant implications, especially with respect to the health needs of nearly 100 million urban poor, many of them migrants, who earn between $4 and $8 per day.[c] While demand has increased exponentially, the expansion of health care services in urban areas has been unable to keep pace with it due to limitations of public resources, restrictions in government processes and constraints in establishing new physical infrastructure.

The Government of India has taken cognizance of this challenge and has identified establishing public–private partnerships (PPPs) as a key intervention in expanding the provision of primary health care services in urban areas across the country. Key policy documents, including the National Urban Health Mission: Framework for Implementation (2013) and the National Health Policy (2017) have consistently emphasized the implementation of a "multi-stakeholder approach with partnership and participation of all non-health ministries and communities. This approach would include partnerships with academic institutions, not for profit agencies, and health care industry as well."

It should be noted that a PPP arrangement is not the same as privatization. Privatization implies the full or partial sale of a public asset to a private entity, or the transfer of the obligation of a public entity to deliver a service to a private entity. In a PPP arrangement, the public entity continues to be involved in the overall management and oversight of the asset or service throughout the period of the contract, and the ownership of the asset or the obligation to provide services reverts to the public entity at the end of the contract.

Several state governments have already established different types of PPP arrangements in primary health care in urban areas. These include contracting out of urban primary health centers (UPHCs) or specific functions thereof; contracting in of specialists; engaging partners to provide diagnostic, emergency, or training services; and providing other nonclinical services such as biomedical waste management, laundry services, etc. However, such efforts are often being carried out without a well-defined policy or detailed guidance in place.

---

a   United Nations Population Division. World Urbanization Prospects: 2018 Revision.
     https://data.worldbank.org/indicator/SP.URB.TOTL.IN.ZS?locations=IN&view=chart (accessed 30 January 2020).
b   The Energy and Resources Institute. Urbanisation. https://www.teriin.org/resilient-cities/urbanisation.php (accessed 30 January 2020).
c   Government of India, Ministry of Housing and Urban Poverty Alleviation. 2009.

The Ministry of Health and Family Welfare (MOHFW) has been making efforts to provide various guidance and tools to support state governments in understanding and utilizing the PPP option more effectively and efficiently. In this context, one of the focus areas identified by MOHFW is the establishment of PPPs in UPHCs where the selected partner takes on all tasks and delivers all services that are typically carried out by a government-run UPHC, including all clinical, diagnostic, outreach, and nonclinical services, whether as individual UPHCs or in a cluster. MOHFW has also emphasized that in the first instance, PPPs in UPHCs may need to focus on contractual arrangements with "not-for-profit" entities (nongovernment organizations, foundations, trusts, faith-based organizations, etc.). Such a focus recognizes health care as a public good, and mitigates any conflict of interest that could arise with the involvement of "for-profit" private entities delivering public health care services. At the same time, while corporate social responsibility (CSR) could be a source of resources, these are less suited to finance "core health care services" as scalability and replicability are important considerations in this context. CSR funds can be better utilized in augmenting specialized clinical services, as well as nonclinical support services.

This *Tool Kit for Public–Private Partnerships in Urban Primary Health Centers in India* is a part of this effort of the government, with technical assistance from the Asian Development Bank (ADB). It has been developed after carrying out a detailed review of existing PPPs on the ground; extensive discussions with government officials, NGO partners with projects on the ground, and other relevant stakeholders; and conducting site visits across the country.

The tool kit is designed to support state governments in assessing the need for PPPs in UPHCs, carrying out feasibility studies, establishing systems and processes to engage partners to run PPPs in UPHCs; and to put in place robust monitoring and evaluation processes to ensure that such PPPs perform consistently and well. The overall purpose of the tool kit is to provide a reference for various state governments in establishing and developing PPPs in UPHCs, with adequate flexibility built in, so that the PPPs can be adapted to suit the needs and contexts of their respective jurisdictions.

Public–Private Partnerships in Urban Primary Health Centers

In UPHCs, PPPs are driven primarily by three factors: (i) rapid urbanization, (ii) limitations of the government in expanding UPHC services at a pace commensurate with the rate of urbanization, and (iii) presence of several nongovernment service providers in urban areas. The first factor leads to an increase in the demand side; the second indicates the limitations in supply when the provisioning is done exclusively by government; and the third points to the possibility of improving supply, by including other types of providers into the urban health care ecosystem.

There are several advantages of using the PPP model in managing and delivering primary health care services through UPHCs. These include

(i) adding capacity to the urban primary health care system relatively quickly as private entities are ordinarily not subject to the same procedural and regulatory restrictions as the government in terms of recruitment, and acquiring and/or leasing physical infrastructure;

(ii) bringing efficiencies in processes and resource management, leading to wider adoption and improvement across the urban primary health care system; and

(iii) bringing innovations in urban health delivery systems, in due course leading to wider adoption and overall improvement of the public health care system.

However, these advantages can be better realized on the ground with the support of structured systems that identify the need, assess the feasibility, and establish transparent and objective norms and processes for each stage of the PPP project lifecycle.

Challenges

Review of existing PPPs, discussions with stakeholders, and site visits have led to the identification of specific challenges that have a direct impact of the establishment and development of PPPs in UPHCs. These pertain to partners—availability of private partners, not-for-profit versus for-profit partners, and size of partner. These also include challenges in procurement, contracts and contract management, costing and budgeting, staff remuneration, and payments. Finally, challenges concerning key performance indicators, monitoring, incentives, and governance are identified.

Key Elements of the Tool Kit

This tool kit provides a series of tasks that need to be carried out by state governments that will assist them in establishing a structured process that can guide the establishment and development of PPPs in UPHCs. Sample documents that can be adapted by each state based on its specific needs and context are provided as appendixes.

Key elements of the tool kit include the rationale and guidelines for the following:

(i)   Establishing a PPP cell
(ii) Carrying out a needs assessment exercise
(iii) Carrying out a feasibility study
(iv) Conducting a project preparation exercise, including the development of requests for proposals and contract documents, which in turn include
  - objectives
  - scope of work
  - estimated value
  - sites of UPHCs
  - physical infrastructure
  - duration of contract
  - financial terms and conditions, including payment mechanisms
  - staffing terms and conditions
  - services to be provided (clinical, outreach, national programs, training, diagnostics)
  - record keeping and reporting
  - norms for infrastructure
  - norms for staffing
  - responsibilities of the government
  - governance (including responsibilities for management, reviews, coordination, reporting, etc.)
  - quality assurance
  - accountability
  - key performance indicators
  - monitoring and evaluation
  - reviews and contract renewal
  - dispute resolution mechanisms
  - eligibility criteria
  - key dates
  - application procedure
  - list of documents to be submitted
  - evaluation criteria and selection process

(v)   Establishing the process for procurement or selection of partner
(vi) Establishing post-procurement processes including
  - reporting
  - communications
  - monitoring and evaluation
  - sanctions
  - dispute resolution

Recommendations

This tool kit also provides recommendations on how the tool kit can be used most effectively, in terms of the following dimensions: institutional, project preparation, costing and budgeting, procurement, payments, performance, staff, and other processes to establish and develop PPPs in UPHCs.

Part 1
Public–Private Partnerships in Urban Health Care: The Context

A. Background

India has witnessed rapid urbanization over the last few decades. Currently, 34% of the population (over 440 million people) lives in urban areas (Figure 1).[1] By 2050, it is projected that India's cities will have added 416 million urban dwellers.[2]

Figure 1: Urban Population as Share of Total Population, India
(%)

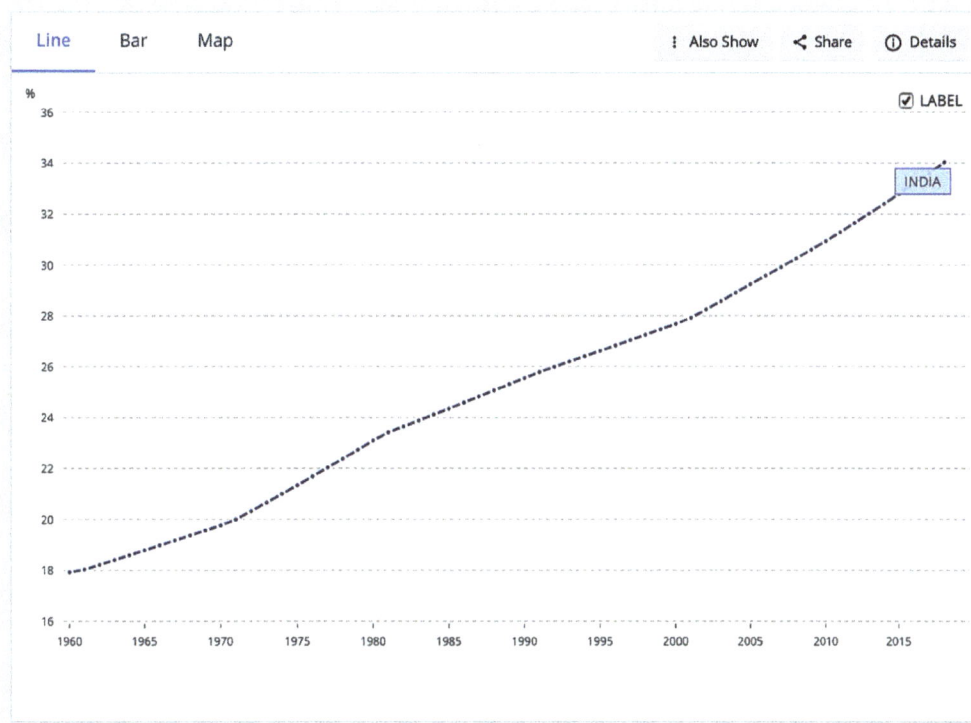

Source: United Nations Population Division. World Urbanization Prospects: 2018 Revision.
https://data.worldbank.org/indicator/SP.URB.TOTL.IN.ZS?locations=IN&view=chart (accessed 30 January 2020).

---

1   United Nations Population Division. World Urbanization Prospects: 2018 Revision.
     https://data.worldbank.org/indicator/SP.URB.TOTL.IN.ZS?locations=IN&view=chart (accessed 30 January 2020).
2   The Energy and Resources Institute. Urbanisation. https://www.teriin.org/resilient-cities/urbanisation.php
     (accessed 30 January 2020).

This rapid urbanization has significant implications, especially with respect to the health needs of nearly 100 million urban poor, many of them migrants, who earn between $4 to $8 per day.[3] While demand has increased exponentially, the expansion of health care services in urban areas has been unable to keep pace with it due to limitations of public resources, restrictions in government processes and constraints in establishing new physical infrastructure. Coupled with a lack of awareness, this has meant that the urban poor often turn to private providers for their health needs. This is reflected in the fact that in urban areas in India, private entities provide over 60% of hospitalization cases.[4]

With private provisioning of health services being largely unregulated, users typically incur significant out-of-pocket (OOP) expenses on their health needs. On average, 70% of OOP expenditure is incurred in obtaining primary health care services, of which 70% is spent on drugs and diagnostics.[5] While such OOP expenses already have a significant economic impact on the urban poor, hospitalization or chronic illnesses can have catastrophic implications. Estimates suggest that more than 40% of the country's population is forced to borrow money or sell assets to pay for medical expenses, and nearly 35% are pushed below the poverty line when such expenses are incurred.[6] Limitations in the availability of accessible and affordable public health services are therefore impacting the government's larger efforts to eradicate poverty.

This is a challenging situation. On the one hand, public health care delivery systems in urban areas are unable to expand at the rate at which the demand for health care services is growing due to rapid urbanization. On the other, private health care providers, which are already providing a significant proportion of health care services in urban areas, possess the capacity and the agility to expand relatively quickly. However, they also bring with them risks such as high OOP expenses that can have a debilitating impact on the lives of the urban poor.

A way out of this seemingly intractable conundrum is by leveraging the respective strengths of both the public and private sectors in mutually supportive and beneficial arrangements. One way this could be done is by establishing appropriate and effective public–private partnership (PPP) arrangements that ensure end users, especially the urban poor, are able to access high-quality health care services at negligible or no cost. PPPs, when designed well, can support the augmentation of health care delivery systems in urban areas while mitigating the risks associated with private provisioning of health care services. It should be noted that PPP arrangements in urban health care do not have to be limited to "for-profit" entities only. With over 7,000 nongovernment organizations (NGOs) providing health care services across the country, "not-for-profit" entities and trusts could play an important role in operationalizing such PPP arrangements.[7]

---

[3] Government of India, Ministry of Housing and Urban Poverty Alleviation. 2009.

[4] See Section 3.5.2.1 in Government of India, Ministry of Statistics and Programme Implementation. 2019. Key Indicators of Social Consumption in India: Health. New Delhi. p. 14.

[5] Government of India, Ministry of Health and Family Welfare. 2019. National Consultation, Road to UHC. New Delhi.

[6] See A. V. Raman and J. W. Björkman. 2008. *Public–Private Partnerships in Health Care in India: Lessons for Developing Countries.* New York: Routledge.

[7] Some studies have shown that NGOs have been able to deliver primary health care services at costs ranging from $0.3 to $1.2 per capita per year.

B. Government Response

The Government of India launched the nationwide Ayushman Bharat scheme in 2018 with the objective of achieving universal health coverage. The scheme adopts a continuum of care approach, comprising two inter-related components: the Ayushman Bharat Health and Wellness Centres (AB-HWCs) and Pradhan Mantri Jan Arogya Yojana (PM-JAY). The first component seeks to transform existing primary health centers and subcenters into health and wellness centers that would deliver comprehensive primary health care services as well essential drugs and diagnostic services at no cost to the end user. The second aims to provide health insurance cover to over 100 million poor and vulnerable families who may require secondary and tertiary care.

Ayushman Bharat builds on the National Health Mission (NHM), which further includes the National Urban Health Mission (NUHM) as a sub-mission. In 2013, the NUHM noted the importance of the private sector in providing health care services in urban areas, especially at the primary level, and highlighted the positive externalities that supported PPPs in primary urban health care: "Urban areas are characterized by presence of large number of for-profit and/or not-for-profit private providers. These providers are frequently visited by the urban poor for meeting their health needs... Partnership with private, charitable, or nongovernment organizations can help in expanding services..."[8]

These observations were reiterated in the NUHM Framework for Implementation, which identified PPPs as a core strategy in improving urban health care services. "In some big cities where credible private sector or other public sector exists, partnerships may be developed with them through public–private partnerships... to augment the urban health care system."[9]

The NUHM Implementation Framework also noted that urban areas had relatively higher capacity in delivering health care services through NGOs and observed that "There is a considerable existing capacity among private providers (NGOs, medical practitioners and other agencies), which should be explored, fruitfully exploited and operationalized." It further stated that "Potential partners should be identified and tapped optimally to improve the quality and standard of health among the urban poor, by capitalizing the skills of potential partners, encouraging pooling of resources, and supplementing the investment burden on the government of India's resources deployed in the health sector."[10]

C. Public–Private Partnerships in the National Health Policy (2017)

The National Health Policy (NHP) of 2017 has built on these observations and specifically refers to leveraging the potential of PPP in public health care. At the very outset, the NHP identifies the development of partnerships in health care as a key policy principle incorporating a "multi-stakeholder approach with partnership and participation of all non-health ministries and communities. This approach would include partnerships with academic institutions, not for profit agencies, and health care industry as well."[11]

---

[8] Section 2.7.7.1 in Government of India, Ministry of Health and Family Welfare. 2013. National Urban Health Mission: Framework for Implementation. New Delhi. p. 21.

[9] Section 5.2 in Government of India, Ministry of Health and Family Welfare. 2013. National Urban Health Mission: Framework for Implementation. New Delhi. p. 29.

[10] Section 12 in Government of India, Ministry of Health and Family Welfare. 2013. National Urban Health Mission: Framework for Implementation. New Delhi. p. 71.

[11] Government of India, Ministry of Health and Family Welfare. 2017. Key Policy Principle VII. In National Health Policy (2017). New Delhi. p. 2.

It further elaborates this principle under policy objective 2.3.1 of "Progressively achiev(ing) Universal Health Coverage" by "Ensuring improved access and affordability, of quality secondary and tertiary care services through a combination of public hospitals and well measured strategic purchasing of services in health care deficit areas, from private care providers, especially the not-for profit providers."[12]

This is reiterated in a subsequent policy objective, to "Enable private sector contribution to making health care systems more effective, efficient, rational, safe, affordable and ethical. Strategic purchasing by the Government to fill critical gaps in public health care facilities would create a demand for private health care sector, in alignment with the public health care goals."[13]

The NHP provides a specific and clear rationale for PPP in urban health care: "Given the large presence of private sector in urban areas, policy recommends exploring the possibilities of developing sustainable models of partnership with for profit and not for profit sector for urban health care delivery."[14]

Finally, an entire section of the NHP (section 13, with 14 sub-sections running into three pages) is dedicated to "Collaboration with Non-Government Sector/Engagement with private sector", stating that "The policy suggests exploring collaboration for primary care services with "not-for-profit" organizations having a track record of public services where critical gaps exist, as a short term measure."[15] Subsequent sub-sections go on to elaborate on the areas in which partnerships with the private sector is envisaged, including capacity building, skill development, mental health care, immunization, disease surveillance, tissue and organ transplants, disaster management, incorporation in referral systems, and health information system. It also identifies corporate social responsibility and "strategic purchasing as stewardship" as critical approaches through which such partnerships would need to be realized.[16] Additionally, it seeks to incentivize private sector participation through a variety of mechanisms including providing training and skill upgradation to private sector health care professionals and institutions, fees and reimbursements, and other ways through which their contribution is publicly recognized.

Importantly, the NHP identifies urban health care as a key area to establish such partnerships. "For achieving the objective of having fully functional primary health care facilities—especially in urban areas to reach under-serviced populations and on a fee basis for middle class populations, Government would collaborate with the private sector for operationalizing such health and wellness centers to provide a larger package of comprehensive primary health care across the country. Partnerships that address specific gaps in public services.. would *inter alia* include diagnostics services, ambulance services, safe blood services, rehabilitative services, palliative services, mental health care, telemedicine services, managing of rare and orphan diseases."[17]

---

[12] Government of India, Ministry of Health and Family Welfare. 2017. Policy Objective 2.3.1 (B), Progressively Achieve Universal Health Coverage. In *National Health Policy (2017)*. New Delhi. p. 3.

[13] Government of India, Ministry of Health and Family Welfare. 2017. Policy Objective 2.3.3, Align the Growth of Private Health Care Sector with Public Health Goals. In *National Health Policy (2017)*. New Delhi. p. 3.

[14] Government of India, Ministry of Health and Family Welfare. 2017. Policy Thrust 3.3.5, Urban Health Care. In *National Health Policy (2017)*. New Delhi. p. 8.

[15] Government of India, Ministry of Health and Family Welfare. 2017. Section 13, Collaboration with Non-Government Sector/ Engagement with Private Sector. In *National Health Policy (2017)*. New Delhi. p. 19.

[16] Section 13, Subsections 13.1-13.14 in Government of India, Ministry of Health and Family Welfare. 2017. *National Health Policy (2017)*. New Delhi. p. 19–22.

[17] Subsection 13.6.3 in Government of India, Ministry of Health and Family Welfare. 2017. *National Health Policy (2017)*. New Delhi. p. 21–22.

In sum, the NHP sees partnerships with the private sector as a key intervention toward achieving the larger goal of universal health care, and has identified several mechanisms, approaches and health care services in which such partnerships are likely to be most effective.

D. What Are Public–Private Partnerships?

With PPPs being considered as a key intervention in strengthening the urban health care system, it is important to first identify what PPPs are, and importantly, what they are not. While there is no single standardized definition, in general, a PPP is a long-term contract between a private party and a government entity to provide a public asset or service, in which the private party bears significant risk and management responsibility, and remuneration is linked to performance. Such a definition of a PPP arrangement can typically be found in the context of infrastructure projects. The Government of India defines PPPs as "an arrangement between a Government / statutory entity / Government owned entity on one side and a private sector entity on the other, for the provision of public assets and/or public services, through investments being made and/or management being undertaken by the private sector entity, for a specified period of time, where there is well defined allocation of risk between the private sector and the public entity and the private entity who is chosen on the basis of open competitive bidding, receives performance linked payments that conform (or are benchmarked) to specified and pre-determined performance standards, measurable by the public entity or its representative."[18]

It should also be noted that a PPP arrangement is not the same as privatization. Privatization implies the full or partial sale of a public asset to a private entity, or the transfer of the obligation of a public entity to deliver a service to a private entity. In a PPP arrangement, the public entity continues to be involved in the overall management and oversight of the asset or service throughout the period of the contract, and the ownership of the asset or the obligation to provide services reverts to the public entity at the end of the contract.

E. Public–Private Partnerships in Urban Health Care

The main reasons for establishing, widening and strengthening PPPs in urban health care are directly related to the constraints of the government in expanding the delivery of health care services in urban areas. First is the issue of resources. The health budget of India (4.1% of gross domestic product) is considerably lower than that of most member countries in the Organisation for Economic Co-operation and Development (OECD). Resource constraints suggest a clear need to explore innovative financing mechanisms and a pooling of resources between the public and private sectors to bring about an overall improvement in public health care.

---

[18] See Public Private Partnerships in India. FAQs. https://www.pppinindia.gov.in/faqs#q1.

Second is the complexity of government processes in establishing new physical infrastructure in response to increased demand for health services. For example, NUHM norms recommend a UPHC be present for every 50,000 population. Given the rate of urbanization, this means that a commensurate increase in the number of UPHCs is necessary. However, identifying and establishing new sites for delivering primary health care is a time-intensive process that can take years to be realized on the ground. Meanwhile, the demand for health care services continues to increase exponentially as migration to urban areas continues unabated.

Third is the issue of human resources. Government recruitment is a complex and time-consuming process, and in many cases is hampered by court restrictions, remuneration levels, and availability of specialists and professionals in a given geography. Further, governments also face a challenge in terms of staff retention due to lower than market salaries and an increasing contractualization in recruitment.

Apart from these push factors, pull factors such as better technologies, processes, and innovations that the private sector is better placed to offer can lead to higher efficiencies and augment the overall quality of and access to health care services.

In the health sector (or other social sectors), infrastructure-oriented PPP arrangements may be in place particularly where building and/or managing physical infrastructure is involved. However, where the delivery of health care services is involved, the term of the contract may not necessarily be long-term. Nevertheless, the key principles of PPP arrangements remain the same regardless of their service orientation: delivering specific health care services benchmarked against clearly defined performance indicators where each partner takes on specific roles and responsibilities for the duration of the contract.

With the NHP having identified PPPs as a policy thrust area, several state governments have introduced a wide range of PPP arrangements to meet the increase in demand for health care services in urban areas. These span different types of services including clinical services, diagnostics, outreach; as well as nonclinical services such as biomedical waste management, emergency ambulance services, conducting auxiliary nurse midwife (ANM) trainings, etc.

Part 2

Public–Private Partnerships in Urban Primary Health Centers

Within a wide spectrum of possibilities, the Ministry of Health and Family Welfare (MOHFW) has identified the development of PPPs in UPHCs as a focus area. This builds on the NHP, which states that the "National health policy prioritizes addressing the primary health care needs of the urban population with special focus on poor populations.... Given the large presence of private sector in urban areas, policy recommends exploring the possibilities of developing sustainable models of partnership with for profit and not for profit sector for urban health care delivery."[19]

Focusing on augmenting primary health care services has multiple objectives, including a reduction in the pressure on secondary and tertiary health care facilities, as well as a movement away from curative, and toward preventive care. The allocation of resources also reflects this approach—the NHP "advocates allocating major proportion (up to two-thirds or more) of resources to primary care followed by secondary and tertiary care."[20]

A. Drivers of Public–Private Partnerships in Urban Primary Health Centers

(i)   Rapid Urbanization

With rapid urbanization, governments at both the central and state levels recognize that the expansion of primary health services in urban areas has not been able to keep pace with the increase in population, which is taking place primarily due to migration from rural to urban areas.

(ii)   Government Limitations

Government efforts to identify and acquire suitable land and then build physical infrastructure to respond to the exponential increase in the demand for primary health services is limited by resource as well as process limitations. State governments are also unable to hire and deploy human resources quickly and in proportion to the increase in demand due to the limitation of resources, as well as the complexity of processes and time required to carry out large-scale recruitment. In some states, courts have also halted recruitment pending the resolution of ongoing cases, which has caused further delays.

---

[19]   Section 3.3.5 in Government of India, Ministry of Health and Family Welfare. 2017. *National Health Policy (2017)*. New Delhi. p. 10.
[20]   Government of India, Ministry of Health and Family Welfare. 2017. Section 12, Financing of Health Care. *National Health Policy (2017)*. New Delhi. p. 18.

(iii)   Availability of Nongovernment Service Providers

While hard data for this is not currently available (MOHFW has already embarked on an exercise to gather the same), it has been noted that urban areas are more likely to have a greater number of private (both for-profit and not-for-profit) health service providers, which could potentially partner with the government in PPP arrangements by putting on the ground various health services that are being provided through UPHCs.

(iv)   Why Public–Private Partnerships in Urban Primary Health Centers

The advantages of using PPPs in managing and delivering primary health services through UPHCs include the following:

(a)   adding capacity to the urban primary health care system relatively quickly as private entities are ordinarily not subject to the same procedural and regulatory restrictions as the government in terms of recruitment, and acquiring and/or leasing physical infrastructure;

(b)   bringing efficiencies in processes and resource management, leading to wider adoption and improvement across the urban public health care system; and

(c)   bringing innovations in urban health delivery systems, in due course leading to wider adoption and overall improvement of the public health care system.

Although risk allocation is an important aspect of PPPs, this may take an atypical form in the context of PPPs in UPHCs. This is discussed in Box 1 below.

**Box 1: Risk Allocation in Public–Private Partnerships
in Urban Primary Health Centers**

It is now widely recognized that risk allocation in public–private partnerships (PPPs) is a key element in structuring a project agreement, as the government and the private party are differentially placed in their respective abilities to absorb financial and other risks, linked to recovery of investment and subsequent gains in revenue. However, in the context of PPPs in urban primary health centers (UPHCs), risk allocation needs to be seen through a different lens. Public health care has been universally recognized as a public good in and of itself. Financial risks, recovery of investment, and revenue gains cannot be seen primarily in monetary terms in this context.

Further, in this type of a PPP, the government defines the site and the service levels, and payments to the private partner are based on agreed performance indicators with no cost to the end user. Here, the risk is primarily borne by the government, which must demonstrate that the investment in PPPs provides value-for-money and achieves the desired public health care outcomes. Mitigating this risk therefore depends on whether the government has identified appropriate sites for establishing PPP UPHCs, provided adequate resources, selected appropriate partners, and efficiently monitored service delivery to ensure desired public health care outcomes are achieved. It is important to note that in PPPs in UPHCs, limiting the duration of the contract to 3–5 years and renewed annually based on performance, greatly mitigates the financial risk to the government.

Source: Asian Development Bank.

Importantly, all services through PPPs in UPHCs are to be provided at no cost to the end user. Discussions with MOHFW also emphasized that in the first instance, PPPs in UPHCs may need to focus on contractual arrangements with not-for-profit entities (NGOs, foundations, trusts, faith-based organizations, etc.). Such a focus recognizes health care as a public good, and also mitigates any conflict of interest that could arise with the involvement of for-profit private entities delivering public health care services.

B. Factors Impacting Public–Private Partnerships in Urban Primary Health Centers

Public–private partnerships in UPHCs can be complex arrangements, with various parameters, including nature and scale of services, procurement process, financing and financial arrangements, asset ownership, and type of partner impacting the final agreement.

Key factors that impact PPP agreements for UPHCs are discussed below.

(i) Service and Function

While each state may have some variations in the bundle of services provided through UPHCs, typically these are premised upon the guidelines developed by the MOHFW, and include clinical services, basic diagnostic services, outreach activities, as well as nonclinical services. Other services may include the implementation of national programs such as those related to tuberculosis, HIV, etc.

(ii) Contract

Public–private partnerships in UPHCs may include an agreement where the operation of a UPHC is contracted out in part to a private entity (for example, contracting out only the diagnostics services to a private party); or an agreement where specific services are contracted in, as with part-time specialists at government-run UPHCs. A PPP arrangement at the UPHC level may also be more comprehensive in nature, where the entire operation and maintenance is carried out by a private party. Another layer of complexity can arise when a UPHC that had been contracted out as a PPP would contract in specialists; or contract out as independent contracts between the private partner managing the UPHC and other private service providers nonclinical services like biomedical waste management. In such a situation, the private partner managing the UPHC would need to raise the required resources from the government or other sources.

(iii) Type of Partner

A PPP arrangement of any of the types above could be carried out with different types of partners, which may include not-for-profit entities such as NGOs, trusts, faith-based organizations; or for-profit ones (private medical care providers). Contractual arrangements, particularly related to costs, are directly impacted by the choice of partner. The scale of operations of a partner also has implications on the type of PPP agreements that could be entered into. A local NGO may be able to manage only a single or at most a small number of UPHCs due to its own capacity and financial constraints. The size of the partner also has an implication on the optimal payment mechanism to be used in a PPP arrangement. Reimbursement of costs by the government is feasible only with large partners with a strong financial base, while advance payments are more effective when partnering with smaller entities.

Using corporate social responsibility (CSR) funds can be an attractive option when developing PPPs in UPHCs. However, this may not be the most efficient use of such resources. This issue is discussed in Box 2 below.

Box 2: Corporate Social Responsibility and Public–Private Partnerships in Urban Health Care

Section 135 of the Companies Act 2013 makes it mandatory for all companies above a certain size to dedicate 2% of their annual profits for corporate social responsibility (CSR) activities. Several such companies see public health care as an important area to channel CSR resources. While CSR resources can indeed be an attractive source of funds to augment urban health care services, this may need to be approached differently from public–private partnership (PPP) arrangements, particularly for urban primary health centers (UPHCs).

The main drivers for establishing and developing PPPs in urban health care is not a lack of funds (the government is willing and able to pay for various health care services being provided by private partners), but in supporting expansion and improvement in the quality of health care services being provided in urban areas. As CSR is primarily a vehicle to bring in resources in the form of funds, these may be utilized differently and strategically in the context of urban health care delivery and PPPs.

Corporate social responsibility funds also have certain specific characteristics, which in turn may or may not support scalability and replicability in PPPs in urban health care. For example, a private hospital chain has entered into an agreement with a state government to finance and manage a UPHC through their CSR resources. The government has handed over an existing UPHC facility to the private party that has taken the responsibility to operate and manage the same at its own cost. In this context, while health care services continue to be provided at no cost to the end user, the private entity remains at liberty to finance the effort without the resource constraints that government-run, or government-financed PPP UPHCs typically operate under.

This model also raises questions on the ways in which the government can carry out oversight activities when it is not providing any finances to the private party. This effectively means that such "partnerships" can at best be seen as one-off efforts that may provide high-quality services, but are not scalable as they do not operate under typical conditions. Scalability and replicability cannot be achieved when pilots and models are established under atypical conditions. This means that CSR funds are less suited to finance "core health care services" as scalability and replicability are important considerations with respect to such services. CSR funds can be better utilized in augmenting specialized clinical services, as well as nonclinical support services.

Table 2a below provides some types of PPP arrangements that may therefore be better suited to utilize CSR funds. These examples are more likely to be replicable and scalable as they focus on specific aspects of health care delivery that could provide systemic benefits over the longer term. These could also be taken up in clusters rather than at individual sites, which in turn makes the activities scalable.

continued on next page

Box 2 *continued*

Box Table 2a: Public–Private Partnership Types Suitable for Corporate Social Responsibility Funds

Type of Public–Private Partnership	Suitability of Corporate Social Responsibility Funds
Diagnostic services (including dialysis)	A corporate entity can enter into an agreement with the government to finance and/or directly provide diagnostic services in specific government-run facilities or cluster of facilities. This will provide financial support and/or technical expertise to augment existing government services.
Training	A corporate entity can undertake to finance or provide regular training to improve the skills of staff at government-run health care facilities. This could also be scaled up to include training of trainers for wider impact.
Ambulance services	A corporate entity provides finance and/or services to run emergency ambulance services attached to government-run facilities.
Process management	A corporate entity provides finances and/or training for government-run facilities to upgrade their management systems and processes.
Provision of specialists	A corporate entity can enter into an agreement to finance and/or provide part-time or full-time services of specialists at government-run facilities.
Telemedicine	A corporate entity can finance and/or provide services for operating telemedicine services (including infrastructure, training, etc.)
Information management systems	A corporate entity can provide finances and/or expertise to upgrade health information management systems (hardware or software) and provide the necessary training for upskilling staff at government-run facilities.

Source: Asian Development Bank.

(iv)   Scale

Scale pertains to whether the PPP agreement for UPHCs is carried out in clusters or for individual UPHCs. Each approach has implications on the efficacy of the PPP arrangements, particularly with respect to the size and capacity of the private partner. For example, smaller, local, NGO partners may be closer to the target population, but may be unable to manage clusters of UPHCs.

(v)   Asset Ownership and Management

Public–private partnership arrangements in UPHCs may include the handing over of existing government-owned premises to the private entity, with regular maintenance being the responsibility of either the government or the private partner (with costs borne by the government in the latter case). Alternately, the arrangement may need to factor in the costs for the private partner to rent premises according to agreed norms.

(vi)   Time Period

Typically, the time period of PPPs in UPHCs is 3–5 years, with annual extensions dependent on achieving agreed service levels as delineated in the contract.

(vii)   Pricing

Public–private partnership agreements to manage UPHCs may have several forms of pricing for end users. At one end of the spectrum is zero cost to end user, with all costs being absorbed by the government and/or the private partner. In other arrangements, a PPP UPHC may offer services to end users at a subsidized cost, with the gap being made up by the government and/or the private partner. In a third type of PPP arrangement, the private partner may cross-subsidize its costs by providing free services to economically weaker sections of the population, while charging fees to those who can afford to pay. However, given that government-run UPHCs typically provide all services at no cost to the end user, PPP UPHCs would be required to replicate this, making the latter two options less practicable.

(viii)   Procurement

The private partner could be selected through a number of ways in a PPP arrangement for UPHCs. This could be either done through a bidding process on pre-identified service levels, where the lowest bidder is selected. Alternately, the government may define the service levels and the payments to be made before the commencement of the selection process, with partners being selected on the basis of their applications submitted through an expression of interest process. In some contexts, the selection process may be more informal, with the government requesting existing partners in other health-related services to manage UPHCs at agreed costs.

(ix)   Payment Mechanisms

Payments mechanisms in PPPs in UPHCs could also be of several types, where the government in some cases regularly reimburses (for example, on a quarterly basis) costs incurred by the private partner in managing a UPHC, subject to caps. Alternately, the government itself may fix the cost of operations of a UPHC at the outset, release partial funds at project commencement to the private partner, and release subsequent tranches based on performance. Another payment mechanism could also be where the user pays (in full or in part) the costs associated with service provision.

These key parameters and their defining characteristics of PPPs in UPHCs are summarized in Table 1.

As indicated in Table 1, each of the parameters directly impact the nature of the final PPP arrangement. However, each parameter has specific strengths and weaknesses, and certain combinations tend to result in more effective PPPs than others. For example, if a state has chosen to contract out UPHCs in clusters, this will have an impact on the choice of potential partners in terms of the size of their operations. A small, local NGO may not have the capacity to manage several UPHCs. This in turn, has a bearing on the payment mechanism to be used. A regional or national level NGO may be able to better absorb delays in payments, and hence the reimbursement method could be used. Conversely, a smaller NGO may not have the capacity to absorb delays in payments, making it imperative for the government to make advance fixed-cost payments to ensure the operational continuity and efficiency of the UPHC is not negatively impacted. It therefore becomes imperative to select an effective combination of options when designing a PPP project, which in turn must be reflected in the contracts.

**Table 1: Public–Private Partnerships in Urban Primary Health Centers—
Key Parameters**

Parameter	Options or Characteristics
Service and/or function	Clinical, diagnostics, outreach, nonclinical
Contract	Contracting out, contracting in, operation and maintenance
Type of partner	For-profit, not-for-profit
Type of partner (scale of operations)	Local, state level, regional, national
Concession scale	Clusters, individual urban primary health center
Asset ownership	Government, private party, mixed
Time period	Short-term (3–5 years), renewed annually
Pricing	Free to end user, subsidized, cross subsidy
Procurement	Lowest bidder, expression of interest, informal
Payment	Reimbursement, fixed cost, user pays (partially or fully)

Source: Asian Development Bank.

C. Challenges in Public–Private Partnerships

Feedback to MOHFW from the states, as well as field missions carried out as a part of this technical support work, have led to the identification of several challenges in ensuring comprehensive, effective and efficient PPPs are established in UPHCs. A thematic discussion on these challenges follows.

(i)   Availability of Private Partners

Several states have reported that the number of NGOs with substantial experience and capacity in the provision of health care services is not large. A small pool of potential partners for PPPs results in lower competition when engaging private partners. The issue of availability can be mitigated by incentivizing the participation of other private actors in the health care ecosystem. For example, teaching institutions, which are growing rapidly across the country, possess an inherent capacity to provide trained human resources, and could therefore become important partners in the establishment and development of PPPs in UPHCs.

(ii)   Not-for-Profit versus For-Profit

Entering into a contractual arrangement with a not-for-profit entity reduces the risk of commercial interests influencing the delivery of a public good. However, these are less likely to bring in innovations in technologies and processes. This could potentially be mitigated by reducing processual burdens, and incentivizing performance and innovations.

Entering into a contractual arrangement with a for-profit entity can help bring in innovations in processes and technologies. However, a for-profit entity using public resources to deliver a public good like health may create a conflict of interest. In addition, engaging for-profit entities in PPPs can be challenging as their operational costs are higher than similar government or not-for-profit entities, even if they operate a UPHC on a no-profit, no-loss basis. Further, such entities tend to find government recruitment rules restrictive in their operations. Some for-profit entities are managing UPHCs but are doing so as a pilot and/or in the context of corporate social responsibility (CSR) activities by putting in substantial resources of their own. While this is not a sustainable approach, the involvement of for-profit entities may need to be investigated further to assess if this could become financially sustainable through scaling up, while comprehensively eliminating all potential conflicts of interest in doing so.

(iii)   Size of Partner

Apart from commitment to the larger cause of social change, smaller entities are interested in partnering with government to manage UPHCs as this helps enhance their credibility, scale, and profile. This in turn allows them to engage with government in other health sector projects, as well as projects in other sectors. However, smaller entities have less financial and human resource capacities and are therefore less able to absorb the costs of process limitations such as delays in payments. They also lack the capacity to provide additional resources for operational expenses or the introduction of innovations. Larger entities, on the other hand, have established credentials and a better capacity to absorb procedural limitations and offset delays using their own resources. They also have greater capacity to raise and deploy additional resources to improve their operational activities and introduce innovations. Larger entities may also possess experience of working across states and bring in lessons learned in one jurisdiction to another. However, all states currently may not have a substantial number of such large entities, pointing to the issue of availability identified above.

(iv)   Procurement

Three different systems of selecting partners are generally in place. In the first, the lowest bidder is selected (L1 process). In practice, especially given the small pool of potential bidders, the estimated cost that the government has planned for is generally known in advance and the bidders bid around it. The lowest bidder procurement process works best where physical infrastructure needs to be developed, where there is a large pool of applicants, and where competitiveness in pricing is an important selection criterion. Since PPPs in UPHCs are primarily service-oriented, major costs are related to human resources, annual budgets are publicly known, and the primary principle is one of not-for-profit, the L1 process is not ideally suited for engaging private partners in PPPs in UPHCs.

In the second system of selection, the partner is selected on the basis of its profile and the strength of its proposal in response to the expression of interest (EOI process). Here, the budget for managing the UPHC is predefined by the government based on its budgets and financial norms. While this process of selection does mitigate the challenges of the L1 process to a large extent, it also presents its own set of challenges. For example, the lack of in-budget flexibility can impact operational effectiveness as partners may have to adhere to very strict expenditure guidelines that may not reflect ground realities such as market-defined salary levels.

A third, less common, procurement process that is present on the ground is more informal. Here, state governments establish PPPs in UPHCs to continue and build existing relationships with NGOs or trusts with whom the government has had a long association in the past. There is no formal competitive selection and/or procurement process in place, and specific UPHCs are handed over to different NGOs through informal, relationship-based processes premised upon the credibility, profile, experience and presence of an NGO in a given area. However, once the decision to engage the NGO is taken, the running of the PPP is managed through a memorandum of understanding signed between the District Health Society and the NGO. Such a system of procurement, which could also be extended to teaching institutions and named centers of excellence, may have value where PPPs in UPHCs are not seen as a major health care intervention, but more in terms of establishing a few centers where innovations could be carried out on a pilot basis for future replication by government-run UPHCs.

While all systems of procurement have their strengths and weaknesses, it was observed that in general, greater transparency in the selection process would add significant value in terms of improving public trust and accountability of PPPs in UPHCs.

(v)   Contracts and Contract Management

The actual contract between the private partner and the government lies at the heart of the PPP arrangement in running UPHCs efficiently. The main challenge that has been faced in the design of the contracts is the approach where the partner is seen as a contractor rather than a partner. This results in an emphasis on financial audits rather than performance audits. In other words, the way the contracts are drafted leads to a focus on processes rather than outcomes. In general, partners are obliged to allocate a significant amount of time and human resources on compliance rather than on bringing in innovations and improving efficiency.

This also has led to contracts allowing limited flexibility in recruitment and UPHC management. An example of the latter is that a partner cannot decide the operating hours of the UPHC it manages. While the number of hours it must remain open must be defined, the partner needs to have some flexibility in terms of the daily timings to respond to on-the-ground user needs as well as staffing patterns. Such small changes can also be termed as innovations, which are currently not possible to be introduced due to the inflexibility of contracts.

The instances above suggest that while one of the stated aims of introducing PPPs in UPHCs is to introduce comparative efficiencies of the private sector, contracts and contract management processes tend to oblige private partners to imitate a government entity.

(vi)   Costing versus Budgeting

The way in which budgetary allocations are made for managing UPHCs have been identified as a major challenge in terms of ensuring operational efficiency of PPPs. While the figure to effectively manage one is premised on a defined number and type of staff and a provision for operational expenses based on specific assumptions (budgeting), taking into account actual expenses incurred in previous time periods (costing) is not taken into consideration when budgeting for succeeding years. For example, travel costs of auxiliary nurse midwives (ANMs) may change due to an increase in coverage area. However, this is not taken into account when budgets are drawn for subsequent years. Hidden costs like collection of medicines for free distribution by the PPP UPHCs are also not adequately covered under operational expense budget lines. This challenge is compounded by the lack of flexibility in the contract itself in the utilization of funds by the private partner.

Doing budgeting without doing costing creates a pressure to perform within potentially unreasonable cost constraints, eventually impacting quality, while the situation on the ground (increases in demand for services due to rapid rate of migration, addition of special campaign responsibilities to regular services, increases in operation costs due to changed requirements, etc.) can change quickly and substantially over short periods of time, especially in urban contexts. The addition of special campaigns to the usual responsibilities of a PPP UPHC may also add costs, which are not accounted for. Instances like the above lead to UPHC staff having to absorb out-of-pocket expenses to discharge their duties. In contrast, additional costs in government-run UPHCs are provided in some form or the other, with no necessity of the staff having to absorb any costs personally.

(vii)   Staff Remuneration

Staff remuneration is another area that was identified as a challenge. While staff strength and profile parameters are set by MOHFW based on population to be served, the actual remuneration costs have several variables that are not appropriately factored in when defining UPHC budgets. These variables include the cost of hiring trained staff in a given state (as some states have a lower availability of trained human resources than others), as well as an increase in footfall due to migration, underestimation of demand, or the relative ease with which users can visit UPHCs outside the predefined catchment area in urban contexts.

Staff remuneration also has limited flexibility leading to difficulties in recruitment and retention of staff. For example, ANMs or medical officers with more experience should be compensated more in comparison to similar staff with less experience. However, financial rules allow very limited flexibility in such situations.

(viii) Payments

Whether the contract mandates payments to the private partner through a reimbursement process or through payments made in advance based on a fixed-cost schedule, PPPs in UPHCs are facing the lack of timely payments as a major challenge. While advance quarterly payments were made in some arrangements, successive tranches could be held up due to delays in approval processes that require several layers of paperwork. Typically, utilization certificates or reimbursement claims (or other required documentation) need to be processed and validated by the UPHC, then the administrative office of the partner, then the Chief Medical Officer, and then the state NUHM office prior to any disbursement. Capacity constraints at each of these stages further exacerbates the problem of delays. Delays in payments in turn leads to problems of staff retention and lack of motivation.

A larger issue is related to the disbursement of funds from the center to the states. Delays in these disbursements have a knock-on impact on payments further down the chain.

(ix)   Performance Indicators, Monitoring, and Incentives

Establishing well-defined, objective performance indicators, along with robust and non-interventionist monitoring systems are essential for the functioning of a PPP. This is another area that has emerged as a challenge in the establishment and development of PPPs in UPHCs. It was observed that performance indicators were at times not very well defined. Often, performance monitoring systems were more process and financial audit based rather than outcome- or performance-based. In other cases, performance indicators that incentivized greater footfall tended to create perverse incentives for partners. Discrepancies between performance indicators and oversight were also found between UPHCs that were run as PPPs and government-run ones. This problem was further exacerbated by the fact that payments to PPP UPHCs were related to performance while no government-run UPHCs face similar financial sanctions should they not perform as per standards, despite the fact that in principle, both government-run and PPP UPHCs need to follow the same standards.

Other challenges also included the lack of institutionalized systems that reward good performance, innovations, and/or improving effectiveness, as well as the lack of institutionalized mechanisms or platforms where learnings gained by private partners could be shared with the government for potential improvements in service delivery across the board.

With respect to monitoring, in most states the responsibility to ensure PPPs in UPHCs were performing as per agreed norms rests with the state public health care officials, with the primary tools for monitoring being regular site visits and validation of financial and other documentation as defined in the contract. However, ensuring monitoring takes place in a timely manner is a challenge. In some states, the officials responsible for monitoring were working beyond their capacity resulting in delays in carrying out their monitoring responsibilities. In others, there was a resistance among mid-level public health care officials toward PPPs in UPHCs, leading to delays in carrying out their monitoring responsibilities. As discussed above, lack of timely monitoring can in turn lead to delays in payments being made to the private partner and may end up disrupting UPHC operations.

Improving performance management and the monitoring system may need to include dynamic performance indicators, perhaps revisited on a yearly basis, to factor in significant changes in user demands in urban settings. This can be supported by putting in place a mechanism to systematically gather user feedback as well as establishing a grievance redressal mechanism. These in turn can be incorporated within the performance indicators to ensure service quality. Additionally, third-party evaluations, developing outcome-based indices for performance monitoring, among others, may also need to be explored. Finally, systems that ensure effective monitoring without impacting payments and operational effectiveness of PPPs in UPHCs need to be developed.

(x)   Governance

A PPP in providing primary health care services is essentially a contractual agreement for a specified period of time between a government and a private entity. However, such a partnership arrangement is not merely a relationship where the private "partner" is simply a contractor. Constant engagement needs to be the norm in such a partnership, with institutionalized mechanisms in place that encourage a mutually supportive relationship. This forms the core of the governance mechanisms that must be in place to ensure PPPs in UPHCs are run effectively and efficiently.

At the institutional level, effective governance was identified as a key challenge. It was observed that there was both a hierarchical as well as generational difference in the approach of government officials to PPPs in UPHCs. While the higher bureaucracy at the state (and national) level was supportive of the idea and its effective implementation, there were instances where state level officials, especially those involved at the operational level, tended to be skeptical and resistant. This in turn also led to a lack of involvement of partners in planning meetings, confusion in the roles of different actors involved, and unclear reporting lines, in some case leading to disputes. These point to an attitudinal inertia where the private entity is not seen as partner but as a contractor. A lack of trust and communication between partners can impact service delivery and increases the possibilities of disputes. This also manifested in the differential approach to ongoing trainings being provided to staff at government-run UPHCs but not to staff at PPP UPHCs.

It was also observed that thus far, a continuity in policies related to PPPs in UPHCs had not developed, in part as these were new arrangements that had not yet stabilized at a systemic level, as well as due to changes in orientation, which come with the transfer of senior officials.

To a large extent, several of these governance and institutional problems can (in some states, have) been mitigated by defining clear processes, as well as roles and responsibilities at the institutional level, coordinated by a dedicated PPP unit or cell embedded within the state NHM directorate. This coordination role is critical as PPPs can be complex because the nature, type, and number of actors are large and more heterogenous.

An overview of the challenges discussed above along with potential solutions are presented in Table 2.

**Table 2: Challenges in Public–Private Partnerships
in Urban Primary Health Centers**

Issue	Challenges	Potential Solution Areas
Availability of private partners	Lack of NGOs with adequate size and capacity to manage UPHCs	Involve teaching institutions
		Incentivize private participation
Not-for-profit versus for-profit partners	Not-for-profit partners may have limited capacity to innovate	Provide training and resources for not-for-profit partners to innovate
	For-profit partners may lead to conflict of interest, and/or find government budgets and processes restrictive	Partner with foundations, trusts, CSR when engaging for-profit partners
Size of partner	Small NGOs have limited capacity to manage UPHCs in clusters, absorb payment delays, and innovate	Engage only with large partners where cluster approach is used
		Engage small partners where individual UPHCs are contracted out
Procurement	L1 selection process is relatively more challenging than EOI in its applicability to PPPs in UPHCs	Choose EOI or L1 as the selection process as per context
		Assess availability of NGOs and then define detailed eligibility criteria
	Selection processes can be opaque	Proactively publish all procurement and performance related information

continued on next page

Table 2 *continued*

Issue	Challenges	Potential Solution Areas
Contracts and contract management	Contractor versus partner	Change language of contract to focus on partnership
	Process versus outcomes	Greater focus on outcomes
	Lack of flexibility	Greater trust
		Involve private partners in trainings and capacity building processes
		Allow operational and budgetary flexibility within the contract
Costing and budgeting	Budgets do not adequately reflect real costs	Annual costing exercise to be carried out and reflected in subsequent budgets
	Additional responsibilities not paid for	All additional responsibilities to be costed and reimbursed.
Staff remuneration	Salary budgets do not take into account market realities	While overall budgets should be fixed, flexibility should be allowed in utilization of funds across budget lines
	Innovation and good performance not rewarded	Introduce performance-based incentives across all roles.
Payments	Payments are often delayed	Rationalize procedures that lead to payment delays
	Staff of smaller NGOs may not receive salaries for months	Delink payment from performance while introducing penalties for nonperformance
		Move from process orientation to performance orientation.
Key performance indicators	KPIs are not uniform and are unclear, which can also lead to needless delays and disruption in payments	Develop objective and verifiable KPIs
		KPIs need to be outcome- and not process-based
	Quick changes to situation on the ground in urban settings make KPIs quickly redundant	Introduce dynamic KPIs to be reviewed annually
	User satisfaction not reflected in KPIs	Establish mandatory process to gather user feedback, as well as grievance redressal policy, and include in KPIs

continued on next page

19

Table 2 *continued*

Issue	Challenges	Potential Solution Areas
Monitoring	Complex monitoring systems that depend solely on government officials can disrupt operations	Simplify monitoring mechanisms
	No institutionalized system for mainstreaming learnings and innovations	Move to a system that favors self-reporting, with heavy sanctions for any breach of trust
		Introduce regular feedback systems to improve the overall efficiency of UPHCs as a whole
		Introduce third-party evaluations
Incentives	No institutionalized system of rewards for good performance	Introduce performance-based incentives for all UPHC staff
Governance	Approach of contractor and not partner	Establish a coordinating entity (PPP unit or cell)
	Resistance at mid-levels of government	Establish clear roles, responsibilities, and reporting lines for all actors
	Mistrust between partners	Reduce government intervention in daily operations
	Differential in resource allocation and behavior toward government-run and PPP UPHCs	Establish institutionalized mechanisms to reinforce mutual trust, review progress, improve services, and resolve differences
		Move from a government–contractor relationship to a partnership approach

CSR = corporate social responsibility, EOI = expression of interest, KPI = key performance indicator, L1 = lowest bidder, NGO = nongovernment organization, PPP = public–private partnership, UPHC = urban primary health center.

Source: Asian Development Bank.

To address some of these challenges, MOHFW is developing guidelines and tool kits to support states in streamlining the process of establishing and developing effective PPPs in UPHCs through budgetary support provided under NUHM. As a part of this effort, MOHFW has indicated that where the PPP option is utilized, state governments should prioritize entering into a comprehensive agreement where all services that are typically offered by a government-run UPHC should be provided through the PPP UPHC. In terms of services and functions of UPHCs being run in the PPP mode, the following characteristics would therefore be desirable.

(i) The entire operation and maintenance of a PPP UPHC should be carried out by the private partner, i.e., the PPP agreement should ideally not be a piecemeal one where only specific services (such as diagnostics) are contracted out as PPPs. It should be comprehensive where the private partner takes on all tasks and delivers all services that are typically carried out by a government-run UPHC, including all clinical, diagnostic, outreach, and nonclinical services.

(ii) As UPHCs are at the frontline of providing public health care services, partners should be not-for-profit entities to mitigate the possibility of any conflict of interest creeping into public health care delivery systems.

(iii) All services delivered through PPP UPHCs must be free to the end user.

(iv) The PPP contract should typically be short-term (3–5 years) and renewed annually based on agreed performance indicators. If required and feasible, budgetary revisions can be incorporated at the time of contract renewal. This will ensure that the fiscal risks and liabilities of the government are mitigated.

(v) The Government of India would provide a specific amount of annual budgetary support to state governments per UPHC, which is calculated in discussion with each state government, and follows the service norms and standards for UPHCs as defined by MOHFW.

(vi) State governments would be at liberty to augment the service levels and/or budgets for UPHCs as per local needs and requirements.

Although this tool kit focuses on PPPs in UPHCs, several other types of PPPs can also exist within urban health care. Some of these are indicated in Box 3 below.

Box 3: Other Types of Existing Public–Private Partnership Arrangements in Urban Health Care

Several other types of public–private partnership (PPP) arrangements exist across the urban health care spectrum. The more popular ones include the following:

Contracting in specialists.[a] The government hires medical specialists on an individual basis in areas such as dermatology; ear, nose and throat; dentistry; gynecology; pediatrics; and medicine. These specialists serve at public health care facilities on specified days for a specific number of hours. The government pays specialists by the number of hours they serve at the public health care facility. Contracting in of specialists could also be carried out in combination with the contracting out of urban primary health centers (UPHCs). In such an arrangement, the private partner managing the UPHC contracts in specialists (this contractual agreement is between the private partner and the specialist), with the costs for this activity built into the contract between the government and the private partner to manage the UPHC, along with relevant key performance indicators (KPIs) for this activity.

Contracting in and contracting out diagnostic services.[b] Private parties bid to run specific (or a range of; or complete contracting out of all) diagnostic services at a public health care facility. The government provides the physical space. All capital, maintenance, and material costs are borne by the private entity. Government pays the private entity on a per capita basis as per the agreed amount based on the winning bid.

Staff training.[c] Government engages a private entity (for example nongovernment organization) to provide training services for staff, which could include auxiliary nurse midwives, support staff, and medical staff.

Outsourcing ancillary services.[d] Government enters into a contractual arrangement with private entities to provide specific ancillary services that lie within the urban health care ecosystem such as biomedical waste management, maintenance of buildings, laundry services, canteen services, etc.

---

[a] A sample contract for contracting in specialists is provided in Appendix 8.
[b] A sample contract for diagnostic services is provided in Appendix 7.
[c] A sample contract for training services is provided in Appendix 9.
[d] A sample contract for outsourcing biomedical waste management is provided in Appendix 6.

Source: Asian Development Bank.

Part 3

Tool Kit

A. Planning for Public–Private Partnerships in Urban Primary Health Centers

(i) Establishment of a PPP Cell

Public–private partnerships are complex processes involving a multitude of stakeholders. Their efficiency is directly related to establishing clearly defined responsibilities, well-defined and objective procurement and performance criteria, and robust yet nonintrusive monitoring systems. The presence of an empowered and agile coordinating entity that ensures that all parties carry out their respective responsibilities in a spirit of partnership therefore becomes an important prerequisite. This can be done through the establishment of a PPP cell or unit within the health department of each state government, embedded within or working closely with the NHM Directorate. The PPP cell could be supported by an advisory board that could consist of representatives of the government (including the health and finance departments at the very least) professional bodies, academia, relevant NGOs, trusts, and the private sector. With PPPs being established across the entire health care delivery continuum, the establishment of a PPP cell—or at the very least allocating appropriate human resources to manage PPPs in health care delivery—is an important prerequisite regardless whether a state government has taken a decision to establish in UPHCs or not.

Where state governments decide to explore the option of PPPs in UPHCs, the responsibilities the PPP cell would include the following:

(a) Identify the rationale for PPPs in UPHCs.
(b) Assess the availability of appropriate NGO partners, including trusts and foundations.
(c) Assess feasibility of establishing and/or developing PPPs in UPHCs.
(d) Draft a short-, medium-, and long-term strategy for PPPs in UPHCs.
(e) Identify the sites where PPPs in UPHCs would be located as per the strategy.
(f) Provide the rationale for and define whether the state should engage private partners though a cluster approach or through individual UPHCs.
(g) Define detailed service levels and performance indicators.
(h) Draft the eligibility and evaluation criteria, as well as the process by which partners would be procured, and define the roles and responsibilities of various actors such as the District Health Societies, Department of Health, Rogi Kalyan Samitis, etc.
(i) Define the performance monitoring processes, including self-reporting.
(j) Define user feedback processes and grievance redressal policy.
(k) Define mechanisms for penalties and sanctions.
(l) Define KPIs and performance incentive mechanisms.
(m) Define payment mechanisms and processes.
(n) Serve as the first point for resolution of any unexpected crisis that requires an immediate response.
(o) Serve as the first point of contact for conflict resolution.

(p) Draft model contracts and/or agreements that incorporate relevant points above.

(q) Create and coordinate institutionalized processes for contract management for the smooth functioning of the partnership, which would include holding regular review meetings, continually improving monitoring systems, encouraging and supporting innovations, providing financial incentives for good performance, and renewal of contracts.

The following steps in the tool kit presume the establishment of a PPP cell within each state health department or NHM mission directorate. Where such a cell has not been or cannot be established, the actions may be taken by the designated officials or team in the health state department that has been tasked with the responsibility of PPPs.

(ii) Needs Assessment

What are the current service delivery gaps in urban primary health care?

As a first step, the state government must assess the level of service delivery gaps in urban primary health care. This would include an analysis of the availability of primary health care services in urban areas in each state, and whether these comply with NUHM norms in terms of presence, size of population being served, accessibility, and quality and range of services being provided by UPHCs (or similar entities). Such an exercise could be supported through data and reports generated by the departments that manage health, urban welfare, women and child development, population, planning, and statistics. District Health Societies would be important sources of data from the field. Data from the MOHFW could also provide important insights into existing service delivery gaps and trends.

Is there a need to expand UPHC coverage? What is the expected rate of increase of UPHC expansion?

Typically, state governments would already have data about the need for expanding UPHC coverage in their jurisdictions. This would be reflected in the strategy and planning documents developed by the department of health in each state. Data may need to be analyzed to assess the requirement and degree to which UPHCs must be expanded.

Does the government have enough financial and human resources to carry out the expansion?

Once the need and extent of UPHC expansion has been assessed, the health department must analyze how this would be financed. The sources of financing would be a combination of state and central funds (especially through NHM and/or NUHM) and discussions with the finance and planning departments would be essential in carrying out this analysis. This process should ideally include estimating the unit cost of running a UPHC as per MOHFW norms in terms of service levels and delivery.

What are the challenges in carrying out the expansion only through government efforts?

Field studies has shown that different states have different challenges in expanding UPHCs only through government efforts. These could include challenges in recruiting appropriate human resources and identifying and developing adequate physical infrastructure. In some states, there could be administrative and legal causes for delays in expanding the government-run UPHC network. The health department would need to identify the impediments in carrying out the expansion of UPHCs at the required rate. This analysis may also result in the finding that the government is well-placed and well-resourced to expand UPHCs only through its own efforts and is achieving its targets.

Can PPPs mitigate these challenges?

Where the health department finds that the government efforts for UPHC expansion requires additional support due to challenges that cannot be resolved quickly, resulting in an increasing gap between demand and supply of primary urban health care services, the government may then take a decision to assess whether PPPs would be an appropriate modality to mitigate these challenges.

(iii) Feasibility

Is there a pool of appropriate NGOs present in the state?

As discussed above, MOHFW has indicated that in the first instance, it would be more advantageous to primarily consider not-for-profit entities as potential partners when considering PPPs in UPHCs. As a first step in establishing the feasibility of PPPs in UPHC, the health department must first assess whether there are adequate number of NGOs, trusts, or other similar organizations that have the experience to be able to manage UPHCs and provide services as per MOHFW norms for UPHCs. Sources for this information would include the health department, District Health Societies, NGOs that were engaged under National Rural Health Mission, and Niti Aayog's Darpan NGO Portal. The assessment would need to include information such as number of registered NGOs that work on health care in the state (or neighboring states); locations; years of experience; nature and quality of prior engagement with government (for example, through NRHM); size (both on the basis of turnover and human resources); sectoral expertise; general credibility, etc. The basic purpose of this exercise would be to assess the size and quality of the pool from which potential partners to run PPP UPHCs would be selected.

Would these NGOs be able to manage more than a single UPHC?

Based on this assessment, the PPP cell would need to assess whether the pool of NGOs or trusts existing in the state have the human and financial resources to manage and run more than one UPHC. This is necessary as this will allow the government to make an informed decision on whether to introduce PPPs in UPHCs in clusters or on an individual UPHC basis. Where the pool of potential partners is primarily made up of small NGOs, a cluster approach may not be the most appropriate as partners may not have the required resources to manage more than a single UPHC. Where the pool of potential NGOs consists of larger entities, a cluster approach may be more effective.

In practice, it may be that a state could have a mix of NGOs, both small and large, in which case the government could devise a mixed policy for establishing PPPs in UPHCs where partnership arrangements could be in a cluster approach with larger NGOs, and on an individual basis with smaller NGOs. The eligibility criteria of potential partners will need to reflect this policy.

Further, the PPP policy may be revisited every 3 years as the situation on the ground can change within a short period of time. For example, even where the pool of relevant NGOs in a state is primarily made up of smaller entities, the capacity of an NGO may grow over a period of time as a result of its growing experience in running individual UPHCs. The overall growth in capacity may then be utilized in a different way over a period of time.

Has the costing of a government-run UPHC been carried out?

Norms of NUHM on staffing and service levels to be delivered through UPHCs have been broadly defined along with corresponding figures for budgetary support. However, the situation in each state may be different (for example, the availability of trained human resources in a given state has an implication on the cost of hiring such professionals) and each state government must undertake a detailed costing exercise based on actual market intelligence to assess the cost of running a UPHC as per NUHM norms.

Conducting such an exercise will help the state government assess whether the budgetary support being provided is adequate and whether flexibility in expenditure is required across different budgetary heads depending on the market reality in each state. For example, while the overall per unit UPHC budgetary support provided through NUHM funds may be adequate, there may be shortfalls for specific line items due to cost variations at the state level. This would indicate whether there is a necessity of cost-neutral budgetary flexibility to be incorporated into PPP contracts.

It should be noted that the costing exercise should be as detailed as possible, with every element of expenditure identified and costed for, including staffing; physical infrastructure acquisition, rental, and maintenance; equipment acquisition and maintenance; operating costs; transport; biomedical waste management costs; performance-based incentives; insurance; contingency funds; and inflation.

Is adequate budgetary support available?

Once the costing exercise has been carried out, the PPP cell will need to assess whether adequate budgetary support is available to establish and develop PPPs in UPHCs. The sources of funds could be the central government (through NHM) supplemented by its own resources where required.

Assessing NGO interest

Once these initial exercises have been carried out, the state government may conduct a market sounding exercise where it engages with potential partners to assess their level of interest in entering into PPP agreements to manage UPHCs at the identified budgetary levels. The government may carry this out as a formal exercise where all potential partners identified above are invited for a meeting where the government presents the broad contours (including estimated number of UPHCs, service-level norms, estimated costs, etc.) of its proposed engagement with NGOs in managing UPHCs and seek their feedback to assess interest levels at the identified budgetary levels. If adequate interest exists, then the government may proceed to the next stage, preprocurement.

B. Project Preparation or Preprocurement

Once the government has decided to proceed with engaging private (NGO) partners in managing UPHCs based on the feasibility exercise described above, it must then prepare for the procurement process by drafting in detail the process that will guide the establishment and development of PPPs in UPHCs. The primary output of this project preparation and/or pre-procurement stage will be a document, or a set of documents called Request for Proposal (RFP).[21] The RFP documents would need to include information as shown in Table 3.[22]

---

21   This is also called the terms of reference (TOR) in some jurisdictions.
22   Sample RFP documents are provided in Appendixes 2 and 3. Sample contracts are provided in Appendixes 4 and 5.

Table 3: Information to Be Included in Requests for Proposals

Information	Description
Objectives	What are the overall objectives of UPHCs being established through PPPs?
Scope of work	This would include high-level information such as the coverage area of each UPHC, timings, types of services to be provided, provision of medicines, costs to end user, etc.
Estimated value	Whether the estimated cost of running each UPHC is made public at this stage or not depends on whether the private partner is procured through an L1 or an EOI process. Where it is the latter, this value should be provided in the RFP documents.
Sites of UPHCs	The sites where the UPHCs are to be located should be provided. Additional information related to whether the PPP contracts will be carried out using a cluster approach or for each individual UPHC should also be included here.
Physical infrastructure	The RFP should make it clear whether the private party is responsible for renting the premises to establish a UPHC, or whether government will provide the premises. This will have a cost implication on the project.
Duration of contract	Refers to date of commencement and duration of contract.
Financial terms and conditions	These include general financial rules and regulations under which the contract will operate, including which partner (government or private party) is financially responsible for which aspect of operations, such as maintenance of physical infrastructure, acquisition and maintenance of medical and diagnostic equipment, costs and supply of consumables and medicines, administrative costs, etc. These must also indicate the degree of flexibility that will be permitted within the contract—both in terms of how the budgetary allocations can be utilized, and how the private party can renegotiate the value and terms of engagement should expectations or conditions change in the future. These must also include the process by which payments will be made, and whether it will be reimbursement-based or performance-based with advance payments.
Staffing terms and conditions	These cover terms and conditions under which staff will be recruited and/or assigned to UPHCs by the partner, including staff profiles and minimum eligibility criteria.
Services to be provided	The services to be provided at each UPHC should be detailed, including clinical services, outreach services, diagnostic services, trainings, participation in national programs, etc.
Record keeping and reporting	These will need to provide in detail the responsibilities of the private partner in keeping records of users and reporting requirements to the government.
Norms for infrastructure	Where the private party is responsible for renting premises, the norms that should be followed in terms of size, location, number of rooms, etc. are indicated.
Norms for staffing	Refers to the number and type of staff to be assigned by the private partner for each UPHC, including part-time specialists. Also indicates if the government will provide any additional staff.
Responsibilities of the government	In this section of the RFP, the government must clearly indicate its responsibilities in the PPP agreement, especially related to the provision and maintenance of physical infrastructure (where government premises are to be used), provision of equipment and consumables, provision of medicines, guarantees of payments, and any other support that the government may be providing.

continued on next page

Table 3 *continued*

Information	Description
Governance (including responsibilities for management, reviews, coordination, reporting, etc.)	This is a critical section of the RFP that will define the roles and responsibilities of each party in terms of the governance of each UPHC. This will include, among others, details of the establishment and functioning of a Rogi Kalyan Samiti, the reporting lines within each UPHC, reporting lines between the UPHC and identified government functionaries, and establishment of norms for communication as well as review meetings.
Quality assurance	This pertains to details of the quality standards and norms that the partner must adhere to.
Accountability	This will provide details of the process by which the partner may maintain public accountability, through proactive information disclosure, creating platforms for user feedback, conducting regular user feedback surveys, and responding to grievances in a sensitive, timely manner (based on a defined grievance redressal policy).
Key performance indicators	These are details of deliverables upon which the private party would be held accountable.
Monitoring and evaluation	This would track how the UPHC is carrying out its tasks and include financial and service-level reporting, site visits, and third-party evaluations. This section should also provide details of performance-based incentives, if any, as well as sanctions on nonperformance.
Reviews and contract renewal	These would provide details of how and under what conditions contracts would be reviewed, renewed, or preterminated.
Dispute resolution mechanisms	These are details of how any disputed between the private parties would be resolved, with a clearly defined escalation ladder.
Eligibility criteria	These would pertain to potential private partners including details related to experience, financial profile, and human resource profile. This would vary significantly based on whether UPHCs are being contracted out in clusters or as individual sites.
Key dates	These are dates in the procurement process, including deadlines for application, evaluation of proposals, procurement, announcement of award, and commencement of contract.
Application procedure	This lays out the details on format of proposal, how and where to apply, etc.
List of documents to be submitted	These are requirements (including any proformas) that the applicant will need to include.
Evaluation criteria and selection process	These are the bases on which proposals will be evaluated and selected. These criteria should be as objective as possible. This section will also include the process that will be followed in evaluating each proposal, including the role and composition of any entities and/or committees that have been constituted for the evaluation and selection process. The government may introduce proposed innovations as an added parameter for selection.
Draft contract	A draft contract incorporating information from all preceding sections to be included with the RFP documents.

EOI = expression of interest, KPI = key performance indicator, L1 = lowest bidder, RFP = request for proposal, UPHC = urban primary health center.

Note: Some of the information in this table may be a part of the contract agreement, a draft of which should ideally be a part of the RFP documents. Sample contracts are provided in Appendixes 4 and 5.

Source: Asian Development Bank.

An important decision that must be taken during the project preparation phase is which procurement method will be used to select PPP partners - the lowest bidder or the expression of interest method. This is discussed in Box 4 below. In addition, a second critical component is the payment mechanism that will be in place. This could be the "reimbursement method" or the "performance method." These are discussed in Box 5.

Box 4: Procurement Method: Lowest Bidder or Expression of Interest?

Currently, public–private partnerships (PPPs) in urban primary health centers (UPHCs) are being procured primarily through two different methods: lowest bidder (L1) and expression of interest (EOI).

Lowest Bidder

In the L1 method, the selection is made through a bidding process, where all else being equal, the lowest bidder is selected. This type of bidding process has long been the norm where the government engages contractors to provide public goods and services, typically in the context of physical infrastructure development. This system of procurement is primarily based on the assumption that the private party seeks to make a profit from the contract, and hence the party willing to provide the same goods or services at the lowest profit margin wins the bid. While this procurement method can be useful from a value-for-money perspective (the government pays as little as possible for a clearly defined output, and the risk of any increase in input costs is primarily borne by the private party) its success depends on several factors, including a large pool of qualified bidders in the market, no leakages in the system, clear and objective performance or output indicators, tight quality control measures and assurances, and robust monitoring systems.

Expression of Interest

An EOI system of procurement implies the government provides detailed project specifications, including estimated value of the project (the budget outlay is therefore largely predefined with market realities factored in), defines clear eligibility criteria for applicants, along with outcomes parameters, and then invites proposals from interested parties. Applicants do not necessarily submit any financial bids as the government has already indicated the broad value of the project. In such a system, proposals are primarily assessed on the profiles of the applicants, including prior experience, financial solvency, credibility and approach, using an objective scoring methodology, with the top scorers being selected. Such a system of procurement is therefore better suited to contexts where the pool of potential applicants is small, where the main concern is not cost-saving (this aspect being already factored in by the government when defining the value of the project), and where the quality of goods or services to be delivered is of critical importance.

In the context of PPPs in UPHCs, NGOs are preferred partners, the pool of applicants is small, the budgets for running a UPHC as a PPP has been broadly predefined (and this information is in the public domain), and the output is service delivery. While this suggests that the EOI system of procurement is better suited to procure PPPs in UPHCs in India, local contexts may require the L1 process to be used. State governments may therefore choose their preferred system of procurement based on local conditions.

continued on next page

Box 4 *continued*

Box Table 4a: Overview of Lowest Bidder versus Expression of Interest Procurement

Parameter	L1	EOI
Size of market	Pool of applicants is large	Pool of applicants is small
Costs	Market-based	Predefined by government
Output	Physical infrastructure	Services; highly specialized physical infrastructure
Financial incentive for private party	Maximizing profit	No profit no loss, or a margin of profit predefined by government
Financial risk	Primarily taken up by the private party	Low risk for all parties as value is predefined by the government
Selection criteria	Lowest bid	Applicant profile with clearly defined eligibility criteria
Relationship	Contractor	Partner

EOI = expression of interest, L1 = lowest bidder.

Source: Asian Development Bank.

Box 5: Payment Mechanism

There are primarily two methods used by governments for funding projects across the globe (including in other parts of Asia and India)—reimbursement of cost method ("**Reimbursement Method**"), and performance-linked payment ("**Performance Method**"). Depending on the nature of the project, either a mix of both, or either one of these payment structures, is used to fund projects by the governments. Both systems necessarily function under the General Financial Rules of the central and relevant state governments.

The Reimbursement Method payment system is one in which the government will fund the actual cost incurred by the private party on the project based on invoices (within certain parameters). On the other hand, the Performance Method payment system is one in which the government will provide the fund periodically based on the performance and objectives achieved by the private party.

The Reimbursement Method is usually used (i.e., the principles for using Reimbursement Method) for financing project where

- the prices of inputs and costs of achieving outputs are likely to vary over the life of a project or are subject to conditions outside of the control of the parties;

- the actual means of accomplishing outcomes are defined in implementation plans or work plans that are prepared after project approval or periodically during the project implementation period; and

- the outcomes cannot be defined and priced with sufficient detail to justify placing the entire financial risk for project completion on the private party.

Therefore, the Reimbursement Method of payment system is more suitable for projects in which actual costs are likely to vary from estimates, as well as when outputs and results depend on factors or events outside the control of the parties.

continued on next page

Box 5 *continued*

In India, most of the funding by the government in infrastructure and energy projects is done through the Performance Method. For example, roads and port projects are funded through the Performance Method. Other infrastructure projects (where funding by the government may not be required) such as international airports, metro, and power projects are also measured by the Performance Method.

One of the methods that could be considered for mitigating delays of payment in primary health care public–private partnerships (PPP) is to move from the Reimbursement Method to Performance Method. The private party could be paid in advance every quarter. The PPP agreement will have key performance indicators (KPIs) or parameters to be achieved by the private party. As long as the private party continues to achieve the minimum KPIs, the private party receives regular funding from the government.

Source: Asian Development Bank.

C. Procurement

Once the RFP documents have been finalized, the procurement process can commence. The government may place advertisements in leading newspapers of the state and/or country and provide all RFP documents on appropriate government websites or portals as per a defined schedule. The government will also need to constitute the evaluation committee (and any other technical committees or entities that are a part of the evaluation process) in line with the evaluation and selection process detailed in the RFP documents.

Before the deadline for proposals has passed, the government may also consider holding an open meeting with all interested parties to discuss the RFP documents and receive feedback on the feasibility of the proposed project. Should the government see fit, it could then take on board any suggestions received and revise and republish the RFP documents accordingly. Should it do so, it may need to revise the deadlines and time schedules for the procurement process accordingly. Adding this step of seeking feedback on the RFP may result in less disputes and smoother contract management once the PPP has been operationalized.

The committee tasked for evaluation will then assess the proposals received as per the criteria and process defined in the RFP. The evaluation committee may choose to make public its report in the interest of transparency.

D. Post-procurement

Once the evaluation of proposals has been completed, the partners selected, and the contracts signed, the PPP will then need to be operationalized as per the plan delineated in the RFP documents. This will include the handing over of premises to the private party (where applicable) as a first step. Once the UPHC has been operationalized, the focus of government activities will shift to contract management and performance monitoring.

(i)   Communication

The key to effective contract management and the effective functioning of PPP UPHCs is regular communication between the government and the implementing partners so that each party is clear about the other's expectations throughout the duration of the contract. It is therefore critical that a well-defined communications strategy is in place for this purpose. This strategy would include a planned schedule of regular and frequent meetings between the government and each individual partner, regular larger meetings between the government and all partners in the state (so that each can learn from the experience of others), open lines of communication so that any problems can be immediately addressed, and clear reporting lines. The critical aspect of an effective communications strategy is to ensure that the private party is engaged as a partner and not a contractor.

(ii) Innovations

The government must encourage private partners to introduce innovations in processes and technologies to improve health care outcomes. Should a partner show an interest in carrying out innovations, the government should facilitate it through additional funding where possible, or by directing the partner to alternate sources of funding through other budgetary provisions and supporting their efforts to access the same. Should the private partner be interested in finding other nongovernment sources of funding to introduce innovations, the government must support such efforts as long as the core activities of the UPHC are not adversely affected.

(iii) Reporting

The government may also consider drafting a reporting protocol where private partners provide regular (daily, weekly, monthly, etc.) self-reported data on all aspects of the functioning of the UPHC, including number of users, services provided, staff attendance, and so on. This could also include details of feedback received from users through regular surveys, as well as information on how grievances, if any, have been addressed. The reporting protocol need to be directly linked to the KPIs identified in the contract documents. Payments would be released on the basis of these reports, along with other oversight mechanisms such as external validations, site visits, and third-party evaluations.

(iv) Monitoring and Evaluation

Continuous yet nonintrusive monitoring and evaluation is another important aspect of contract management. The government would also need to develop a monitoring and evaluation protocol that defines the timelines, responsibilities, and processes of continuous evaluation, set against performance indicators identified in the RFP documents. These evaluations can be of a regular nature throughout the contract duration, and also include third-party evaluations at the end of the contract to assess whether it should be renewed, and how improvements could be made.

While payments could be linked to the private party delivering as per the performance indicators, in practice this can result in delays in payments to processual delays on the part of the government. This can be mitigated by isolating the payment schedule from performance indicators. However, clear sanctions in terms of financial penalties in case of nonachievement of performance levels would also need to be in place.

(v) Payments

As discussed above, delays in payments can be highly debilitating in a context where relatively small NGOs working on a not-for-profit basis are not provided adequate finances in time to carry out the operations of a UPHC. To ensure this does not happen, an advance payment system needs to be put in place. A well-defined protocol of performance-based incentives may also be put in place to encourage better health care outcomes.

(vi) Sanctions

Situations may arise where the private party does not or is unable to deliver as per the performance indicators. In such cases, the government needs to have a clear protocol for sanctions, which could include providing grace periods with support and additional oversight, financial penalties in case of consistent nonperformance, and where improvements are not forthcoming, terminating contracts, recovering costs, and backlisting for any future engagement with government where necessary.

(vii) Dispute Resolutions

While clear and well-defined contracts mitigate this to a large extent, disputes may occur between the government and the private party. The contract documents should include a section on how disputes would be addressed with a clearly defined escalation ladder (including arbitration) with the matter being taken to the judicial system only as a matter of last resort.

While these are the specific tasks at the post-procurement stage, governments at different levels have specific roles and responsibilities throughout the PPP lifecycle. These are discussed in Box 6 below.

Box 6: Roles of Central, State, and Municipal Governments in Public–Private Partnerships in Urban Primary Health Centers

The degrees of responsibility among the central, state, and municipal governments in the establishment and development of public–private partnerships (PPPs) in urban primary health centers (UPHCs) will be different depending on the nature of the task and phase in the PPP process.

Box Table 6a: Roles of Governments in the PPP Process

Task/Phase	Central	State	Municipal[a]
Budgetary support	Primary	Secondary	Secondary
Tools and guidelines	Primary	Primary	Secondary
Laws, policies, and rules	Secondary	Primary	Secondary
Planning for PPPs in UPHCs	Secondary	Primary	Secondary
Project preparation and/or Preprocurement		Primary	Secondary
Procurement		Primary	Secondary
Contract signing and management		Secondary	Primary
Post-procurement		Secondary	Primary

PPP = public–private partnership, UPHC = urban primary health center.

[a] Municipal bodies in large metropolitan cities would play a primary role in the budgetary, planning and procurement processes as they have significantly greater resources and autonomy than urban local bodies in smaller cities.

Source: Asian Development Bank.

A summary of the tool kit to establish and develop PPPs in UPHCs is provided in Table 4.

**Table 4: Tool Kit for Public–Private Partnerships
in Urban Primary Health Centers—Overview**

Phase/Step	Key Elements	Outputs
Needs assessment	Current service delivery gaps; need for UPHC expansion; availability of resources; challenges in UPHC expansion; value addition of PPPs	Needs assessment done; if assessment suggests that public–private partnerships may offer benefits, then move to next stage
Feasibility	Availability of appropriate partners; profiling of potential partners; costing or budgeting of UPHCs; assessment of market interest	Feasibility study done; if assessment is positive, then move to next stage
Project preparation or preprocurement	Development of RFP documents Information to include objectives; scope; estimated value (where applicable); locations; clusters or individual UPHCs; financial terms; staffing terms; services to be provided; record keeping and reporting; norms for infrastructure, staffing and biomedical waste management; responsibilities of government; quality norms; accountability; key performance indicators; monitoring and evaluation; contract renewal; dispute resolution; eligibility criteria; dates; application procedures; selection criteria and process; draft contract	Relevant committees and entities established; RFP documents finalized; RFP published as per schedule
Procurement	Place advertisements in leading newspapers; publish RFP documents on appropriate website; hold open meeting with partners to take feedback on RFP and revise if necessary; evaluate proposals received	Proposals evaluated; evaluation report published; selected partners announced as per schedule
Post-procurement	Establish channels and processes for effective communication; institutionalize support for innovations; establish systems for reporting with a focus on self-reporting rather than external validation; establish efficient payment processes; operationalize the monitoring and evaluation plan; have in a place clear protocols for dispute resolution and sanctions	Partnership is established; runs smoothly and efficiently based on mutual respect and support

RFP = request for proposal, UPHC = urban primary health center.

Source: Asian Development Bank.

An overview of the work flow suggested above is provided in Figure 2.

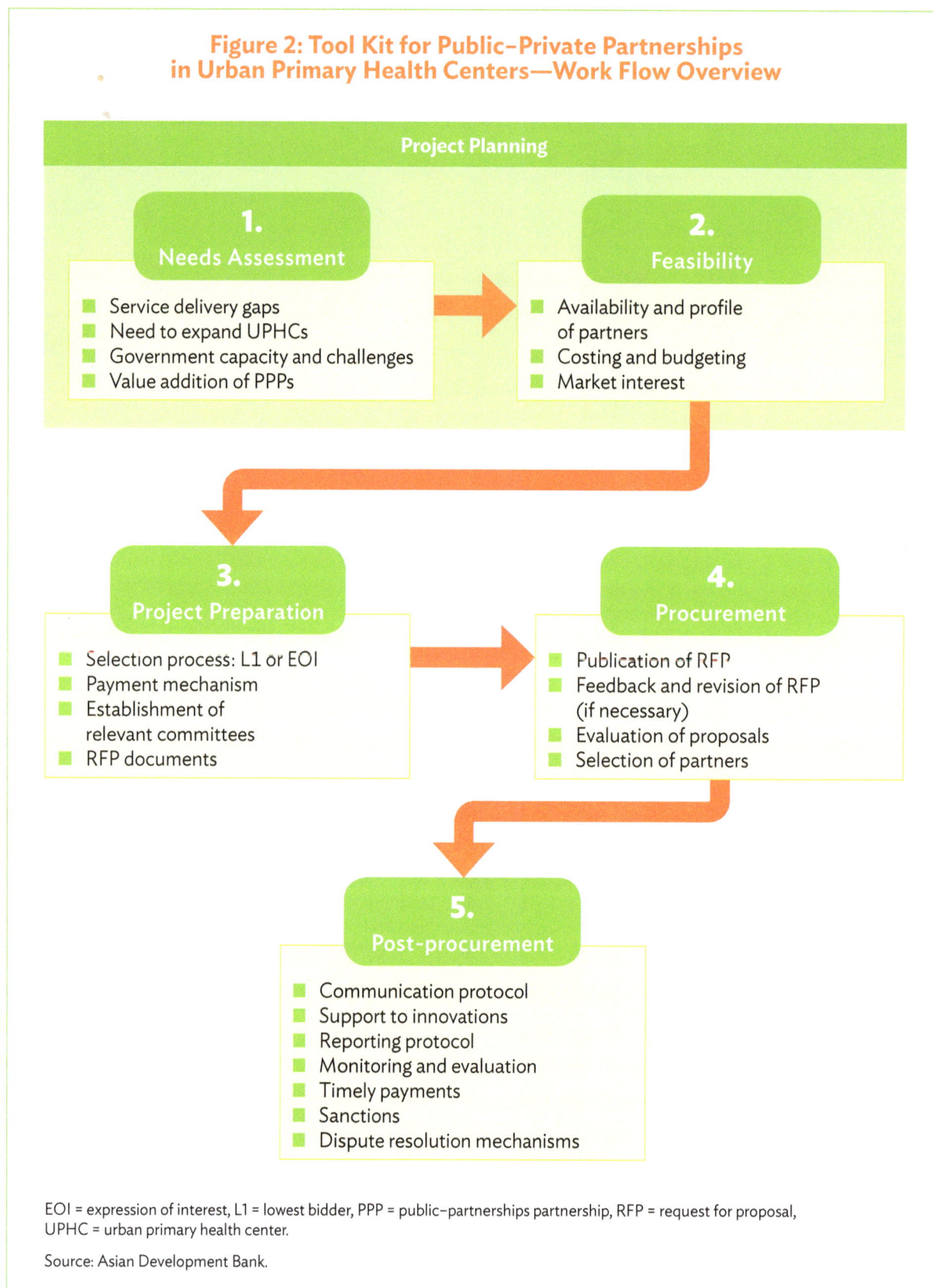

Figure 2: Tool Kit for Public–Private Partnerships in Urban Primary Health Centers—Work Flow Overview

Project Planning

1. Needs Assessment

- Service delivery gaps
- Need to expand UPHCs
- Government capacity and challenges
- Value addition of PPPs

2. Feasibility

- Availability and profile of partners
- Costing and budgeting
- Market interest

3. Project Preparation

- Selection process: L1 or EOI
- Payment mechanism
- Establishment of relevant committees
- RFP documents

4. Procurement

- Publication of RFP
- Feedback and revision of RFP (if necessary)
- Evaluation of proposals
- Selection of partners

5. Post-procurement

- Communication protocol
- Support to innovations
- Reporting protocol
- Monitoring and evaluation
- Timely payments
- Sanctions
- Dispute resolution mechanisms

EOI = expression of interest, L1 = lowest bidder, PPP = public–partnerships partnership, RFP = request for proposal, UPHC = urban primary health center.

Source: Asian Development Bank.

Part 4

Recommendations

Based on the discussion above, the following recommendations will support the institutionalization of a systematic and efficient process to establish and develop PPPs in UPHCs across different states in the country.

A. Institutional

(i) Given that PPPs are becoming increasingly common in the delivery of public health care services it is recommended that state governments establish a PPP cell or unit embedded within the state health department. This entity is essential for guiding, regulating, and coordinating all PPP activities related to health care in each state.

(ii) State governments may also consider establishing a PPP advisory board for health care comprising experts from the government (including the departments of health and finance), private sector, academia, relevant NGOs, trusts, and foundations to provide overall guidance to the evolution of PPPs in the state.

(iii) Each state must also establish technical evaluation committees for different types of PPPs in health care. These committees could be comprised of ex-officio members so that these could be quickly called upon to evaluate proposals and bids when the need arises. In any event, at the very least, PPP cells in each state must develop the norms for establishing technical evaluation committees for various existing and/or potential PPPs in health care.

(iv) In line with the technical evaluation committees, each state PPP cell must also establish approval committees and/or approval protocols that would review and provide approvals to the decision taken by the technical evaluation committees.

(v) State PPP cells must also identify and establish a PPP health care arbitration committee to resolve any disputes arising in any partnership. Such committees could also be set up on a project basis where the members of the committee are jointly selected by the parties concerned.

B. Project Preparation

Currently, many states are carrying out PPP projects in health care without conducting a thorough feasibility study. It is recommended that the PPP cell carries out detailed feasibility studies to assess the suitability of establishing and developing PPPs in UPHCs.

C. Costing and Budgeting

(i) Feasibility studies must necessarily include a thorough costing exercise of government-run UPHCs to establish the level of budgetary support required to establish PPPs in UPHCs. The costing exercise must identify each element of expenditure in detail as some expenses (such as travel, insurance and infrastructure maintenance costs) may be hidden in government-run UPHCs.

(ii) Feasibility studies must also include a budget for a PPP UPHC based on this costing exercise. The budget should ensure that all projected expenditures for the regular operation and maintenance of a UPHC are factored in. This includes costs such as biomedical waste management, infrastructure maintenance or security, which in many cases is being met through RKS funds.

(iii) RKS funds should not be used for the regular maintenance and operations of PPP UPHCs. Rather, these could be best utilized for bringing in innovations informed by the local context.

(iv) Specific one-time costs for initial setting up or upgrading facilities should be factored in.

(v) Administrative costs should be added to the budget as percentage of the total outlay.

(vi) Budgets should be pegged against an appropriate inflation index and revised on an annual basis accordingly.

(vii) When PPP UPHCs are required to provide services extraneous to the original agreement, such as participation in any health emergency, or in newly launched national programs, adequate additional budgetary support must be provided to them to carry out the same.

(viii) Partners should be allowed flexibility across budget line items to allow for variations in costs. While certain budgetary elements, such as rent, must be fixed for the year (as these are predictable), other costs such as salary may vary due to local conditions impacting availability of appropriate human resources.

D. Procurement

(i) Depending on the context, governments may use the EOI or L1 process to select partners when establishing PPPs in UPHCs.

(ii) Where the EOI is process is used, detailed eligibility criteria along with transparent and objective selection criteria should be used.

E. Payments

(i) It is recommended that the government make advance payments on a quarterly basis to ensure that the PPP UPHC operations continue uninterrupted.

(ii) While there can be delays in the disbursement of funds from the central government to the states, state governments must ensure that this does not impact advance payments to ensure uninterrupted services.

(iii) Payment procedures can be cumbersome and may lead to delays, which in turn negatively affect the regular operations of PPP UPHCs. It is recommended that the payment mechanisms shift to a "trust, verify, support, sanction" approach to mitigate this challenge. Payments must therefore not be directly linked to KPIs. However, financial penalties must be imposed where the KPIs fall below predefined levels, despite efforts to improve performance. Such a system will ensure a predictable cash flow for the partner, provide support and build capacity to improve performance where necessary, and ensure compliance to KPIs through the imposition of penalties should the need arise.

F. Performance

The PPP cell must develop objective and measurable KPIs for effective monitoring and evaluation.[23]

G. Staff

Governments must consider PPP UPHC staff at par with staff at government-run UPHCs in terms of meetings, trainings, and all other staff development programs.

H. Other Processes to Establish and Develop Public–Private Partnerships in Urban Primary Health Centers

In addition to the recommendations above, Table 5 provides the recommended process to establish and develop PPPs in UPHCs.

Table 5: Recommended Process to Establish and Develop Public–Private Partnerships in Urban Primary Health Centers

Activity	Output (if applicable)	Responsible Entity
Preprocurement		
Needs Assessment		
■ What are the current service delivery gaps in primary urban health care?	Needs assessment report	PPP cell
■ Is there a need to expand UPHC coverage? What is the expected rate of increase of UPHC expansion?		
■ Does the government have enough financial and human resources to carry out the expansion?		
■ What are the challenges in carrying out the expansion only through government efforts?		
■ Can PPPs mitigate these challenges?		

continued on next page

---

23 Sample KPIs that can be adapted based on local needs and context are provided in Appendix 10.

Table 5 *continued*

Activity	Output (if applicable)	Responsible Entity
Feasibility		
■ Is there a pool of appropriate NGOs present in the state?	Feasibility report	PPP cell
■ Would these NGOs be able to manage more than a single UPHC?		
■ Carry out a costing of a government-run UPHC		
■ Assess NGO interest; conduct a market -sounding exercise		
Project preparation		
■ Prepare RFP including: Objectives; Scope of work; Estimated value; Sites of UPHCs; Physical infrastructure; Duration of contract; Financial terms and conditions; Staffing terms and conditions; Services to be provided (clinical, outreach, national programs, training, diagnostics); Record keeping and reporting; Norms for infrastructure; Norms for staffing; Norms for biomedical waste management; Responsibilities of the government; Governance (including responsibilities for management, reviews, coordination, reporting, etc.); Quality assurance; Accountability (including user feedback and grievance redressal mechanisms); Key Performance Indicators; Monitoring and evaluation; Reviews and Contract renewal; Dispute resolution mechanisms; Eligibility criteria; Key dates; Application procedure; List of documents to be submitted; Evaluation criteria and selection process; Draft contract	RFP	PPP cell
Procurement		
Publish RFP document	RFP	PPP cell
Conduct pre-bid meeting		PPP cell
Change and republish RFP documents (if needed)		PPP cell
Receive bids		PPP cell
Evaluation of bids		
■ Document scrutiny		PPP cell
■ Request additional information (if necessary)		
■ Rejection of incomplete and/or late bids (provide reasons)		
■ Technical evaluation of proposal based on objective criteria		
■ Evaluation of financial bid (where L1 process is followed)	Technical evaluation report Financial evaluation report	Evaluation Committee
Approval		Approving authority and/or committee
Announce award	Letter of award	PPP cell

continued on next page

Table 5 *continued*

Activity	Output (if applicable)	Responsible Entity
Sign agreement	Agreement	PPP cell and/or District Health Society and private party
Post-Procurement		
Facility handover to private party (where applicable)		DHO
Inventory of assets		DHO
Inspection of rented premises (where applicable) and approval		DHO
Commencement of operations		Private party
Reporting ■ Daily reports of services provided, drugs offtake, staff attendance (through MIS) ■ Consolidated monthly reports ■ Monthly patient feedback reports ■ Quarterly financial reports		Private party
Governance ■ Monthly review meetings with each UPHC and/or cluster under one private party		PPP cell, DHO and private party
■ Quarterly review meetings with all PPP partners in state		PPP cell and all private partners
■ Rogi Kalyan Samiti meetings as per norms		Rogi Kalyan Samiti
Monitoring and evaluation ■ Quarterly site visits ■ Unscheduled site visits		DHO
■ Annual third-party evaluation		Third-party selected by PPP cell
Dispute Resolution ■ Level 1: Resolution through dialogue		PPP cell and private party
■ Level 2: Escalate to Principal Secretary (Health)		PS (H) and private party
■ Level 3: Escalate to Arbitration Committee		Arbitration committee and private party
■ Level 4: Courts		Courts and all relevant parties

DHO = district health officer, EOI = expression of interest, L1 = lowest bidder, MIS = management information system, NGO = nongovernment organization, PPP = public–private partnership, RFP = request for proposal, UPHC = urban primary health center.

Source: Asian Development Bank.

Appendixes

Appendix 1
Sample Budget Sheet

[Delete initial setup costs where not applicable]

Budget Item	units	Support Received from National Urban Health Mission (Annual)	Actual Cost (Annual)	Difference (if any)	Shortfall Met Through (if applicable)
A: One-off costs (if applicable; typically at commencement of contract)					
Infrastructure and/or site upgradation					
Equipment					
Other					
Subtotal (A)					
B: Staff					
Medical officer					
Staff nurse					
Pharmacist					
Laboratory technician					
Data assistant and/or accountant					
Support staff					
Part-time specialists (add row per specialist)					
Auxiliary nurse midwives					
Other staff (if applicable; add row per staff)					
Subtotal (B)					
C: Infrastructure					
Rental of premises (if applicable)					
Maintenance of premises (rented or government)					
Biomedical waste management					
IT equipment maintenance					
Subtotal (C)					

Budget Item	units	Support Received from National Urban Health Mission (Annual)	Actual Cost (Annual)	Difference (if any)	Shortfall Met Through (if applicable)
D: Other costs					
Transport and/or Mobility					
Internet connectivity					
Office expenses					
Miscellaneous					
Subtotal (D)					
E: Overhead					
Overhead provided to partner as percentage of total budget (if applicable)					
Subtotal (E)					
Total (A+B+C+D+E)					

Sample Request for Proposal Document (Competitive Bidding)

This request for proposal for competitive bidding template has the following volumes:

Volume I   -   Instructions to Bidders
Volume II   -   Information Memorandum
Volume III -   Terms of Reference
Volume IV   -   Concession Agreement
Volume V   -   Information Memorandum
Volume VI   -   Scope of Work
Volume VII -   Health Center and Draft Concession Agreement

Volume I:
Instructions to Bidders

(This section specifies procedures to be followed by Bidders in preparation and submission of their proposals and provides information on submission, opening, evaluation of proposals and on award of concession.)

Date of release of documents:
Deadline for submission:
Pre-bid meeting - Date and time:
Issuing office:
Name and designation of issuing officer:
Address of correspondence:
Phone:
Fax number:
E-mail:

DISCLAIMER

The information contained in this Request for Proposal document (the "**RFP**") or subsequently provided to Bidder(s), whether verbally or in documentary or any other form by or on behalf of the Authority or any of their employees or advisors, is provided to Bidder(s) on the terms and conditions set out in this RFP and such other terms and conditions subject to which such information is provided. This RFP is not an agreement and is neither an offer nor invitation by the Authority to the prospective Bidders or any other person. The purpose of this RFP is to provide interested parties with information that may be useful to them in making their financial offers pursuant to this RFP (the "**Bid**"). This RFP includes statements, which reflect various assumptions and assessments arrived at by the Authority in relation to the Project. Such assumptions, assessments and statements do not purport to contain all the information that each Bidder may require. The information given is not an exhaustive account of statutory requirements and should not be regarded as a complete or authoritative statement of law. The Authority accepts no responsibility for the accuracy or otherwise for any interpretation or opinion on law expressed herein. The Authority may in its absolute discretion, but without being under any obligation to do so, update, amend or supplement the information, assessment or assumptions contained in this RFP. The issue of this RFP does not imply that the Authority is bound to select a Bidder or to appoint the Selected Bidder or Concessionaire, as the case may be, for the Project and the Authority reserves the right to reject all or any of the Bidders or Bids without assigning any reason whatsoever.

1. Introduction

1.1. Background

1.1.1. The Authority is desirous of implementing certain health care services (the "**Project**") for the [*Particular*] City through private participation and has decided to carry out the bidding process for selection of the bidder to whom the Project may be awarded.

Brief particulars of the Project are as follows:

S.N	Project Name, Site and Area, Components	Indicative Annual Project Cost (in ₹)	Project Coverage

1.1.2. The details of the Terms of Reference are provided in Volumes II and III of this RFP document, which set forth the detailed scope of work for the Selected Bidder.

1.1.3. The Selected Bidder and the Authority will execute a Concession Agreement (**Volume IV of this RFP template**) sets forth the detailed terms and conditions for grant of the concession to the Concessionaire, including the scope of the Concessionaire's services and obligations (the "**Concession**").

1.1.4. The statements and explanations contained in this RFP are intended to provide a proper understanding to the Bidders about the subject matter of this RFP and should not be construed or interpreted as limiting in any way or manner the scope of services and obligations of the Concessionaire set forth in the Concession Agreement.

1.2. Minimum Eligibility Criteria

The minimum qualification required for participating in this Project:

S.N	Particulars
1.	[Must have minimum experience of [_____] years in managing social services.]
2.	[Must have minimum experience of [_____] years in providing, managing, implementing health care services.]
3.	Must have at least done [_____] number of health care projects of value [_____]
4.	Financial [_____]
5.	[_____]
6.	[_____]

1.3. Brief Description of Bidding Process

1.3.1. The Authority has adopted a one-stage process ("**Bidding Process**") for selection of the Bidder for award of the Project.

1.3.2. The Authority will evaluate the Bid, including the Technical and Financial Bid in accordance with the RFP. The preferred Bidder shall be the lowest Bidder. The Bid shall be valid for a period of not less than 120 (One Hundred Twenty) days from the date specified in Clause 1.4 for submission of bids (the "**Bid Due Date**").

1.3.3. The Technical Bid should be furnished in the format in Annex I, clearly indicating the components as per this RFP document and signed by the Bidder's authorized signatory.

1.3.4. The Financial Bid should be furnished in the format in Annex II, clearly indicating the Bid amount in both figures and words, in Indian Rupees (₹), and signed by the Bidder's authorized signatory. In the event of any difference between figures and words, the amount indicated in words shall be taken into account.

1.3.5. The Bidding Documents include the Information Memorandum, Scope of Work, Details related to Health Center and Draft Concession Agreement for the Project are attached as Volume II, Volume III, and Volume IV. The aforesaid documents and any addenda issued subsequent to this RFP Document, but before the Bid Due Date, will be deemed to form part of the Bidding Documents.

1.3.6. Bidders are strongly recommended to examine the Project in greater detail, and to carry out, at their cost, such studies as may be required for submitting their respective Bids for award of the Concession including implementation of the Project. The Authority will not be held responsible for any incorrect decision arrived at by the bidder based on the data provided in this RFP document.

1.3.7. The Bid documents shall consist of:
(a) Formats for technical proposal
(b) Formats for financial offer

1.4. Schedule of Bidding Process

The Authority shall endeavor to adhere to the bidding schedule:

S.N	Event Description	Estimated Date
1.	Submission of query by the perspective applicants	*[Deadline should be at least 1 month after the publication of RFP]*
2.	Pre-bid meeting	
3.	Authority response to queries	
4.	Bid Submission Due Date	
5.	Opening of Bids	
6.	Letter of Intent	
7.	Signing of Concession Agreement	

2. Instructions to Bidders

2.1. General Terms of Bidding

2.1.1. A Bidder is eligible to submit only one Bid for the Project. A Bidder will bid individually and not as a member of a Consortium.

2.1.2. Notwithstanding anything to the contrary contained in this RFP, the detailed terms specified in the draft Concession Agreement shall have overriding effect; provided, however, that any conditions or obligations imposed on the Bidder hereunder shall continue to have effect in addition to its obligations under the Concession Agreement.

2.1.3. A Bidder shall not have a conflict of interest (the "**Conflict of Interest**") that affects the Bidding Process. Any Bidder found to have a Conflict of Interest shall be disqualified. Without limiting the generality of the above, a Bidder shall be considered to have a Conflict of Interest that affects the Bidding Process, if such Bidder (a) has the same legal representative for purposes of this Bid as any other Bidder; or (b) a relationship with another Bidder, directly or through common third parties, that puts them in a position to have access to each other's information about, or to influence the Bid of either or each of the other Bidder.

2.1.4. Any award of concession pursuant to this RFP shall be subject to the terms of Bidding Documents.

2.2. Change in Control

By submitting the Bid, the Bidder shall also be deemed to have acknowledged and agreed that in the management of the (NGO, Trust, society) will not change from those who were taken into consideration for the purposes of shortlisting and pre-qualification under and in accordance with the RFP, the Bidder shall inform the Authority forthwith along with all relevant particulars about the same and the Authority may, in its sole discretion disqualify the Bidder or withdraw the LOA from the Selected Bidder, as the case may be.

2.3. Site Visit and Verification of Information

Prior to submitting the proposal, the Bidder is advised to visit and examine the project site and its surroundings, obtain and ascertain for themselves all technical data, and other information necessary for preparing their proposal (bid) including carrying out necessary technical surveys, field investigations, market and demand assessment (for waste processing), assets condition assessment, etc. at its own cost and risk. Bidders are encouraged to submit their respective Bids after visiting the Project site or area to ascertain the ground situation, coverage, quality of assets or any other matter considered relevant by it. The Bidder shall be deemed to have full knowledge of the site conditions, whether physically inspected or not, if Bidder submits a Proposal for this Project.

[THIS PART IS ONLY APPLICABLE IF THE GOVERNMENT IS PROVIDING THE HEALTH CENTER; IF NOT, THIS PART IS TO BE DELETED]

2.4. Right to Accept and to Reject Any or All Bids

Notwithstanding anything contained in this RFP, the Authority reserves the right to accept or reject any Bid and to annul the Bidding Process and reject all Bids at any time without any liability or any obligation for such acceptance, rejection or annulment, and without assigning any reasons thereof.

2.5. Clarifications

2.5.1. Bidders requiring any clarification on the RFP may notify the Authority in writing or by e-mail and should send in their queries before the date mentioned in the Schedule of Bidding Process specified in Clause 1.4. The Authority shall endeavor to respond to the questions raised or clarifications sought by the Bidders within the specified time therein, but no later than 15 (fifteen) days prior to the Bid Due Date. The responses will be sent by e-mail. The Authority will forward all the queries and its responses thereto, to all Bidders without identifying the source of queries.

2.5.2. The Authority shall endeavor to respond to the questions raised or clarifications sought by the Bidders. However, the Authority reserves the right not to respond to any question or provide any clarification, in its sole discretion, and nothing in this Clause shall be taken or read as compelling or requiring the Authority to respond to any question or to provide any clarification, which will have material adverse effect on the bidding outcome.

2.6. Amendment of RFP

At any time prior to the deadline for submission of Bids, the Authority may, for any reason, whether at its own initiative or in response to clarifications requested by a Bidder, modify the RFP by the issuance of Addenda.

2.7. Format and Signing of Bid

2.7.1. The Bidder shall provide all the information sought under this RFP. The Authority will evaluate only those Bids that are received in the required formats and complete in all respects. Those bids which are not in the required formats will be termed as "non-responsive".

2.7.2. The Bid shall be typed or written in indelible ink and signed by the authorized signatory of the Bidder who shall also initial each page, in blue ink. All the alterations, omissions, additions or any other amendments made to the Bid shall be initialed by the person(s) signing the Bid.

2.8. Sealing and Marking of Bids

The Bidder shall submit 2 (two) copies of the Proposal in separate envelopes marked "Original" and "Copy" respectively. In the event of any discrepancy between the original and the copy, the Original shall prevail.

2.9. Bid Due Date

Bids should be submitted before 1600 hours IST on the Bid Due Date. The Authority may, in its sole discretion, extend the Bid Due Date by issuing an Addendum for all Bidders.

2.10. Late Bids

Bids received by the Authority after the specified time on the Bid Due Date shall not be eligible for consideration and shall be summarily rejected.

2.11. Modifications, Substitution, and Withdrawal of Bids

The Bidders may modify, substitute or withdraw its Bids after submission, provided that written notice of the modification, substitution or withdrawal is received by the Authority prior to Bid Due Date. No Bid shall be modified, substituted or withdrawn by the Bidder after the Bid Due Date.

2.12. Rejection of Bid

The Authority reserves the right to accept or reject all or any of the Bids without assigning any reason whatsoever. It is not obligatory for the Authority to accept any Bid or to give any reasons for their decision. The Authority reserves the right not to proceed with the Bidding Process at any time, without notice or liability, and to reject any Bid without assigning any reasons.

2.13. Validity of Bids

The Bids shall be valid for a period of not less than [120 (One hundred Twenty)] days from the Bid Due Date. The validity of Bids may be extended by mutual consent of the respective Bidders and the Authority.

2.14. Confidentiality

Information relating to the examination, clarification, evaluation and recommendation for the Bidders shall not be disclosed to any person who is not officially concerned with the process or is not a retained professional advisor advising the Authority in relation to or matters arising out of, or concerning the Bidding Process. The Authority will treat all information, submitted as part of the Bid, in confidence and will require all those who have access to such material to treat the same in confidence. The Authority may not divulge any such information unless it is directed to do so by any statutory entity that has the power under law to require its disclosure or is to enforce or assert any right or privilege of the statutory entity and/or the Authority.

2.15. Correspondence with the Bidder

The Authority shall not entertain any correspondence with any Bidder in relation to acceptance or rejection of any Bid; however, to maintain transparency it will publish and/or send the evaluation report to all the Bidders.

3. Evaluation of Bids

3.1. Evaluation

The Authority shall ensure that the rules for the bidding proceedings for the Project are applied in a non-discriminatory, transparent and objective manner. The Authority shall not provide to any Bidder information with regard to the Project or the bidding proceedings, which may have the effect of restricting competition.

3.2. Clarifications

3.2.1. To facilitate evaluation of Proposals the Authority may, at its sole discretion, seek clarifications from any Bidder during the evaluation period. Such clarification(s) shall be provided within the time specified by the Authority for this purpose. Any request for clarification(s) and all clarification(s) shall be in writing. If a Bidder does not provide clarifications sought within the prescribed time, its Proposal shall be liable to be rejected. In case the Proposal is not rejected, the Authority may proceed to evaluate the Proposal by construing the particulars requiring clarification to the best of its understanding, and the Bidder shall be barred from subsequently questioning such interpretation of the Authority.

3.2.2. Bidders are advised that the evaluation of Proposals will be entirely at the discretion of the Authority. Bidders will be deemed to have understood and agreed that no explanation or justification on any aspect of the Bidding Process or selection will be given.

3.3. Proposal Evaluation – Part I – Technical Proposal

3.3.1. **Test of responsiveness**: As part of the evaluation, the Proposals shall first be checked for responsiveness with the requirements of the RFP and only those Proposals that are found to be responsive would be further evaluated in accordance with the criteria set out in this RFP document. The Proposal would be considered to be responsive if it meets the following conditions it is received (a) as per the format; (b) by the Bid Due; (c) signed, sealed, hardbound, and marked; and (d) accompanied with all the information as requested in this RFP and/or Bidding Documents (in formats same as those specified).

3.3.2. **Technical Evaluation of Proposal** - The areas of scrutiny and the basis of marking for the Technical Evaluation are given below:

Sr. No.	Technical Evaluation	Weights
	Total	100

3.3.3. Only Bidders scoring more than [***in general in the range of 60-70***] marks in the Technical Evaluation would qualify for opening of Part II - Financial Offer. Part II – Financial Offer of Bidders not qualifying post evaluation of Part I-Technical Offer would be returned unopened to the Bidders.

3.4. Proposal Evaluation – Part II – Financial Offer

3.4.1. Financial proposal of short-listed Bidders who qualify after evaluation of Part I – Technical Offer shall be opened in the presence of the representatives of shortlisted Bidders, who choose to attend. The Financial Bid of the shortlisted Bidders shall be read out and recorded.

3.4.2. The financial proposals would then be ranked in descending order of the validated financial bid parameter, with the Bidder quoting the [**lowest**] shall be ranked First as [L1] and the Bidder quoting the second lowest Financial Bid Parameter shall be ranked Second as [L2] and so on.

3.4.3. The Bidder ranked "First" in accordance with the above procedure would be declared as the Preferred and/or Selected Bidder.

3.4.4. In the event that two or more Bidders quote exactly the same lowest validated Financial Bid Parameter for the project, then the Authority reserves the right either to, (a) invite fresh Proposals from these Bidders; or (b) take any such measure as may be deemed fit in its sole discretion, including annulment of the bidding process; or (c) identify the selected Bidder by draw of lots, which shall be conducted, with prior notice, in the presence of the tie Bidders who choose to attend.

3.5. Notification and Issue of Letter of Award

The Selected Bidder shall be notified in writing by the Authority as evidenced by issue of Letter of Award (LOA) to the Selected Bidder. The Selected Bidder shall confirm his acceptance of the LOA issued by the Authority within 7 (seven) days as evidenced by signing and sending a copy of the LOA issued.

4. Termination

4.1. Event of Default

In addition to the default and remedies provided in the Concession Agreement, the Authority reserves the right to terminate the Concession entered into with the Selected Bidder under the following circumstances:

4.1.1. If the Selected Bidder fails to initiate the Project, as per the timelines prescribed or, fails to initiate the assignment, even after extension, if any, allowed by the Authority.

4.1.2. The Selected Bidder sells or transfers any proprietary rights or entrust to any other third party for running the proposed Project, the duration for which the Concession has been signed.

4.1.3. If the human resource deployed, by the Selected Bidder is/are found indulging in any criminal activity, illegal, immoral activity or found indulging in action affecting the dignity of women or children including but not limited to direct or indirect harassment, or sexual abuse and misdemeanor. The Selected Bidder shall terminate the concerned employee immediately, or the Concession will be liable for termination.

4.2. Process of Termination

The Authority, reserves the right to terminate the Concession by following processes:

4.2.1. The Authority will issue a show cause notice in writing upon the occurrence of any of the termination event.

4.2.2. The Selected Bidder will have to submit and provide road map and action plan within 10 days of receipt of the notice to the Authority on his proposed plan to ratify such termination event. If the Authority is not satisfied with the road map or the plan, or the Selected Bidder fails to execute and/or initiate the action plan within the stipulated time, the Authority at its sole discretion may terminate the Concession or take such other action as may be deemed appropriate.

5. Fraud and Corrupt Practices

The Bidders and their respective officers, employees, agents and advisers shall observe the highest standard of ethics during the Bidding Process and subsequent to the issue of the LOA and during the subsistence of the Concession Agreement. Notwithstanding anything to the contrary contained herein, or in the LOA or the Concession Agreement, the Authority shall reject a Bid, withdraw the LOA, or terminate the Concession Agreement, as the case may be, without being liable in any manner whatsoever to the Bidder or Concessionaire, as the case may be, if it determines that the Bidder or Concessionaire, as the case may be, has, directly or indirectly or through an agent, engaged in corrupt practice, fraudulent practice, coercive practice, undesirable practice or restrictive practice in the Bidding Process.

6. Pre-Bid Conference

Pre-Bid conferences shall be convened at the designated date, time and place. During the course of Pre-Bid conferences, the Bidders will be free to seek clarifications and make suggestions for considerations of the Authority. The Authority shall endeavor to provide clarifications and such further information as it may, in its sole discretion, consider appropriate for facilitating a fair, transparent and competitive Bidding Process.

7. Miscellaneous

The Bidding Process shall be governed by, and construed in accordance with, the laws of India and the Courts at [____] shall have exclusive jurisdiction over all disputes arising under, pursuant to and/ or in connection with the Bidding Process.

Annex I
Formats for Technical Proposal

[please insert the format of the technical proposal]

Annex II
Formats for Financial Offer

(To be submitted separately on the Letter Head)

Date: [____]
To: [____]
Sub: RFP Reference No. [____] dated [____] for the Project

Dear Sir,

Having gone through this RFP document and the draft Concession Agreement and having fully understood the Scope of Work for the Project as set out by the Authority in the RFP document.

1. I/We are pleased to inform that I/We would charge /or pay the following [____] for carrying out the Project envisaged under the Scope of Work indicated in this RFP document and as set out below:

Project Name	Amount (INR)

2. We confirm that in case of discrepancy in Figures and Words for the Amount Quoted the [Lowest or the amount in words] will be considered.

3. We confirm that the Financial Proposal conforms to all the terms and conditions stipulated in the Request for Proposal (RFP) Document.

4. We confirm that our Financial Proposal is final in all respects and is unconditional.

5. We confirm that, the information submitted in our Financial Proposal is complete and is correct to the best of our knowledge and understanding. We would be solely responsible for any errors or omissions in our Proposal.

6. We confirm that we have studied the provisions of relevant Indian laws and regulations required to enable us to prepare this Financial Proposal and as required for the Project, in the event that we are finally selected.

Thanking you,
For and on behalf of (name of Bidder)
Duly signed by the Authorized signatory of the Bidder

(Name, Designation, and Address of the Authorized Signatory)

Annex III
Letter of Award

[Letter Head of the Authority]
Letter No.:_____   Date: _____
To:
(Name and Address of the Preferred Bidder)

Dear Sir,

Subject: Letter of Award for development of the Project

1. This in reference to your Project proposal submitted by (Name of the firm) in response to the Request for Proposal issued to your firm on ...... (date).

2. Following the submission of your Project proposal, the proposal was considered and evaluated by the bid evaluation and/or tender committee constituted this purpose for the Project.

3. Following this process, the Authority is pleased to inform you that your firm has been selected as the "Successful Bidder" (as per section provisions of the RFP document) for the Project.

4. This letter is intended to convey the Authority acceptance of your proposal. Accordingly, you are hereby requested to acknowledge the receipt of this letter within 7 (seven) days of receipt.

5. The LOA and award of work is subject to the terms and conditions set out in the RFP issued to you and would further be subject to the conditions set out in the Concession Agreement to be executed between the Authority and your firm.

This "Letter of Award" is based on the following conditions:

1. (Bidder Name) shall enter into a Concession Agreement with the Authority at the earliest [to be specified by the Authority], detailing the Terms and Conditions of implementing and managing the Project.

2. [Bidder name] shall be governed by the Terms and Conditions stated in the RFP and Concession Agreement. [Bidder name] shall not attach any condition on any of its obligations as stipulated in the RFP document and Concession Agreement.

3. Kindly be informed that this communication by itself does not create any rights or contractual relationship with the Authority. Any such right or relationship shall come into effect only after the approval of the Authority, furnishing the acceptance of LOA, and the execution of the Concession Agreement. This letter is awarded in duplicate. The duplicate copy of this letter may be signed and returned along with the LOA authorizing the person to sign on behalf of [bidder name], as a token of acceptance of the above terms and conditions.

With best regards,

[The Authority Name and Address]

We confirm that the terms and conditions outlined in this Letter of Award are acceptable to us

Signature:
Name:
Designation:
Date and seal

Volume II:
Information Memorandum

[please insert information memorandum of the Project, i.e., information related to the Project to be provided to the Bidders]

Volume III:
Scope of Work, Details Related to Health Center, and Proposed Fee Structure or Budget

Part 1: Scope of Work

[scope of work should be same as provided in the Concession Agreement]

Part 2: Details Related to Health Center

[- if the health center is provided by the government, then the details of the health center.

- If the health center is not provided by the government then (i) the area in which the health center to be opened by the concessionaire and (ii) requirements of the health center]

Part 3: Proposed Fee Structure or Budget

[include this part if we are providing indicative figure, or else please delete part 3]

Volume IV:
Draft Concession Agreement

[please insert the concession agreement]

Sample Request for Proposal Document (Expression of Interest Selection Process)

This request for proposal for competitive bidding template has the following volumes:

Volume I   –   Instructions to Bidders
Volume II   –   Information Memorandum
Volume III   –   Terms of Reference
Volume IV   –   Concession Agreement
Volume V   –   Information Memorandum
Volume VI   –   Scope of Work
Volume VII   –   Health Center and Draft Concession Agreement

Volume I:
Instructions to Bidders

(This section specifies procedures to be followed by Bidders in preparation and submission of their proposals and provides information on submission, opening, evaluation of proposals and on award of concession.)

Date of release of documents:
Deadline for submission:
Pre-bid meeting - Date and time:
Issuing Office:
Name and designation of issuing officer:
Address of correspondence:
Phone:
Fax number:
E-mail:

DISCLAIMER

The information contained in this Request for Proposal document (the "**RFP**") or subsequently provided to Bidder(s), whether verbally or in documentary or any other form by or on behalf of the Authority or any of their employees or advisors, is provided to Bidder(s) on the terms and conditions set out in this RFP and such other terms and conditions subject to which such information is provided. This RFP is not an agreement and is neither an offer nor invitation by the Authority to the prospective Bidders or any other person. The purpose of this RFP is to provide interested parties with information that may be useful to them in making their financial offers pursuant to this RFP (the "**Bid**"). This RFP includes statements, which reflect various assumptions and assessments arrived at by the Authority in relation to the Project. Such assumptions, assessments and statements do not purport to contain all the information that each Bidder may require. The information given is not an exhaustive account of statutory requirements and should not be regarded as a complete or authoritative statement of law. The Authority accepts no responsibility for the accuracy or otherwise for any interpretation or opinion on law expressed herein. The Authority may in its absolute discretion, but without being under any obligation to do so, update, amend or supplement the information, assessment or assumptions contained in this RFP. The issue of this RFP does not imply that the Authority is bound to select a Bidder or to appoint the Selected Bidder or Concessionaire, as the case may be, for the Project and the Authority reserves the right to reject all or any of the Bidders or Bids without assigning any reason whatsoever.

1. Introduction

1.1. Background

1.1.1. The Authority is desirous of implementing certain health care services (the "**Project**") for the [*Particular*] City through private participation and has decided to carry out the bidding process for selection of the bidder to whom the Project may be awarded.

Brief particulars of the Project are as follows:

S.N	Project Name, Site and Area, Components	Indicative Annual Project Cost (in ₹)	Project Coverage

1.1.2. The details of the Terms of Reference are provided in Volume II and III of this RFP document, which set forth the detailed scope of work for the Selected Bidder.

1.1.3. The Selected Bidder and the Authority will execute a Concession Agreement (**Volume IV of this RFP document**) sets forth the detailed terms and conditions for grant of the concession to the Concessionaire, including the scope of the Concessionaire's services and obligations (the "**Concession**").

1.1.4. The statements and explanations contained in this RFP are intended to provide a proper understanding to the Bidders about the subject matter of this RFP and should not be construed or interpreted as limiting in any way or manner the scope of services and obligations of the Concessionaire set forth in the Concession Agreement.

1.2. Minimum Eligibility Criteria

The minimum qualification required for participating in this Project:

S.N	Particulars
1.	[Must have minimum experience of [_____] years in managing social services.]
2.	[Must have minimum experience of [_____] years in providing, managing, and implementing health care services.]
3.	Must have at least done [_____] number of health care projects of value [_____]
4.	Financial [_____]
5.	[_____]
6.	[_____]

1.3. Brief Description of Bidding Process

1.3.1. The Authority has adopted a one-stage process ("**Bidding Process**") for selection of the Bidder for award of the Project.

1.3.2. The Authority will evaluate the Bid, including the Technical and Financial Bid in accordance with the RFP. The preferred Bidder shall be the lowest Bidder. The Bid shall be valid for a period of not less than 120 (One Hundred Twenty) days from the date specified in Clause 1.4 for submission of bids (the "**Bid Due Date**").

1.3.3. The Technical Bid should be furnished in the format presented in Annex I, clearly indicating the components as per this RFP document and signed by the Bidder's authorized signatory.

1.3.4. The Financial Bid should be furnished in the format presented in Annex II, clearly indicating the Bid amount in both figures and words, in Indian Rupees (₹), and signed by the Bidder's authorized signatory. In the event of any difference between figures and words, the amount indicated in words shall be taken into account.

1.3.5. The Bidding Documents include the Information Memorandum, Scope of Work, Details related to Health Center and Draft Concession Agreement for the Project are attached as Volume II, Volume III, and Volume IV. The aforesaid documents and any addenda issued subsequent to this RFP document, but before the Bid Due Date, will be deemed to form part of the Bidding Documents.

1.3.6. Bidders are strongly recommended to examine the Project in greater detail, and to carry out, at their cost, such studies as may be required for submitting their respective Bids for award of the Concession including implementation of the Project. The Authority will not be held responsible for any incorrect decision arrived at by the bidder based on the data provided in this RFP document.

1.3.7. The Bid documents shall consist of:
(a) Formats for technical proposal

1.4. Schedule of Bidding Process

The Authority shall endeavor to adhere to the bidding schedule:

S.N	Event Description	Estimated Date
1.	Submission of query by the perspective applicants	*[Deadline should be at least 1 month after the publication of RFP]*
2.	Pre-bid meeting	
3.	Authority response to queries	
4.	Bid Submission Due Date	
5.	Opening of Bids	
6.	Letter of Intent	
7.	Signing of Concession Agreement	

2. Instructions to Bidders

2.1. General Terms of Bidding

2.1.1. A Bidder is eligible to submit only one Bid for the Project. A Bidder will bid individually and not as a member of a Consortium.

2.1.2. Notwithstanding anything to the contrary contained in this RFP, the detailed terms specified in the draft Concession Agreement shall have overriding effect; provided, however, that any conditions or obligations imposed on the Bidder hereunder shall continue to have effect in addition to its obligations under the Concession Agreement.

2.1.3. A Bidder shall not have a conflict of interest (the "**Conflict of Interest**") that affects the Bidding Process. Any Bidder found to have a Conflict of Interest shall be disqualified. Without limiting the generality of the above, a Bidder shall be considered to have a Conflict of Interest that affects the Bidding Process, if such Bidder (a) has the same legal representative for purposes of this Bid as any other Bidder; or (b) a relationship with another Bidder, directly or through common third parties, that puts them in a position to have access to each other's information about, or to influence the Bid of either or each of the other Bidder.

2.1.4. Any award of concession pursuant to this RFP shall be subject to the terms of Bidding Documents.

2.2. Change in Control

By submitting the Bid, the Bidder shall also be deemed to have acknowledged and agreed that in the management of the (NGO, Trust, society) will not change from those who were taken into consideration for the purposes of shortlisting and pre-qualification under and in accordance with the RFP, the Bidder shall inform the Authority forthwith along with all relevant particulars about the same and the Authority may, in its sole discretion disqualify the Bidder or withdraw the LOA from the Selected Bidder, as the case may be.

2.3. Site Visit and Verification of Information

Prior to submitting the proposal, the Bidder is advised to visit and examine the project site and its surroundings, obtain and ascertain for themselves all technical data, and other information necessary for preparing their proposal (bid) including carrying out necessary technical surveys, field investigations, market and demand assessment (for waste processing), assets condition assessment, etc. at its own cost and risk. Bidders are encouraged to submit their respective Bids after visiting the Project site or area to ascertain the ground situation, coverage, quality of assets or any other matter considered relevant by it. The Bidder shall be deemed to have full knowledge of the site conditions, whether physically inspected or not, if Bidder submits a Proposal for this Project.

[THIS PART IS ONLY APPLICABLE IF THE GOVERNMENT IS PROVIDING THE HEALTH CENTER; IF NOT, THIS PART IS TO BE DELETED]

2.4. Right to Accept and to Reject Any or All Bids

Notwithstanding anything contained in this RFP, the Authority reserves the right to accept or reject any Bid and to annul the Bidding Process and reject all Bids at any time without any liability or any obligation for such acceptance, rejection or annulment, and without assigning any reasons thereof.

2.5. Clarifications

2.5.1. Bidders requiring any clarification on the RFP may notify the Authority in writing or by e-mail and should send in their queries before the date mentioned in the Schedule of Bidding Process specified in Clause 1.4. The Authority shall endeavor to respond to the questions raised or clarifications sought by the Bidders within the specified time therein, but no later than 15 (fifteen) days prior to the Bid Due Date. The responses will be sent by e-mail. The Authority will forward all the queries and its responses thereto, to all Bidders without identifying the source of queries.

2.5.2. The Authority shall endeavor to respond to the questions raised or clarifications sought by the Bidders. However, the Authority reserves the right not to respond to any question or provide any clarification, in its sole discretion, and nothing in this Clause shall be taken or read as compelling or requiring the Authority to respond to any question or to provide any clarification that will have material adverse effect on the bidding outcome.

2.6. Amendment of RFP

At any time prior to the deadline for submission of Bids, the Authority may, for any reason, whether at its own initiative or in response to clarifications requested by a Bidder, modify the RFP by the issuance of Addenda.

2.7. Format and Signing of Bid

2.7.1. The Bidder shall provide all the information sought under this RFP. The Authority will evaluate only those Bids that are received in the required formats and complete in all respects. Those bids that are not in the required formats will be termed as "non-responsive".

2.7.2. The Bid shall be typed or written in indelible ink and signed by the authorized signatory of the Bidder who shall also initial each page, in blue ink. All the alterations, omissions, additions or any other amendments made to the Bid shall be initialed by the person(s) signing the Bid.

2.8. Sealing and Marking of Bids

The Bidder shall submit 2 (two) copies of the Proposal in separate envelopes marked "Original" and "Copy", respectively. In the event of any discrepancy between the original and the copy, the Original shall prevail.

2.9. Bid Due Date

Bids should be submitted before 1600 hours IST on the Bid Due Date. The Authority may, in its sole discretion, extend the Bid Due Date by issuing an Addendum for all Bidders.

2.10. Late Bids

Bids received by the Authority after the specified time on the Bid Due Date shall not be eligible for consideration and shall be summarily rejected.

2.11. Modifications, Substitution, and Withdrawal of Bids

The Bidders may modify, substitute or withdraw its Bids after submission, provided that written notice of the modification, substitution or withdrawal is received by the Authority prior to Bid Due Date. No Bid shall be modified, substituted or withdrawn by the Bidder after the Bid Due Date.

2.12. Rejection of Bid

The Authority reserves the right to accept or reject all or any of the Bids without assigning any reason whatsoever. It is not obligatory for the Authority to accept any Bid or to give any reasons for their decision. The Authority reserves the right not to proceed with the Bidding Process at any time, without notice or liability, and to reject any Bid without assigning any reasons.

2.13. Validity of Bids

The Bids shall be valid for a period of not less than [120 (One hundred Twenty)] days from the Bid Due Date. The validity of Bids may be extended by mutual consent of the respective Bidders and the Authority.

2.14. Confidentiality

Information relating to the examination, clarification, evaluation and recommendation for the Bidders shall not be disclosed to any person who is not officially concerned with the process or is not a retained professional advisor advising the Authority in relation to or matters arising out of, or concerning the Bidding Process. The Authority will treat all information, submitted as part of the Bid, in confidence and will require all those who have access to such material to treat the same in confidence. The Authority may not divulge any such information unless it is directed to do so by any statutory entity that has the power under law to require its disclosure or is to enforce or assert any right or privilege of the statutory entity and/or the Authority.

2.15. Correspondence with the Bidder

The Authority shall not entertain any correspondence with any Bidder in relation to acceptance or rejection of any Bid; however, to maintain transparency it will publish or send the evaluation report to all the Bidders.

3. Evaluation of Bids

3.1. Evaluation

The Authority shall ensure that the rules for the bidding proceedings for the Project are applied in a non-discriminatory, transparent and objective manner. The Authority shall not provide to any Bidder information with regard to the Project or the bidding proceedings, which may have the effect of restricting competition.

3.2. Clarifications

3.2.1. To facilitate evaluation of Proposals the Authority may, at its sole discretion, seek clarifications from any Bidder during the evaluation period. Such clarification(s) shall be provided within the time specified by the Authority for this purpose. Any request for clarification(s) and all clarification(s) shall be in writing. If a Bidder does not provide clarifications sought within the prescribed time, its Proposal shall be liable to be rejected. In case the Proposal is not rejected, the Authority may proceed to evaluate the Proposal by construing the particulars requiring clarification to the best of its understanding, and the Bidder shall be barred from subsequently questioning such interpretation of the Authority.

3.2.2. Bidders are advised that the evaluation of Proposals will be entirely at the discretion of the Authority. Bidders will be deemed to have understood and agreed that no explanation or justification on any aspect of the Bidding Process or selection will be given.

3.3. Proposal Evaluation – Part I – Technical Proposal

3.3.1. **Test of responsiveness**: As part of the evaluation, the Proposals shall first be checked for responsiveness with the requirements of the RFP and only those Proposals that are found to be responsive would be further evaluated in accordance with the criteria set out in this RFP document. The Proposal would be considered to be responsive if it meets the following conditions it is received (a) as per the format; (b) by the Bid Due (c) signed, sealed, hardbound, and marked; and (d) accompanied with all the information as requested in this RFP and/or Bidding Documents (in formats same as those specified).

3.3.2. **Technical Evaluation of Proposal** - The areas of scrutiny and the basis of marking for the Technical Evaluation are given below:

Sr. No.	Technical Evaluation	Weights
	Total	100

3.3.3. The Bidders scoring highest score in the Technical Evaluation would be the preferred or Selected Bidder.

3.4. Notification and Issue of Letter of Award

The Selected Bidder shall be notified in writing by the Authority as evidenced by issue of Letter of Award (LOA) to the Selected Bidder. The Selected Bidder shall confirm his acceptance of the LOA issued by the Authority within 7 (seven) days as evidenced by signing and sending a copy of the LOA issued.

4. Termination

4.1. Event of Default

In addition to the default and remedies provided in the Concession Agreement, the Authority reserves the right to terminate the Concession entered into with the Selected Bidder under the following circumstances:

4.1.1.   If the Selected Bidder fails to initiate the Project, as per the timelines prescribed or, fails to initiate the assignment, even after extension, if any, allowed by the Authority.

4.1.2.   The Selected Bidder sells or transfers any proprietary rights or entrust to any other third party for running the proposed Project, the duration for which the Concession has been signed.

4.1.3.   If the human resource(s) deployed, by the Selected Bidder is or are found indulging in any criminal activity, illegal, immoral activity or found indulging in action affecting the dignity of women or children including but not limited to direct or indirect harassment, or sexual abuse and misdemeanor. The Selected Bidder shall terminate the concerned employee immediately, or the Concession will be liable for termination.

4.2. Process of Termination

The Authority, reserves the right to terminate the Concession by following processes:

4.2.1.   The Authority will issue a show cause notice in writing upon the occurrence of any of the termination event.

4.2.2.   The Selected Bidder will have to submit and provide road map and action plan within 10 days of receipt of the notice to the Authority on his proposed plan to ratify such termination event. If the Authority is not satisfied with the road map or the plan, or the Selected Bidder fails to execute and/or initiate the action plan within the stipulated time, the Authority at its sole discretion may terminate the Concession or take such other action as may be deemed appropriate.

5. Fraud and Corrupt Practices

The Bidders and their respective officers, employees, agents and advisers shall observe the highest standard of ethics during the Bidding Process and subsequent to the issue of the LOA and during the subsistence of the Concession Agreement. Notwithstanding anything to the contrary contained herein, or in the LOA or the Concession Agreement, the Authority shall reject a Bid, withdraw the LOA, or terminate the Concession Agreement, as the case may be, without being liable in any manner whatsoever to the Bidder or Concessionaire, as the case may be, if it determines that the Bidder or Concessionaire, as the case may be, has, directly or indirectly or through an agent, engaged in corrupt practice, fraudulent practice, coercive practice, undesirable practice or restrictive practice in the Bidding Process.

6. Pre-Bid Conference

Pre-Bid conferences shall be convened at the designated date, time, and place. During the course of Pre-Bid conferences, the Bidders will be free to seek clarifications and make suggestions for considerations of the Authority. The Authority shall endeavor to provide clarifications and such further information as it may, in its sole discretion, consider appropriate for facilitating a fair, transparent, and competitive Bidding Process.

7. Miscellaneous

The Bidding Process shall be governed by, and construed in accordance with, the laws of India and the Courts at [_____] shall have exclusive jurisdiction over all disputes arising under, pursuant to and/ or in connection with the Bidding Process.

Annex I
Formats for Technical Proposal

[please insert the format of the technical proposal]

Annex II
Letter of Award

[Letter Head of the Authority]
Letter No.:_____   Date: _____
To:
(Name and Address of the Preferred Bidder)

Dear Sir,

Subject: Letter of Award for development of the Project

1.   This in reference to your Project proposal submitted by (Name of the firm) in response to the Request for Proposal issued to your firm on ...... (date).

2.   Following the submission of your Project proposal, the proposal was considered and evaluated by the bid evaluation and/or tender committee constituted this purpose for the Project.

3.   Following this process, the Authority is pleased to inform you that your firm has been selected as the "Successful Bidder" (as per section provisions of the RFP document) for the Project.

4.   This letter is intended to convey the Authority acceptance of your proposal. Accordingly, you are hereby requested to acknowledge the receipt of this letter within 7 (seven) days of receipt.

5.   The LOA and award of work is subject to the terms and conditions set out in the RFP issued to you and would further be subject to the conditions set out in the Concession Agreement to be executed between the Authority and your firm.

This "Letter of Award" is based on the following conditions:

1. (Bidder name) shall enter into a Concession Agreement with the Authority at the earliest [to be specified by the Authority], detailing the Terms and Conditions of implementing and managing the Project.

2. [Bidder name] shall be governed by the Terms and Conditions stated in the RFP and Concession Agreement. [Bidder name] shall not attach any condition on any of its obligations as stipulated in the RFP document and Concession Agreement.

3. Kindly be informed that this communication by itself does not create any rights or contractual relationship with the Authority. Any such right or relationship shall come into effect only after the approval of the Authority, furnishing the acceptance of LOA, and the execution of the Concession Agreement. This letter is awarded in duplicate. The duplicate copy of this letter may be signed and returned along with the LOA authorizing the person to sign on behalf of [bidder name], as a token of acceptance of the above terms and conditions.

With best regards,

[The Authority Name and Address]

We confirm that the terms and conditions outlined in this Letter of Award are acceptable to us

_____

Signature:
Name:
Designation:
Date and seal

Volume II:
Information Memorandum

[please insert information memorandum of the Project, i.e., information related to the Project to be

Volume III:
Scope of Work, Details Related to Health Center, and Proposed Fee Structure or Budget

Part 1: Scope of Work

[scope of work should be same as provided in the Concession Agreement]

Part 2: Details Related to Health Center

[- if the health center is provided by the government, then the details of the health center.

- If the health center is not provided by the government then (i) the area in which the health center to be opened by the concessionaire and (ii) requirements of the health center]

Part 3: Proposed Fee Structure or Budget

Volume IV:
Request for Proposal Document Draft Concession Agreement

[please insert the concession agreement]

Sample Concession Agreement (Government-Owned Urban Primary Health Center)

CONCESSION AGREEMENT

FOR

URBAN PRIMARY HEALTH CENTER PUBLIC-PRIVATE PARTNERSHIP PROJECTS

(WITH HEALTH CENTER)

Between

Department of [_____]

And

[_____]

Concessionaire

For

Public–Private Partnership for Urban Primary Health Center in

[_____]

[We understand that (i) this concession agreement will be used to execute or implement multiple low value health care project (less than Rs. 50 lacs), and (ii) the service provider will mostly be an NGO with limited access to legal advice. In light of this, we have kept the agreement as simple and short as possible.]

URBAN PRIMARY HEALTH CENTER PUBLIC-PRIVATE PARTNERSHIP CONCESSION AGREEMENT (WITH HEALTH CENTER)

This agreement is entered into on this [__] day of [__], 2020 at [_____] ("**Agreement**"):

BETWEEN

1.   [_____], represented by [_____] and having its principal office at [_____] (hereinafter referred to as the "Authority" which expression shall, unless repugnant to the context or meaning thereof, include its administrators, successors and assigns);

AND

2.   [please insert name of the NGO], is a section 8 company, incorporated under the provisions of Companies Act, 2013 and having its registered office at [__] (hereinafter referred to as the "Concessionaire" which expression shall, unless repugnant to the context or meaning thereof, include its successors and permitted assigns and substitutes).

Or

2.   [please insert name of the Trust], is a trust created by a trust deed dated [____], having its office at [·] (hereinafter referred to as the "Concessionaire" which expression shall, unless repugnant to the context or meaning thereof, include its successors and permitted assigns and substitutes).

Or

2.   [please insert name of the Society], is society created under the Societies Registration Act, 1860, having its office at [____] (hereinafter referred to as the "Concessionaire" which expression shall, unless repugnant to the context or meaning thereof, include its successors and permitted assigns and substitutes).]

"**Authority**" and "**Concessionaire**" will be referred to individually as the "**Party**" and collectively as the "**Parties**".

[Comment: We have been given to understand that the Concessionaire will be an NGO/TRUST/SOCIETY, and they will be executing the project directly and not through a separate legal entity.]

WHEREAS:

A.   The Government of India has launched National Urban Health Mission ("NUHM") for providing primary health care services to the urban population with special focus on slum and other vulnerable sections of the society. As a part of NUHM, the Government of [____] ("State Government") has decided to establish and/or upgrade urban primary health centers ("UPHCs") in the State through private sector participation.

B.   The Authority had accordingly invited bids through its Request for Proposal No. [_____] dated [_____] ("**RFP**") for the selection of an entity for the operation and maintenance of the UPHCs in accordance with the terms and conditions of this Agreement ("Project").

C.   After evaluation of the bids received, the Authority accepted the [bid or EOI] of the Concessionaire in accordance with the terms of the RFP and issued the Letter of Acceptance No. [_____] dated [_____] ("**LOA**") requiring, *inter alia*, the execution of this Agreement within 30 (thirty) days of the date of the issue of LOA.

D.   The Authority is accordingly entering into this Agreement with the Concessionaire for implementation of the Project, subject to and on the terms and conditions as set forth hereinafter.

NOW, THEREFORE, in consideration of the foregoing and the respective covenants and agreements set forth in this Agreement, the receipt and sufficiency of which is hereby acknowledged, and intending to be legally bound hereby, the Parties agree as follows:

1.   Definitions and Interpretation

1.1.   Definitions

The following words and expressions shall, unless the context otherwise requires, have the following meanings:

1.1.1.   "**Authority Inspection Report**" will have the meaning as provided in Clause 12.2.

1.1.2.   "**Additional Service**s" will have the meaning as provided in Clause 2.5 and Schedule 1.

1.1.3.   "**Authority Services**" will have the meaning as provided in Schedule 3.

1.1.4.   "**Award**" will have the meaning as provided in Clause 19.3.3.

1.1.5.   "**Confidential Information**" will have the meaning as provided in Clause 13.1.1.

1.1.6.   "**Conditions Precedent**" will have the meaning as provided in Clause 3.1.

1.1.7.   "**CP Satisfaction Date**" will have the meaning as provided in Clause 3.2.

1.1.8.   "**CP Satisfaction Notice**" will have the meaning as provided in Clause 3.3.

1.1.9.   "**Concession Period**" will have the meaning as provided in Clause 2.3.

1.1.10.   "**Dispute**" will have the meaning as provided in Clause 19.1.1.

1.1.11. **"Documents for Payment"** will have the meaning as provided in Schedule 4.

1.1.12. **"Effective Date"** will have the meaning as provided in Clause 3.4.

1.1.13. **"Extended CP Satisfaction Date"** will have the meaning as provided in Clause 3.5.
[This definition will only be incorporated in the Agreement when Health Center does require fixing or upgradation.]

1.1.14. **"Failure Notice"** will have the meaning as provided in Clause 3.5.
[This definition will only be incorporated in the Agreement when the Health Center requires fixing or upgradation.]

1.1.15. **"Force Majeure"** will have the meaning as provided in Clause 16.1.1.

1.1.16. **"Good Industry Practice"** means the practices, methods, techniques, designs, standards, skills, diligence, efficiency, reliability, and prudence, which are generally and reasonably expected from a reasonably skilled and experienced operator engaged in the same type of undertaking as envisaged under this Agreement and which would be expected to result in the performance of its obligations by the Concessionaire in accordance with this Agreement and applicable laws in reliable, safe, economical and efficient manner.

1.1.17. **"Government Instrumentality"** means any department, division or sub-division of the Government of India or the State Government and includes any commission, board, authority, agency or municipal and other local authority or statutory body including Panchayat under the control of the Government of India or the State Government, as the case may be, and having jurisdiction over all or any part of the Project or the performance of all or any of the Services or obligations of the Concessionaire under or pursuant to this Agreement.

1.1.18. **"Handover Date"** will have the meaning as provided in Clause 3.1.
[This definition will only be incorporated in the Agreement when the Health Center requires fixing or upgradation.]

1.1.19. **"Health Center"** will have the meaning as provided in Schedule 2.

1.1.20. **"Indemnified Part**y" will have the meaning as provided in Clause 18.2.

1.1.21. **"Indemnifying Party"** will have the meaning as provided in Clause 18.2.

1.1.22. **"KPIs"** will have the meaning as provided in Clause 7 and Schedule 5.

1.1.23. **"LOA"** will have the meaning as provided in Recital C.

1.1.24. **"Nominated Person"** will have the meaning as provided in Clause 3.1.3.

1.1.25. "**NUHM**" will have the meaning provided in Recital A.

1.1.26. "**Personal Data**" will have the meaning as provided in Clause 13.2.2.

1.1.27. "**Project**" will have the meaning as provided in Recital B.

1.1.28. "**RFP**" will have the meaning as provided in Recital B.

1.1.29. "**Rules**" will have the meaning as provided in Clause 19.3.1.

1.1.30. "**Services**" will have the meaning as provided in Schedule 1.

1.1.31. "**Service Fees**" will have the meaning as provided in Clause 6.1 and Schedule 4.

1.1.32. "**Signing Date**" will mean the date of execution of this Agreement.

1.1.33. "**State Government**" will have the meaning as provided in Recital A.

1.1.34. "**Third-Party Inspection**" will have the meaning as provided in Clause 12.3.

1.1.35. "**UPHCs**" will have the meaning as provided in Recital A.

1.2. Interpretation

In this Agreement, unless the context specifies otherwise:

1.2.1. headings are used for convenience only and shall not affect the interpretation of this Agreement;

1.2.2. reference to the singular includes a reference to the plural and vice versa, and reference to any gender includes a reference to all other genders;

1.2.3. references to the Recitals, Clauses and Schedules shall deemed to be a reference to the recitals, clauses and schedules of this Agreement;

1.2.4. the expression "this Clause" shall, unless followed by reference to a specific provision, be deemed to refer respectively to the whole Clause, not merely the sub-clause, paragraph or other provision in which the expression occurs;

1.2.5. references to any enactment are to be construed as referring also to any amendment or re-enactment (whether before or after the date of this Agreement), any previous enactment, which such enactment has replaced (with or without amendment) and to any regulation or order made under it;

1.2.6. references to "include" and "including" shall be construed without limitation.

2. Scope of the Project

Primary Scope of Work

2.1. Subject to the terms and conditions of this Concession Agreement, the Authority grants to the Concessionaire the exclusive right during the Concession Period to (i) provide the Services identified in Schedule 1 (**Services**); and (ii) collect the Service Fees from the Authority, all in accordance with the terms and conditions of this Agreement.

2.2. The Health Center and assets to be handed over to the Concessionaire are identified in Schedule 2 (**Health Center**).

2.3. This Agreement will become effective on the Signing Date and will continue for a period of [____] months or years from the Effective Date ("**Concession Period**"), unless otherwise extended or terminated in accordance with this Agreement.

2.4. This Agreement may be extended by the Authority for a further period of [___] months or years if the Concessionaire achieves an average minimum KPI score of [X] during the initial Concession Period.

Variation to the Scope of Work

2.5. If the Concessionaire is required to provide any service in addition to the Services identified in Schedule 1 (**Services**) ("**Additional Service**"), then the Parties will mutually agree on fees for such Additional Service before commencement of the Additional Service by the Concessionaire. If the Parties are unable to mutually agree on the scope of the Additional Service to be provided by the Concessionaire and/or the fees associated with the Additional Service, then the Concessionaire will not be required to provide the Additional Service, and the Parties will continue to fulfil its obligations under this Agreement.

3. Handover of the Health Center

Applicable where Health Center Does Not Require Fixing/Upgradation

3.1. [The Concessionaire is required to fulfil the following obligations (as these are required for operation of the Health Center) before handover of the Health Center by the Authority to the Concessionaire ("**Conditions Precedent**"):

3.1.1. Obtain all consents and approvals required for providing the Services;

3.1.2. Appoint consultants, employees and doctors for providing the Services;

3.1.3. The Concessionaire will nominate 1 person as its point of contact for co-ordinating with the Authority ("**Nominated Person**");

3.1.4. *[please incorporate any other conditions that the private party will be required to fulfil before the Health Center will be handed over to the private party]*

3.2. The Conditions Precedent are to be fulfilled by the Concessionaire within [30] of the Signing Date ("**CP Satisfaction Date**").

3.3. Upon fulfilling the Conditions Precedent, the Concessionaire will inform the Authority by written notice that it has fulfilled the Conditions Precedent ("**CP Satisfaction Notice**").

3.4. Upon receiving the above notice and being satisfied that the Concessionaire has fulfilled the Conditions Precedent, the Authority, within [30] days of receipt of CP Satisfaction Notice, will hand over the Health Center to the Concessionaire. The Concessionaire will commence providing the Services from the date of handover of the Health Center by the Authority to the Concessionaire ("**Effective Date**").

3.5. If the condition precedents are not fulfilled by the Concessionaire by the CP Satisfaction Date, then the Authority at its discretion, at the request of the Concessionaire, may extend the CP Satisfaction Date by [30] days ("**Extended CP Satisfaction Date**").

3.6. If the Concessionaire is unable to fulfil its obligations within the CP Satisfaction Date or the Extended CP Satisfaction Date, as the case may be, then the Authority will be entitled to terminate this Agreement.

3.7. If the Authority is unable to hand over the Health Center to the Concessionaire within [30] days of the issuance of the CP Satisfaction Notice by the Concessionaire, then the Authority will be given additional [30] days to hand over the Health Center to the Concessionaire. If the Authority fails to hand over the Health Center after the extended handover period, then Concessionaire will be entitled to terminate this Agreement.

Or

Applicable where Health Center Requires Fixing/Upgradation

3.1 [Within [15] days of the Signing Date, the Authority will (i) hand over the Health Center to the Concessionaire, and (ii) pay to the Concessionaire the Upgradation Fees ("**Handover Date**"). Handover Date will be the date when both the above obligations are fulfilled by the Authority. The Concessionaire will fulfil the following obligations ("**Conditions Precedent**"):

  3.1.1 Obtain all consents and approvals required for providing the Services;

  3.1.2 Appoint consultants, employees and doctors for providing the Services;

  3.1.3 The Concessionaire will nominate 1 person as its point of contact for coordinating with the Authority ("**Nominated Person**");

  3.1.4 Fix or upgrade the Health Center in accordance with Schedule 2 (**Health Center**).

  3.1.5 *[please incorporate any other conditions that the private party will be required to fulfil before the Health Center will be handed over to the private party]*

3.2 The Conditions Precedent are to be fulfilled by the Concessionaire within [30] of the Handover Date ("**CP Satisfaction Date**").

3.3 Upon fulfilling the Conditions Precedent, the Concessionaire will inform the Authority by written notice that it has fulfilled the Conditions Precedent ("**CP Satisfaction Notice**").

3.4 Within [15] days of receiving the CP Satisfaction Notice, (i) the Authority will inspect and confirm (if the Authority is satisfied that the Conditions Precedent have been fulfilled) that the Conditions Precedent have been fulfilled, or (ii) if the Authority fails to convey to the Concessionaire within the aforesaid period either fulfilment or failure to fulfil the Conditions Precedent, then it will be deemed that the Concessionaire has fulfilled the Conditions Precedent. On the date of either of the above event, the Concessionaire will commence providing the Services at the Health Center in accordance with this Agreement ("**Effective Date**").

3.5 If within the period provided in Clause 3.4 above, the Authority identifies that the Concessionaire has failed fulfil the Conditions Precedent, then the Authority will provide a written notice to the Concessionaire identifying the failures ("**Failure Notice**"). Upon receiving the Failure Notice, the Concessionaire will rectify the failures identified by the Authority within a period of [15] days and give notice to the Authority as provided in Clause 3.3 above and the procedure provided in Clause 3.4 will be followed. Every time a Failure Notice is issued by the Authority, the process provided in Clause 3.3, 3.4, and 3.5 above will be followed.

3.6 If the Concessionaire fails to achieve Effective Date within a period of [90] of the Handover Date, then the Authority will be entitled to termination this Agreement and claim refund of the Upgradation Fees.

3.7 If the Authority is unable to hand over the Health Center to the Concessionaire within [15] days of the Signing Date, then the Authority will be given additional [15] days to hand over the Health Center to the Concessionaire. If the Authority fails to hand over the Health Center after the extended handover period, then then Concessionaire will be entitled to terminate this Agreement.]

4. Roles and Responsibilities of the Concessionaire

4.1 The Concessionaire will provide the Services during the Concession Period in accordance with the terms of this Agreement. Without prejudice to the generality of the foregoing, the Concessionaire

4.1.1 will obtain and maintain all consents and approvals necessary for providing the Services;

4.1.2 comply with the provisions of this Agreement, applicable laws and conform to Good Industry Practice for securing the safety and hygiene of the patients, visitors and staff;

4.1.3   ensure that the Nominated Person will report, attend meetings and provide all reasonable information as required by the district medical officer from time to time;

4.1.4   pay all taxes and duties applicable by the Concessionaire under the applicable laws;

4.1.5   ensure that the Health Center is in good working condition at all times in accordance with the provisions of this Agreement including, without any limitation, at the time of handing over to the Authority.

5.   Role and Responsibilities of the Authority

5.1   The Authority will provide the services as identified in Schedule 3 (**Authority Services**) during the Concession Period.

5.2   The Authority agrees to provide support to the Concessionaire and undertakes to observe, comply with and perform, subject to and in accordance with the provisions of this Agreement, the following:

5.2.1   upon written request from the Concessionaire, and subject to the Concessionaire complying with applicable laws, provide reasonable support and assistance to the Concessionaire in procuring applicable permits required from any Government Instrumentality for implementation of the Project;

5.2.2   upon written request from the Concessionaire, provide reasonable assistance to the Concessionaire in obtaining access to all necessary infrastructure facilities and utilities, including water and electricity at rates and on terms no less favorable to the Concessionaire than those generally available to public hospitals and such other facilities receiving substantially equivalent services;

5.2.3   assist the Concessionaire in procuring police assistance for dealing with medico-legal cases that are brought to the Health Center, if any;

5.2.4   hand over the Health Center to the Concessionaire in accordance with Clause 3, Clause 9, and Clause 10;

5.2.5   will extend the training provided under the NUHM to the employees and consultants of the Concessionaire engaged in providing the Services in the Health Center;

5.2.6   make all payments to the Concessionaire in the manner and within the time period specified in this Agreement.

6. Payments

6.1 For the Services to be performed by the Concessionaire under this Agreement, the Authority will pay to the Concessionaire the Service Fees in accordance with Schedule 4 ("**Service Fees and Documents for Payment**").

6.2 On the Effective Date, the Authority will pay to the Concessionaire in advance the estimated Service Fees for the Services to be provided by the Concessionaire in the coming quarter. The Service Fees will be paid by the Authority on the Effective Date and on each quarter thereafter until the expiry or termination of the Agreement.

6.3 The Concessionaire will provide to the Authority between [30] day and [15] days before each quarter (i) an invoice for the Service Fees for the following quarter (which will also include adjustment of any unutilized fees from the previous quarter or any excess spend by the Concessionaire) based on Schedule 4 (**Service Fees and Documents for Payments**), and (ii) the documents listed in Schedule 4 (**Service Fees and Documents for Payments**).

6.4 Within [15] days of receipt of the documents by the Authority as identified in Clause 6.3 above, the Authority will pay the Service Fees for the following year to the Concessionaire.

7. Key Performance Indicators

7.1 Without prejudice to the obligations specified in this Agreement, the Concessionaire will operate the Health Center and provide the Services such that it meets the key performance indicators provide In Schedule 5 ("**KPIs**").

7.2 The Concessionaire will during the Concession Period, furnish to the Authority, a report, setting out the details provided in Clause 7.3, no later than 7 (seven) days after the close of each quarter of providing the Services.

7.3 The report specified in Clause 7.2 will state in reasonable detail the compliance with all the KPIs specified in Schedule 5 (**KPIs**) along with an analysis of the reasons for failures, if any, and the strategies for addressing the same and for otherwise improving the performance of the Health Center.

7.4 The Concessionaire will ensure compliance of each of the KPIs specified in Schedule 5 (**KPIs**) and for any shortfall in performance, it will pay damages within 30 (thirty) days of every quarter in which the shortfall occurred. The damages due and payable under this Clause 7.4 will be determined in accordance with Schedule 5 (**KPIs**).

7.5 If the Concessionaire fails to achieve KPI scope of [X] for two consecutive quarters, then the Authority will be entitled to terminate this Agreement.

8. Grievance Redressal Policy

Unless a Grievance Redressal Policy is provided by the Authority, the Concessionaire will monitor and address any issues or complaints regarding quality of services, denial of services, staff behaviour, etc. with respect to the patients in accordance with the principles related to Grievance Redressal Policy provided in Schedule 6 (**Salient Feature of Grievance Redressal Policy**).

9. Right of Way

9.1   The Health Center will comprise of the real estate and assets described in Schedule 2 (**Health Center**) and in respect of which the right of way and license will be granted by the Authority to the Concessionaire in accordance with this Agreement.

9.2   Subject to Clause 3, the Authority grants to the Concessionaire access and license to the Health Center for providing the Services during the Concession Period.

9.3   It is expressly agreed that the license granted to the Concessionaire in relation to the Health Center (including assets provided by the Authority and/or any asset added or infrastructure upgraded by the Concessionaire) will terminate and revert to the Authority automatically without the need for any action to be taken by the Authority to terminate the license, upon the termination or expiry of this Agreement for any reason whatsoever.

9.4   Within [5] days of the Signing Date, the Authority and the Concessionaire will, on a mutually agreed date and time, inspect the Health Center (including assets) and prepare a memorandum containing an inventory of the Health Center including the vacant and unencumbered land, buildings, structures, road works, trees, any other immovable property on or attached to the Health Center, movable assets, equipment, machinery. Such memorandum will specify in reasonable detail those parts of the Health Center (including assets) to which license is granted to the Concessionaire. Signing of the memorandum by the authorized representatives of the Parties will be deemed to constitute a valid license to the Concessionaire for the use of the Health Center (including assets) during the Concession Period in accordance with the provisions of this Agreement.

9.5   On and after signing the memorandum referred to in Clause 9.4 above, and until handover of the Health Center (including assets provided by the Authority and/or any asset added or infrastructure upgraded by the Concessionaire), the Concessionaire will maintain a round-the-clock vigil over the Health Center and will ensure that no encroachment and destruction takes place, and in the event of any encroachment, occupation or destruction of any part of the Health Center (including assets provided by the Authority and/or any asset added or infrastructure upgraded by the Concessionaire), the Concessionaire will report such encroachment, occupation or destruction forthwith to the Authority.

10. Management of Assets

10.1 Immovable Assets

10.1.1 The Concessionaire will be responsible for maintaining the Health Center in accordance with Clause 4.

10.1.2 The Authority will be responsible for any capital expenditure that may be required for the maintenance of the immovable assets in the Health Center.

10.2 Movable Assets

10.2.1 Save and except any movable assets identified in Schedule 3 (**Authority Services**), all the other movable assets required for providing the Services will be provided by the Concessionaire.

10.2.2 Any movable asset provided by the Authority will be operated and maintained by the Concessionaire is accordance with the Good Industry Practice.

11. Subcontract

The Concessionaire will not assign or sub-contract any of its rights or obligations under this Agreement without the prior written consent of the Authority.

12. Information Obligation in Relation to Operation of UPHC

12.1 During Concession Period, the Concessionaire will, no later than 7 (seven) days after the close of each month, furnish to the Authority, a monthly report in a form acceptable to the Authority, stating in reasonable detail the information identified in Schedule 7 ("**Monthly Report**").

12.2 The Authority will have right to inspect the Health Centers from time to time. The Authority will make a report of such inspection ("**Authority Inspection Report**") stating in reasonable detail the defects or deficiencies, if any, in relation to the Services, and send a copy thereof to the Concessionaire. The Concessionaire will rectify the defects or deficiencies, if any, set forth in the Authority Inspection Report, and furnish a report to the Authority within 15 days of the aforesaid reports.

12.3 The Authority may, once in each year, appoint an independent third party to conduct independent inspection of the Services provided by the Concessionaire ("**Third-Party Inspection**"). The Concessionaire will provide all reasonable assistance and access to the Health Center to third party for the Third-Party Inspection.

13. Confidentiality and Data Protection

13.1 Confidentiality

13.1.1 Each Party will maintain in strict confidence and protect the confidentiality of all information, reports, data, software or other material, whether written or oral, in electronic or magnetic format, and the contents thereof and any reports, digests or summaries created or derived from any of the foregoing that is provided by one Party to the other Party in relation to this Agreement ("**Confidential Information**"), and will not disclose any such Confidential Information to any third party without the prior written consent of the other Party; provided that each Party will be entitled to use Confidential Information for any and all lawful purposes.

13.1.2 Notwithstanding Clause 13.1.1, each Party may disclose Confidential Information to the extent that such Confidential Information:
   (a) was properly in the possession of the receiving Party prior to disclosure thereof by the other Party;
   (b) was in the public domain prior to its delivery to such Party or after such delivery if it becomes part of the public domain without breach of any confidentiality obligations by the receiving Party under this Agreement;
   (c) was obtained from a third party with no known duty to maintain its confidentiality;
   (d) is required to be disclosed by applicable law or judicial or administrative or arbitral process, provided that for any such disclosure, the disclosing Party will give the other Party prompt written notice, where possible, and use reasonable efforts to ensure that such disclosure is accorded confidential treatment and also to enable such other Party to seek a protective order or other appropriate remedy at such other Party's sole costs; and
   (e) lawfully becomes available without any limitation as to its disclosure.

13.1.3 The Parties agree that upon termination of this Agreement, the receiving Party will promptly deliver to the disclosing Party the Confidential Information and copies thereof in its possession or under its direct or indirect control, and will destroy all memoranda, notes and other writings prepared by the receiving Party or directors, officers, employees or advisors, based on Confidential Information.

13.2 Data Protection

13.2.1 The Concessionaire represents that it will abide by and observe all laws, rules, regulations including but not limited to the data protection laws of India while performing its obligations under this Agreement.

13.2.2 The Concessionaire will protect the personal data which it receives in connection with the provision of the Services ("**Personal Data**") by making security arrangements (as required under law) to prevent unauthorized or accidental access, collection, use, disclosure, copying, modification, disposal or destruction of Personal Data, or other similar risks.

13.2.3   The Concessionaire will only permit the authorized personnel to access Personal Data on a need to know basis.

13.2.4   The Concessionaire will not retain Personal Data (or any documents or records containing Personal Data, electronic or otherwise) for any period of time longer than that is necessary to serve the purposes of this Agreement or as may be provided under law.

13.2.5   The Concessionaire will immediately notify the Authority when the Concessionaire becomes aware of any breach of Personal Data.

13.2.6   The Concessionaire will indemnify the Authority against all actions, claims, demands, losses, damages, statutory penalties, expenses and cost in respect of breach of obligation under this Clauses 13.2.

14. Insurance

14.1 The Concessionaire will Maintain the Following Insurance:

14.1.1   comprehensive third-party liability insurance including professional liability insurance;

14.1.2   the Concessionaire's general liability arising out of the Concession;

14.1.3   liability to third parties for goods or property damage;

14.1.4   workmen's compensation insurance; and

14.1.5   any other insurance that may be necessary to protect the Concessionaire and its employees, [including all Force Majeure Events that are insurable at commercially reasonable premiums and not otherwise covered in Clauses 14.1.1 to 14.1.4 above.] *[Comment: The cost aspect of the insurance needs to be included in the Service Fees]*

14.2 The Authority will Maintain the Following Insurance:

14.2.1   insurance for the immovable properties at the Health Center;

14.2.2   [any other insurance depending on the nature of the project].

15. Representations and Warranties

Each Party Hereby Represents and Warrants to the Other Party That:

15.1.   it is duly organized and validly existing under the laws of the jurisdiction of its establishment or incorporation;

15.2   it has all necessary approvals, powers, licenses and authorities to enter into and perform its obligations under this Agreement;

15.3   its representative whose signature is affixed below hereto is fully authorized to sign this Agreement and to bind it pursuant to a valid power of attorney or resolution passed by its board of directors;

15.4   this Agreement constitutes legal, valid and binding obligations of such Party, enforceable against it in accordance with its terms;

15.5   it is not insolvent, and no receiver, liquidator, trustee, administrator, custodian or similar official has been appointed in respect of the whole or any substantial part of the business or assets of such Party;

15.6   the execution, delivery and performance of this Agreement by such Party will not (i) violate any provision of the constitutional documents of such Party; or (ii) require such Party to obtain any approvals or action of, or make any filing with or give any notice to, any governmental authority or any other person pursuant to any instrument, contract or other agreement to which such Party is a party or by which such Party is bound; (iii) conflict with or result in any material breach or violation of any of the terms and conditions of, or constitute a default under, any instrument, contract or other agreement to which such Party is a party or by which such Party is bound; (iv) to its knowledge, violate any order, judgment or decree against, or binding upon, such Party or upon its respective securities, properties or businesses; or (v) to its knowledge, violate any applicable laws; and

15.7   there is no lawsuit, arbitration, or legal, administrative or other proceedings or governmental investigation pending or, to the best of the knowledge of such Party, threatened, against it with respect to the subject matter of this Agreement or that would affect in any way its ability to enter into or perform its obligations under this Agreement.

16. Force Majeure

16.1 Definition of Force Majeure

16.1.1 In this Clause, "**Force Majeure**" means an exceptional event or circumstance:
(a)   which is beyond a Party's control,
(b)   which such Party could not reasonably have provided against before entering into the Agreement,
(c)   which, having arisen, such Party could not reasonably have avoided or overcome,
(d)   which is not substantially attributable to the other Party, and
(e)   which has a material adverse effect.

16.1.2 Force Majeure event will include (i) change in law and (ii) political events, which increases cost or makes it difficult for the Concessionaire to perform its obligations under this Agreement.

16.2 Notice of Force Majeure

16.2.1 If a Party is or will be prevented from performing any of its obligations under the Agreement by Force Majeure, then it will give notice to the other Party of the event or circumstances constituting the Force Majeure and will specify the obligations, the performance of which is or will be affected. The notice will be given within 14 days after the Party became aware, or should have become aware, of the relevant event or circumstance constituting Force Majeure.

16.2.2 The Party will, having given notice, be excused from performance of such obligations for so long as such Force Majeure prevents it from performing them.

16.2.3 Notwithstanding any other provision of this Clause, Force Majeure will not apply to obligations of either Party to make payments to the other Party under the Agreement.

16.3 Duty to Minimize Delay

16.3.1 Each Party will at all times use all reasonable endeavours to minimize any delay in the performance of the Agreement as a result of Force Majeure.

16.3.2 A Party will give notice to the other Party when it ceases to be affected by the Force Majeure.

16.4 Consequences of Force Majeure

If the Concessionaire is prevented from performing any of his obligations under the Agreement by Force Majeure of which notice has been given under Clause 16.2, and suffers delay and/or incurs cost by reason of such Force Majeure, then the Concessionaire will be entitled to payment of increased cost, which needs to be mutually agreed by the Parties, failing which, the cost will be determined by the Parties in accordance with the dispute resolution mechanism provided in Clause 19.

16.5 Optional Termination and Payment

16.5.1 If the Service is prevented for a continuous period of 90 days by reason of Force Majeure of which notice has been given under Clause 16.2, or for multiple periods which totals more than 140 days, then either Party may give to the other Party a notice of termination of the Agreement. In this event, the termination will take effect 7 days after the notice is given.

16.5.2 Upon such termination, the Concessionaire will determine the value of the Service provided and issue a payment notice or refund the excess of advance payments, received by the Concessionaire.

17. Default and Termination

17.1 Termination Events

17.1.1 Without limiting any other rights or remedies, the Authority reserves the right to terminate this Agreement, if the Concessionaire:
(a) fails to achieve KPI scores in accordance with Clause 7.5;
(b) is in default under any material obligation hereunder and the default has not been cured within 15 days after receipt of notice of such breach or default, unless the Parties otherwise mutually agree; or
(c) becomes insolvent, makes a general assignment for the benefit of creditors, files a voluntary petition in bankruptcy, or suffers or permits the appointment of a receiver for its business or assets.

17.1.2 Without limiting any other rights or remedies, the Concessionaire reserves the right to terminate this Agreement, if the Authority:
(a) fails to pay any invoice in accordance with Clause 6;
(b) is in default under any material obligation hereunder that has not been cured within 15 days after receipt of notice of such breach or default, unless the Parties otherwise mutually agree.

17.2 Consequence of Termination

17.2.1 Then termination of this Agreement in whole or in part for any reason under this Clause 17 will not affect (i) any liabilities or obligations of either Party arising before such termination or out of the events causing such termination; or (ii) any damages or other remedies to which a Party may be entitled under this Agreement, at law or in equity, arising from any breaches of such liabilities or obligations.

17.2.2 Upon termination, the Concessionaire will hand over the Health Center to the Authority. If required by the Authority, the Concessionaire will continue to operate and maintain the Health Center and provide the Services for a maximum further period of 3 months after termination in accordance with the terms and conditions of this Agreement.

18. Indemnity

18.1 General Indemnity

18.1.1 The Concessionaire will indemnify, defend and hold the Authority harmless against any and all proceedings, actions and third-party claims for any loss, damage, cost and expense of whatever kind and nature arising out of any act of the Concessionaire including failure of the Concessionaire to comply with applicable laws.

18.1.2 The Authority will indemnify, defend and hold the Concessionaire harmless against any and all proceedings, actions and third-party claims for any loss, damage, cost and expense of whatever kind and nature arising out of any act of the Authority.

18.2 Notice and Contest of Claims

If any Party receives a claim from a third-party in respect of which it is entitled to the benefit of an indemnity under Clause 18.1 above ("**Indemnified Party**"), then such Party will notify the other Party responsible for indemnifying such claim hereunder ("**Indemnifying Party**") within 15 (fifteen) days of receipt of the claim and will not settle or pay the claim without the prior approval of the Indemnifying Party, which approval not to be unreasonably withheld or delayed. If the Indemnifying Party wishes to contest or dispute the claim, it may conduct the proceedings in the name of the Indemnified Party and will bear all costs involved in contesting the same. The Indemnified Party will provide all cooperation and assistance in contesting any claim and will sign all such writings and documents as the Indemnifying Party may reasonably require.

19. Dispute Resolution

19.1 Dispute

19.1.1 Any dispute, difference or controversy of whatever nature howsoever arising under or out of or in relation to this Agreement between the Parties, and so notified in writing by either Party to the other Party ("Dispute") will, in the first instance, be attempted to be resolved amicably in accordance with the conciliation procedure set forth in Clause 19.1.2.

19.1.2 The Parties agree to use their best efforts for resolving all Disputes arising under or in respect of this Agreement promptly, equitably and in good faith, and further agree to provide each other with reasonable access during normal business hours to all non-privileged records, information and data pertaining to any Dispute.

19.2 Conciliation

If any Dispute between the Parties cannot be amicable settled, then such Dispute may be referred to the [Chairman of the District or State Health Care Department] and the CEO of the Concessionaire for amicable settlement, and upon such reference, the said persons will meet no later than 14 days from the date of reference to discuss and attempt to amicably resolve the Dispute. If such meeting does not take place within the 14 day period or the Dispute is not amicably settled within 30 days of the meeting or such longer period as may be mutually agreed by the Parties, either Party may refer the Dispute to arbitration in accordance with the provisions of Clause 19.3.

19.3 Arbitration

19.3.1 Any Dispute that is not resolved amicably by conciliation, as provided in Clause 19.2, will be finally decided by reference to arbitration by a board of arbitrators appointed in accordance with Clause 19.3.2 below. Such arbitration will be held in accordance with the Rules of Arbitration of the International Center for Alternative Dispute Resolution, New Delhi ("Rules"), or such other rules as may be mutually agreed by the Parties, and shall be subject to the provisions of the Arbitration and Conciliation Act, 1996. The venue of such arbitration will be [_____].

19.3.2 There will be a board of 3 arbitrators, of whom each Party will select 1, and the 3rd arbitrator will be appointed by the 2 arbitrators so selected and in the event of disagreement between the 2 arbitrators, the appointment will be made in accordance with the Rules.

19.3.3 The arbitrators will make a reasoned award ("**Award**"). Any Award made in any arbitration will be final and binding on the Parties as from the date it is made, and the Concessionaire and the Authority agree and undertake to carry out such Award without delay.

19.3.4 This Agreement and the rights and obligations of the Parties shall remain in full force and effect, pending the Award in any arbitration proceedings hereunder.

19.4 Adjudication by Regulatory Authority or Commission

In the event of constitution of a statutory Regulatory Authority or Commission with powers to adjudicate upon disputes between the Concessionaire and the Authority, all Disputes arising after such constitution shall, instead of reference to arbitration under Clause 19.3, be adjudicated upon by such Regulatory Authority or Commission in accordance with the applicable law and all references to Dispute Resolution Procedure will be construed accordingly.

20. Miscellaneous

20.1 Governing Law and Jurisdiction

This Agreement will be construed and interpreted in accordance with and governed by the laws of India, and the courts at [___] will have exclusive jurisdiction over matters arising out of or relating to this Agreement.

20.2 Waiver of immunity

Each Party unconditionally and irrevocably:

(a) agrees that the execution, delivery and performance by it of this Agreement constitute commercial acts done and performed for commercial purpose;

(b) agrees that, should any proceedings be brought against it or its assets, property or revenues in any jurisdiction in relation to this Agreement or any transaction contemplated by this Agreement, no immunity (whether by reason of sovereignty or otherwise) from such proceedings shall be claimed by or on behalf of the Party with respect to its assets;

(c) waives any right of immunity that it or its assets, property, or revenues it now has, or may acquire in the future, or which may be attributed to it in any jurisdiction; and

(d) consents generally in respect of the enforcement of any judgment or award against it in any such proceedings to the giving of any relief or the issue of any process in any jurisdiction in connection with such proceedings (including the making, enforcement or execution against it or in respect of any assets, property or revenues whatsoever irrespective of their use or intended use of any order or judgment that may be made or given in connection therewith).

20.3 Delayed Payments

The Parties hereto agree that payments due from one Party to the other Party under the provisions of this Agreement shall be made within the period set forth therein, and if no such period is specified, within 30 (thirty) days of receiving a demand along with the necessary particulars. In the event of delay beyond such period, the defaulting Party will pay interest for the period of delay calculated at a rate equal to 10% per annum, and recovery thereof will be without prejudice to the rights of the Parties under this Agreement including termination thereof.

20.4 Waiver

No waiver of any provision of this Agreement will constitute a waiver of any other provision(s) or of the same provision on another occasion. Failure of either Party to enforce any provision of this Agreement will not constitute a waiver of such provision or any other provision(s) of this Agreement.

20.5 Survival

Termination will not relieve the Concessionaire or the Authority, as the case may be, of any obligations hereunder which expressly or by implication survive termination hereof.

20.6 Entire Agreement

This Agreement together constitute the entire agreement between the Parties on the subject hereof, and no amendment or modification will be valid and effective unless such modification or amendment is agreed to in writing by the Parties. All prior written or oral understandings, offers or other communications of every kind pertaining to this Agreement are abrogated and withdrawn. For the avoidance of doubt, the Parties hereto agree that any obligations of the Concessionaire arising from the RFP will be deemed to form part of this Agreement.

20.7 Severability

Should any provision of this Agreement be held by a court of competent jurisdiction to be illegal, invalid or unenforceable, such provision may be modified by such court in compliance with the law giving effect to the intent of the Parties and enforced as modified. All other terms and conditions of this Client Agreement remain in full force and effect and will be construed in accordance with the modified provision.

20.8 Relationship of Parties

This Agreement will not be interpreted or construed to create an association, joint venture or partnership agreement between the Parties, or to impose any partnership obligation or liability upon either Party, and neither Party shall have any right, power or authority to enter into any agreement or undertaking for, or act on behalf of, or to act as or be an agent or representative of, or to otherwise bind, the other Party.

20.9 Third Parties

This Agreement is intended solely for the benefit of the Parties, and their respective successors and permitted assigns, and nothing in this Agreement shall be construed to create any duty to, standard of care with reference to, or any liability to, any person not a Party to this Agreement.

20.10 Notices

Notice to the Parties shall be in writing and shall be sent at the addresses first hereinabove mentioned (email accepted). In case, there is any change in the addresses of a Party, the same shall be communicated immediately to the other Party, failing which any notice sent to the earlier address of the said Party shall be deemed to be valid service of such notice.

Authority
Address:
Email:
Phone:
Kind Attention:

Concessionaire
Address:
Email:
Phone:
Kind Attention:

IN WITNESS WHEREOF, and intending to be legally bound, the Parties have duly executed this Agreement as of the date first written above.

Signed for and on behalf of
[*insert name of the Authority*]

Signed for and on behalf of
[*insert name of the Concessionaire*]

_____
By:
Name:
Title:

_____
By:
Name:
Title:

SCHEDULE 1 – SERVICES

[Please incorporate the standard services which are provided by UPHC including services related to operation and maintenance of the UPHC (cleanliness, operation hours, etc), who will maintain the security of UPHC, with a note that the Services may be modify in accordance with the requirement of the project.

Further, the Authority to identify the norms which will be followed by the Concessionaire in providing the Services (for example any norms listed by NUHM).]

SCHEDULE 2 – HEALTH CENTER

[Details of the health center and the assets to be handed over to the Concessionaire to be inserted in this schedule.]

SCHEDULE 3 – AUTHORITY SERVICES

[Any services that the Authority will provide should be included here, for example, if the Authority will provide medical supplies, ambulance, etc.]

SCHEDULE 4 – SERVICE FEES AND DOCUMENTS FOR PAYMENT

Part A: Fees
Upgradation Fees: [_____] (if any)

Service Fees:
[_____]

Part B: Documents for Payment

[Government to include in this schedule the list of documents (including formats) to be provided by the Concessionaire for claiming payment.]

SCHEDULE 5 – KEY PERFORMANCE INDICATORS

[Please incorporate standard KPIs that are required for UPHCs in accordance with the project.]

SCHEDULE 6 – SALIENT FEATURES OF GRIEVANCE REDRESSAL POLICY

1.1.   The Health Center will have a provision of complaint drop box at suitable and visible location where any aggrieved patient can register his/her complaint. Patient can also raise the concern/complaint orally.

1.2.   The process of grievance handling will be displayed at reception in local language and English for patient information. It will also mention the concerned authorized person name and phone number.

1.3.   The Concessionaire will act promptly on receiving any complaint and the same should be addressed within 48 hours.

1.4.   The Concessionaire will ensure that preventive mechanisms are in place so that complaints are not repeated again.

1.5.   All patient complaints should be captured in digitised way and feed into the Health Management Information System (HMIS). The Concessionaire will produce quarterly reports on patient feedback received from the patients and share with the Authority.

SCHEDULE 7 – MONTHLY REPORT

[The information for monthly report to be identified here.]

Sample Concession Agreement
(Rented Urban Primary Health Center)

CONCESSION AGREEMENT

FOR

URBAN PRIMARY HEALTH CENTER PUBLIC–PRIVATE PARTNERSHIP PROJECTS

(WITH HEALTH CENTER)

Between

Department of [_____]

And

[_____]

Concessionaire

For

Public–Private Partnership for Urban Primary Health Center in

[_____]

[We understand that (i) this concession agreement will be used to execute/implement multiple low value health care project (less than Rs. 50 lacs), and (ii) the service provider will mostly be an NGO with limited access to legal advice. In light of this, we have kept the agreement as simple and short as possible.]

URBAN PRIMARY HEALTH CENTER PUBLIC–PRIVATE PARTNERSHIP CONCESSION AGREEMENT (WITH HEALTH CENTER)

This agreement is entered into on this [__] day of [__], 2020 at [_____] ("**Agreement**"):

BETWEEN

1. [_____], represented by [_____] and having its principal office at [_____] (hereinafter referred to as the "**Authority**" which expression shall, unless repugnant to the context or meaning thereof, include its administrators, successors and assigns);

AND

2. [*please insert name of the NGO*], is a section 8 company, incorporated under the provisions of Companies Act, 2013 and having its registered office at [__] (hereinafter referred to as the "Concessionaire" which expression shall, unless repugnant to the context or meaning thereof, include its successors and permitted assigns and substitutes).

Or

2. [*please insert name of the Trust*], is a trust created by a trust deed dated [____], having its office at [*] (hereinafter referred to as the "**Concessionaire**" which expression shall, unless repugnant to the context or meaning thereof, include its successors and permitted assigns and substitutes).

Or

2. [*please insert name of the Society*], is society created under the Societies Registration Act, 1860, having its office at [____] (hereinafter referred to as the "**Concessionaire**" which expression shall, unless repugnant to the context or meaning thereof, include its successors and permitted assigns and substitutes).]

"**Authority**" and "**Concessionaire**" will be referred to individually as the "**Party**" and collectively as the "**Parties**".

[Comment: We have been given to understand that the Concessionaire will be an NGO/TRUST/ SOCIETY, and they will be executing the project directly and not through a separate legal entity.]

WHEREAS:

A. The Government of India has launched National Urban Health Mission ("**NUHM**") for providing primary health care services to the urban population with special focus on slum and other vulnerable sections of the society. As a part of NUHM, the Government of [____] ("**State Government**") has decide to establish/upgrade urban primary health centers ("**UPHCs**") in the State through private sector participation.

B.   The Authority had accordingly invited bids through its Request for Proposal No. [_____] dated [_____] ("**RFP**") for the selection of an entity for the operation and maintenance of the UPHCs in accordance with the terms and conditions of this Agreement ("**Project**").

C.   After evaluation of the bids received, the Authority accepted the [bid/EOI] of the Concessionaire in accordance with the terms of the RFP and issued the Letter of Acceptance No. [_____] dated [_____] ("**LOA**") requiring, *inter alia*, the execution of this Agreement within 30 (thirty) days of the date of the issue of LOA.

D.   The Authority is accordingly entering into this Agreement with the Concessionaire for implementation of the Project, subject to and on the terms and conditions as set forth hereinafter.

NOW, THEREFORE, in consideration of the foregoing and the respective covenants and agreements set forth in this Agreement, the receipt and sufficiency of which is hereby acknowledged, and intending to be legally bound hereby, the Parties agree as follows:

1.   Definitions and Interpretation

1.1.   Definitions

The following words and expressions shall, unless the context otherwise requires, have the following meanings:

1.1.1.   "**Authority Inspection Report**" will have the meaning as provided in Clause 12.2.

1.1.2.   "**Additional Service**s" will have the meaning as provided in Clause 2.5 and Schedule 1.

1.1.3.   "**Authority Services**" will have the meaning as provided in Schedule 3.

1.1.4.   "**Award**" will have the meaning as provided in Clause 19.3.3.

1.1.5.   "**Confidential Information**" will have the meaning as provided in Clause 13.1.1.

1.1.6.   "**Conditions Precedent**" will have the meaning as provided in Clause 3.1.

1.1.7.   "**CP Satisfaction Date**" will have the meaning as provided in Clause 3.2.

1.1.8.   "**CP Satisfaction Notice**" will have the meaning as provided in Clause 3.3.

1.1.9.   "**Concession Period**" will have the meaning as provided in Clause 2.3.

1.1.10. "**Dispute**" will have the meaning as provided in Clause 19.1.1.

1.1.11. **"Documents for Payment"** will have the meaning as provided in Schedule 4.

1.1.12. **"Effective Date"** will have the meaning as provided in Clause 3.4.

1.1.13. **"Failure Notice"** will have the meaning as provided in Clause 3.5.

1.1.14. **"Force Majeure"** will have the meaning as provided in Clause 16.1.1.

1.1.15. **"Good Industry Practice"** means the practices, methods, techniques, designs, standards, skills, diligence, efficiency, reliability and prudence which are generally and reasonably expected from a reasonably skilled and experienced operator engaged in the same type of undertaking as envisaged under this Agreement and which would be expected to result in the performance of its obligations by the Concessionaire in accordance with this Agreement and applicable laws in reliable, safe, economical and efficient manner.

1.1.16. **"Government Instrumentality"** means any department, division or sub-division of the Government of India or the State Government and includes any commission, board, authority, agency or municipal and other local authority or statutory body including Panchayat under the control of the Government of India or the State Government, as the case may be, and having jurisdiction over all or any part of the Project or the performance of all or any of the Services or obligations of the Concessionaire under or pursuant to this Agreement.

1.1.17. **"Health Center"** will have the meaning as provided in Schedule 2.

1.1.18. **"Health Center Procurement Fee"** will have the meaning as provided in Schedule 4.

1.1.19. **"Indemnified Part**y" will have the meaning as provided in Clause 18.2.

1.1.20. **"Indemnifying Party"** will have the meaning as provided in Clause 18.2.

1.1.21. **"KPIs"** will have the meaning as provided in Clause 7 and Schedule 5.

1.1.22. **"LOA"** will have the meaning as provided in Recital C.

1.1.23. **"Nominated Person"** will have the meaning as provided in Clause 3.1.3.

1.1.24. **"NUHM"** will have the meaning provided in Recital A.

1.1.25. **"Personal Data"** will have the meaning as provided in Clause 13.2.2.

1.1.26. **"Project"** will have the meaning as provided in Recital B.

1.1.27. **"RFP"** will have the meaning as provided in Recital B.

1.1.28. "**Rules**" will have the meaning as provided in Clause 19.3.1.

1.1.29. "**Services**" will have the meaning as provided in Schedule 1.

1.1.30. "**Service Fees**" will have the meaning as provided in Clause 6.1 and Schedule 4.

1.1.31. "**Signing Date**" will mean the date of execution of this Agreement.

1.1.32. "**State Government**" will have the meaning as provided in Recital A.

1.1.33. "**Third-Party Inspection**" will have the meaning as provided in Clause 12.3.

1.1.34. "**UPHCs**" will have the meaning as provided in Recital A.

1.2. Interpretation

In this Agreement, unless the context specifies otherwise:

1.2.1. headings are used for convenience only and shall not affect the interpretation of this Agreement;

1.2.2. reference to the singular includes a reference to the plural and vice versa, and reference to any gender includes a reference to all other genders;

1.2.3. references to the Recitals, Clauses and Schedules shall deemed to be a reference to the recitals, clauses and schedules of this Agreement;

1.2.4. the expression "this Clause" shall, unless followed by reference to a specific provision, be deemed to refer respectively to the whole Clause, not merely the sub-clause, paragraph or other provision in which the expression occurs;

1.2.5. references to any enactment are to be construed as referring also to any amendment or re-enactment (whether before or after the date of this Agreement), any previous enactment, which such enactment has replaced (with or without amendment) and to any regulation or order made under it;

1.2.6. references to "include" and "including" shall be construed without limitation.

2. Scope of the Project

Primary Scope of Work

2.1. Subject to the terms and conditions of this Concession Agreement, the Authority grants to the Concessionaire the exclusive right during the Concession Period to (i) provide the Services identified in Schedule 1 (**Services**); and (ii) collect the Service Fees from the Authority, all in accordance with the terms and conditions of this Agreement.

2.2. The Health Center and assets to be handed over to the Concessionaire are identified in Schedule 2 (**Health Center**).

2.3. This Agreement will become effective on the Signing Date and will continue for a period of [_____] months or years from the Effective Date ("**Concession Period**"), unless otherwise extended or terminated in accordance with this Agreement.

2.4. This Agreement may be extended by the Authority for a further period of [____] months or years if the Concessionaire achieves an average minimum KPI score of [X] during the initial Concession Period.

Variation to the Scope of Work

2.5. If the Concessionaire is required to provide any service in addition to the Services identified in Schedule 1 (**Services**) ("**Additional Service**"), then the Parties will mutually agree on fees for such Additional Service before commencement of the Additional Service by the Concessionaire. If the Parties are unable to mutually agree on the scope of the Additional Service to be provided by the Concessionaire and/or the fees associated with the Additional Service, then the Concessionaire will not be required to provide the Additional Service, and the Parties will continue to fulfil its obligations under this Agreement.

3. Conditions Precedent

Applicable where Health Center Does Not Require Fixing/Upgradation

3.1. The Concessionaire is required to fulfil the following obligations before the Effective Date (as these are required for operation of the Health Center) ("**Conditions Precedent**"):

   3.1.1. Obtain all consents and approvals required for providing the Services;

   3.1.2. Appoint consultants, employees and doctors for providing the Services;

   3.1.3. The Concessionaire will nominate 1 person as its point of contact for co-ordinating with the Authority ("**Nominated Person**");

   3.1.4 Procure the Health Center in accordance with Schedule 2 (**Health Center**).

   3.1.5 *[please incorporate any other conditions that the private party will be required to fulfil before the Health Center will be handed over to the private party]*

3.2. The Conditions Precedent are to be fulfilled by the Concessionaire within [90] of the Signing Date ("**CP Satisfaction Date**").

3.3 Upon fulfilling the Conditions Precedent, the Concessionaire will inform the Authority by written notice that it has fulfilled the Conditions Precedent ("**CP Satisfaction Notice**").

3.4   Within [15] days of receiving the CP Satisfaction Notice, (i) the Authority will inspect and confirm (if the Authority is satisfied that the Conditions Precedent have been fulfilled) that the Conditions Precedent have been fulfilled, or (ii) if the Authority fails to convey to the Concessionaire within the aforesaid period either fulfilment or failure to fulfil the Conditions Precedent, then it will be deemed that the Concessionaire has fulfilled the Conditions Precedent. On the date of either of the above event, the Concessionaire will commence providing the Services at the Health Center in accordance with this Agreement ("Effective Date").

3.5   If within the period provided in Clause 3.4 above, the Authority identifies that the Concessionaire has failed to fulfil the Conditions Precedent, then the Authority will provide a written notice to the Concessionaire identifying the failures ("**Failure Notice**"). Upon receiving the Failure Notice, the Concessionaire will rectify the failures identified by the Authority within a period of [15] days and give notice to the Authority as provided in Clause 3.3 above and the procedure provided in Clause 3.4 will be followed. Every time a Failure Notice is issued by the Authority, the process provided in Clause 3.3, 3.4 and 3.5 above will be followed.

3.6   If the Concessionaire fails to achieve Effective Date within a period of [150] of the Signing Date, then the Authority will be entitled to termination this Agreement.

4.   Roles and Responsibilities of the Concessionaire

4.1   The Concessionaire will provide the Services during the Concession Period in accordance with the terms of this Agreement. Without prejudice to the generality of the foregoing, the Concessionaire:

4.1.1   will obtain and maintain all consents and approvals necessary for providing the Services;

4.1.2   comply with the provisions of this Agreement, applicable laws and conform to Good Industry Practice for securing the safety and hygiene of the patients, visitors and staff;

4.1.3   ensure that the Nominated Person will report, attend meetings and provide all reasonable information as required by the district medical officer from time to time;

4.1.4   pay all taxes and duties applicable by the Concessionaire under the applicable laws;

4.1.5   ensure that the Health Center is in good working condition at all times in accordance with the provisions of this Agreement including, without any limitation, at the time of handing over to the Authority.

5.   Role and Responsibilities of the Authority

5.1   The Authority will provide the services as identified in Schedule 3 (**Authority Services**) during the Concession Period.

5.2 The Authority agrees to provide support to the Concessionaire and undertakes to observe, comply with and perform, subject to and in accordance with the provisions of this Agreement, the following:

  5.2.1 upon written request from the Concessionaire, and subject to the Concessionaire complying with applicable laws, provide reasonable support and assistance to the Concessionaire in procuring applicable permits required from any Government Instrumentality for implementation of the Project;

  5.2.2 upon written request from the Concessionaire, provide reasonable assistance to the Concessionaire in obtaining access to all necessary infrastructure facilities and utilities, including water and electricity at rates and on terms no less favorable to the Concessionaire than those generally available to public hospitals and such other facilities receiving substantially equivalent services;

  5.2.3 assist the Concessionaire in procuring police assistance for dealing with medico-legal cases which are brought to the Health Center, if any;

  5.2.4 will extend the training provided under the NUHM to the employees and consultants of the Concessionaire engaged in providing the Services in the Health Center;

  5.2.5 make all payments to the Concessionaire in the manner and within the time period specified in this Agreement.

6. Payments

6.1 For the Services to be performed by the Concessionaire under this Agreement, the Authority will pay to the Concessionaire the Service Fees in accordance with Schedule 4 (**"Service Fees and Documents for Payment"**).

6.2 The Authority will provide to the Concessionaire a one-time Health Center Procurement Fee on the [Signing Date/Effective Date.]

6.3 On the Effective Date, the Authority will pay to the Concessionaire in advance the estimated Service Fees for the Services to be provided by the Concessionaire in the coming quarter. The Service Fees will be paid by the Authority on the Effective Date and on each quarter thereafter until the expiry or termination of the Agreement.

6.4 The Concessionaire will provide to the Authority between [30] day and [15] days before each quarter (i) an invoice for the Service Fees for the following quarter (which will also include adjustment of any unutilised fees from the previous quarter or any excess spend by the Concessionaire) based on Schedule 4 (**Service Fees and Documents for Payments**), and (ii) the documents listed in Schedule 4 (**Service Fees and Documents for Payments**).

6.5 Within [15] days of receipt of the documents by the Authority as identified in Clause 6.4 above, the Authority will pay the Service Fees for the following year to the Concessionaire.

7. Key Performance Indicators

7.1   Without prejudice to the obligations specified in this Agreement, the Concessionaire will operate the Health Center and provide the Services such that it meets the key performance indicators provide in Schedule 5 ("**KPIs**").

7.2   The Concessionaire will during the Concession Period, furnish to the Authority, a report, setting out the details provided in Clause 7.3, no later than 7 (seven) days after the close of each quarter of providing the Services.

7.3   The report specified in Clause 7.2 will state in reasonable detail the compliance with all the KPIs specified in Schedule 5 (**KPIs**) along with an analysis of the reasons for failures, if any, and the strategies for addressing the same and for otherwise improving the performance of the Health Center.

7.4   The Concessionaire will ensure compliance of each of the KPIs specified in Schedule 5 (**KPIs**) and for any shortfall in performance, it will pay damages within 30 (thirty) days of every quarter in which the shortfall occurred. The damages due and payable under this Clause 7.4 will be determined in accordance with Schedule 5 (**KPIs**).

7.5   If the Concessionaire fails to achieve KPI scope of [X] for two consecutive quarters, then the Authority will be entitled to terminate this Agreement.

8. Grievance Redressal Policy

Unless a Grievance Redressal Policy is provided by the Authority, the Concessionaire will monitor and address any issues or complaints regarding quality of services, denial of services, staff behaviour, etc. with respect to the patients in accordance with the principles related to Grievance Redressal Policy provided in Schedule 6 (**Salient Feature of Grievance Redressal Policy**).

9. Intentionally Left Blank

10. Assets

Except the building of the Health Center, any asset including equipment and medicine (i) created or procured by the Concessionaire or provided by the Authority for providing the Services during the Concession Period or (ii) remaining at the expiry or termination of this Agreement, will be handed over by the Concessionaire to the Authority at the expiry or termination of this Agreement.

11. Subcontract

The Concessionaire will not assign or sub-contract any of its rights or obligations under this Agreement without the prior written consent of the Authority.

12. Information Obligation in Relation to Operation of UPHC

12.1 During Concession Period, the Concessionaire will, no later than 7 (seven) days after the close of each month, furnish to the Authority, a monthly report in a form acceptable to the Authority, stating in reasonable detail the information identified in Schedule 7 ("**Monthly Report**").

12.2 The Authority will have right to inspect the Health Centers from time to time. The Authority will make a report of such inspection ("**Authority Inspection Report**") stating in reasonable detail the defects or deficiencies, if any, in relation to the Services, and send a copy thereof to the Concessionaire. The Concessionaire will rectify the defects or deficiencies, if any, set forth in the Authority Inspection Report, and furnish a report to the Authority within 15 days of the aforesaid reports.

12.3 The Authority may, once in each year, appoint an independent third party to conduct independent inspection of the Services provided by the Concessionaire ("**Third-Party Inspection**"). The Concessionaire will provide all reasonable assistance and access to the Health Center to third party for the Third-Party Inspection.

13. Confidentiality and Data Protection

13.1 Confidentiality

13.1.1 Each Party will maintain in strict confidence and protect the confidentiality of all information, reports, data, software or other material, whether written or oral, in electronic or magnetic format, and the contents thereof and any reports, digests or summaries created or derived from any of the foregoing that is provided by one Party to the other Party in relation to this Agreement ("**Confidential Information**"), and will not disclose any such Confidential Information to any third party without the prior written consent of the other Party; provided that each Party will be entitled to use Confidential Information for any and all lawful purposes.

13.1.2 Notwithstanding Clause 13.1.1, each Party may disclose Confidential Information to the extent that such Confidential Information:
  (a) was properly in the possession of the receiving Party prior to disclosure thereof by the other Party;
  (b) was in the public domain prior to its delivery to such Party or after such delivery if it becomes part of the public domain without breach of any confidentiality obligations by the receiving Party under this Agreement;
  (c) was obtained from a third party with no known duty to maintain its confidentiality;
  (d) is required to be disclosed by applicable law or judicial or administrative or arbitral process, provided that for any such disclosure, the disclosing Party will give the other Party prompt written notice, where possible, and use reasonable efforts to ensure that such disclosure is accorded confidential treatment and also to enable such other Party to seek a protective order or other appropriate remedy at such other Party's sole costs; and
  (e) lawfully becomes available without any limitation as to its disclosure.

13.1.3 The Parties agree that upon termination of this Agreement, the receiving Party will promptly deliver to the disclosing Party the Confidential Information and copies thereof in its possession or under its direct or indirect control, and will destroy all memoranda, notes and other writings prepared by the receiving Party or directors, officers, employees or advisors, based on Confidential Information.

13.2 Data Protection

13.2.1 The Concessionaire represents that it will abide by and observe all laws, rules, regulations including but not limited to the data protection laws of India while performing its obligations under this Agreement.

13.2.2 The Concessionaire will protect the personal data which it receives in connection with the provision of the Services ("**Personal Data**") by making security arrangements (as required under law) to prevent unauthorized or accidental access, collection, use, disclosure, copying, modification, disposal or destruction of Personal Data, or other similar risks.

13.2.3 The Concessionaire will only permit the authorized personnel to access Personal Data on a need to know basis.

13.2.4 The Concessionaire will not retain Personal Data (or any documents or records containing Personal Data, electronic or otherwise) for any period of time longer than that is necessary to serve the purposes of this Agreement or as may be provided under law.

13.2.5 The Concessionaire will immediately notify the Authority when the Concessionaire becomes aware of any breach of Personal Data.

13.2.6 The Concessionaire will indemnify the Authority against all actions, claims, demands, losses, damages, statutory penalties, expenses and cost in respect of breach of obligation under this Clause 13.2.

14. Insurance

14.1 The Concessionaire will Maintain the Following Insurance:

14.1.1 comprehensive third-party liability insurance including professional liability insurance;

14.1.2 the Concessionaire's general liability arising out of the Concession;

14.1.3 liability to third parties for goods or property damage;

14.1.4 workmen's compensation insurance;

14.1.5   insurance for the immovable properties at the Health Center; and

14.1.6   any other insurance that may be necessary to protect the Concessionaire and its employees, [including all Force Majeure Events that are insurable at commercially reasonable premiums and not otherwise covered in Clauses 14.1.1 to 14.1.4 above.] *[Comment: The cost aspect of the insurance needs to be included in the Service Fees]*

15. Representations and Warranties

Each Party Hereby Represents and Warrants to the Other Party That:

15.1   it is duly organized and validly existing under the laws of the jurisdiction of its establishment or incorporation;

15.2   it has all necessary approvals, powers, licenses and authorities to enter into and perform its obligations under this Agreement;

15.3   its representative whose signature is affixed below hereto is fully authorized to sign this Agreement and to bind it pursuant to a valid power of attorney or resolution passed by its board of directors;

15.4   this Agreement constitutes legal, valid and binding obligations of such Party, enforceable against it in accordance with its terms;

15.5   it is not insolvent, and no receiver, liquidator, trustee, administrator, custodian or similar official has been appointed in respect of the whole or any substantial part of the business or assets of such Party;

15.6   the execution, delivery and performance of this Agreement by such Party will not (i) violate any provision of the constitutional documents of such Party; or (ii) require such Party to obtain any approvals or action of, or make any filing with or give any notice to, any governmental authority or any other person pursuant to any instrument, contract or other agreement to which such Party is a party or by which such Party is bound; (iii) conflict with or result in any material breach or violation of any of the terms and conditions of, or constitute a default under, any instrument, contract or other agreement to which such Party is a party or by which such Party is bound; (iv) to its knowledge, violate any order, judgment or decree against, or binding upon, such Party or upon its respective securities, properties or businesses; or (v) to its knowledge, violate any applicable laws; and

15.7   there is no lawsuit, arbitration, or legal, administrative or other proceedings or governmental investigation pending or, to the best of the knowledge of such Party, threatened, against it with respect to the subject matter of this Agreement or that would affect in any way its ability to enter into or perform its obligations under this Agreement.

16. Force Majeure

16.1 Definition of Force Majeure

16.1.1 In this Clause, "Force Majeure" means an exceptional event or circumstance:
   (a) which is beyond a Party's control,
   (b) which such Party could not reasonably have provided against before entering into the Agreement,
   (c) which, having arisen, such Party could not reasonably have avoided or overcome,
   (d) which is not substantially attributable to the other Party, and
   (e) which has a material adverse effect.

16.1.2 Force Majeure event will include (i) change in law and (ii) political events, which increases cost or makes it difficult for the Concessionaire to perform its obligations under this Agreement.

16.2 Notice of Force Majeure

16.2.1 If a Party is or will be prevented from performing any of its obligations under the Agreement by Force Majeure, then it will give notice to the other Party of the event or circumstances constituting the Force Majeure and will specify the obligations, the performance of which is or will be affected. The notice will be given within 14 days after the Party became aware, or should have become aware, of the relevant event or circumstance constituting Force Majeure.

16.2.2 The Party will, having given notice, be excused from performance of such obligations for so long as such Force Majeure prevents it from performing them.

16.2.3 Notwithstanding any other provision of this Clause, Force Majeure will not apply to obligations of either Party to make payments to the other Party under the Agreement.

16.3 Duty to Minimize Delay

16.3.1 Each Party will at all times use all reasonable endeavours to minimize any delay in the performance of the Agreement as a result of Force Majeure.

16.3.2 A Party will give notice to the other Party when it ceases to be affected by the Force Majeure.

16.4 Consequences of Force Majeure

If the Concessionaire is prevented from performing any of his obligations under the Agreement by Force Majeure of which notice has been given under Clause 16.2, and suffers delay and/or incurs cost by reason of such Force Majeure, then the Concessionaire will be entitled to payment of increased cost, which needs to be mutually agreed by the Parties, failing which, the cost will be determined by the Parties in accordance with the dispute resolution mechanism provided in Clause 19.

16.5 Optional Termination and Payment

16.5.1   If the Service is prevented for a continuous period of 90 days by reason of Force Majeure of which notice has been given under Clause 16.2, or for multiple periods which totals more than 140 days, then either Party may give to the other Party a notice of termination of the Agreement. In this event, the termination will take effect 7 days after the notice is given.

16.5.2   Upon such termination, the Concessionaire will determine the value of the Service provided and issue a payment notice or refund the excess of advance payments, received by the Concessionaire.

17. Default and Termination

17.1 Termination Events

17.1.1   Without limiting any other rights or remedies, the Authority reserves the right to terminate this Agreement, if the Concessionaire:
   (a)   fails to achieve KPI scores in accordance with Clause 7.5;
   (b)   is in default under any material obligation hereunder and the default has not been cured within 15 days after receipt of notice of such breach or default, unless the Parties otherwise mutually agree; or
   (c)   becomes insolvent, makes a general assignment for the benefit of creditors, files a voluntary petition in bankruptcy, or suffers or permits the appointment of a receiver for its business or assets.

17.1.2   Without limiting any other rights or remedies, the Concessionaire reserves the right to terminate this Agreement, if the Authority:
   (a)   fails to pay any invoice in accordance with Clause 6;
   (b)   is in default under any material obligation hereunder that has not been cured within 15 days after receipt of notice of such breach or default, unless the Parties otherwise mutually agree.

17.2 Consequence of Termination

17.2.1   Then termination of this Agreement in whole or in part for any reason under this Clause 17 will not affect (i) any liabilities or obligations of either Party arising before such termination or out of the events causing such termination; or (ii) any damages or other remedies to which a Party may be entitled under this Agreement, at law or in equity, arising from any breaches of such liabilities or obligations.

17.2.2   Upon termination, the Concessionaire will hand over the Health Center to the Authority. If required by the Authority, the Concessionaire will continue to operate and maintain the Health Center and provide the Services for a maximum further period of 3 months after termination in accordance with the terms and conditions of this Agreement.

18. Indemnity

18.1 General Indemnity

18.1.1   The Concessionaire will indemnify, defend and hold the Authority harmless against any and all proceedings, actions and third-party claims for any loss, damage, cost and expense of whatever kind and nature arising out of any act of the Concessionaire including failure of the Concessionaire to comply with applicable laws.

18.1.2   The Authority will indemnify, defend and hold the Concessionaire harmless against any and all proceedings, actions and third-party claims for any loss, damage, cost and expense of whatever kind and nature arising out of any act of the Authority.

18.2 Notice and Contest of Claims

If any Party receives a claim from a third-party in respect of which it is entitled to the benefit of an indemnity under Clause 18.1 above ("**Indemnified Party**"), then such Party will notify the other Party responsible for indemnifying such claim hereunder ("**Indemnifying Party**") within 15 (fifteen) days of receipt of the claim and will not settle or pay the claim without the prior approval of the Indemnifying Party, which approval not to be unreasonably withheld or delayed. If the Indemnifying Party wishes to contest or dispute the claim, it may conduct the proceedings in the name of the Indemnified Party and will bear all costs involved in contesting the same. The Indemnified Party will provide all cooperation and assistance in contesting any claim and will sign all such writings and documents as the Indemnifying Party may reasonably require.

19. Dispute Resolution

19.1 Dispute

19.1.1   Any dispute, difference or controversy of whatever nature howsoever arising under or out of or in relation to this Agreement between the Parties, and so notified in writing by either Party to the other Party ("**Dispute**") will, in the first instance, be attempted to be resolved amicably in accordance with the conciliation procedure set forth in Clause 19.1.2.

19.1.2   The Parties agree to use their best efforts for resolving all Disputes arising under or in respect of this Agreement promptly, equitably and in good faith, and further agree to provide each other with reasonable access during normal business hours to all non-privileged records, information and data pertaining to any Dispute.

19.2 Conciliation

If any Dispute between the Parties cannot be amicable settled, then such Dispute may be referred to the [Chairman of the District/State Health Care Department] and the CEO of the Concessionaire for amicable settlement, and upon such reference, the said persons will meet no later than 14 days from the date of reference to discuss and attempt to amicably resolve the Dispute. If such meeting does not take place within the 14 day period or the Dispute is not amicably settled within 30 days of the meeting or such longer period as may be mutually agreed by the Parties, either Party may refer the Dispute to arbitration in accordance with the provisions of Clause 19.3.

19.3 Arbitration

19.3.1 Any Dispute which is not resolved amicably by conciliation, as provided in Clause 19.2, will be finally decided by reference to arbitration by a board of arbitrators appointed in accordance with Clause 19.3.2 below. Such arbitration will be held in accordance with the Rules of Arbitration of the International Center for Alternative Dispute Resolution, New Delhi ("**Rules**"), or such other rules as may be mutually agreed by the Parties, and shall be subject to the provisions of the Arbitration and Conciliation Act, 1996. The venue of such arbitration will be [_____].

19.3.2 There will be a board of 3 arbitrators, of whom each Party will select 1, and the 3rd arbitrator will be appointed by the 2 arbitrators so selected and in the event of disagreement between the 2 arbitrators, the appointment will be made in accordance with the Rules.

19.3.3 The arbitrators will make a reasoned award ("Award"). Any Award made in any arbitration will be final and binding on the Parties as from the date it is made, and the Concessionaire and the Authority agree and undertake to carry out such Award without delay.

19.3.4 This Agreement and the rights and obligations of the Parties shall remain in full force and effect, pending the Award in any arbitration proceedings hereunder.

19.4 Adjudication by Regulatory Authority or Commission

In the event of constitution of a statutory Regulatory Authority or Commission with powers to adjudicate upon disputes between the Concessionaire and the Authority, all Disputes arising after such constitution shall, instead of reference to arbitration under Clause 19.3, be adjudicated upon by such Regulatory Authority or Commission in accordance with the applicable law and all references to Dispute Resolution Procedure will be construed accordingly.

20. Miscellaneous

20.1 Governing Law and Jurisdiction

This Agreement will be construed and interpreted in accordance with and governed by the laws of India, and the courts at [___] will have exclusive jurisdiction over matters arising out of or relating to this Agreement.

20.2 Waiver of Immunity

Each Party unconditionally and irrevocably:

(a) agrees that the execution, delivery and performance by it of this Agreement constitute commercial acts done and performed for commercial purpose;

(b) agrees that, should any proceedings be brought against it or its assets, property or revenues in any jurisdiction in relation to this Agreement or any transaction contemplated by this Agreement, no immunity (whether by reason of sovereignty or otherwise) from such proceedings shall be claimed by or on behalf of the Party with respect to its assets;

(c) waives any right of immunity which it or its assets, property or revenues now has, may acquire in the future or which may be attributed to it in any jurisdiction; and

(d) consents generally in respect of the enforcement of any judgment or award against it in any such proceedings to the giving of any relief or the issue of any process in any jurisdiction in connection with such proceedings (including the making, enforcement or execution against it or in respect of any assets, property or revenues whatsoever irrespective of their use or intended use of any order or judgment that may be made or given in connection therewith).

20.3 Delayed Payments

The Parties hereto agree that payments due from one Party to the other Party under the provisions of this Agreement shall be made within the period set forth therein, and if no such period is specified, within 30 (thirty) days of receiving a demand along with the necessary particulars. In the event of delay beyond such period, the defaulting Party will pay interest for the period of delay calculated at a rate equal to 10% per annum, and recovery thereof will be without prejudice to the rights of the Parties under this Agreement including termination thereof.

20.4 Waiver

No waiver of any provision of this Agreement will constitute a waiver of any other provision(s) or of the same provision on another occasion. Failure of either Party to enforce any provision of this Agreement will not constitute a waiver of such provision or any other provision(s) of this Agreement.

20.5 Survival

Termination will not relieve the Concessionaire or the Authority, as the case may be, of any obligations hereunder which expressly or by implication survive termination hereof.

20.6 Entire Agreement

This Agreement together constitute the entire agreement between the Parties on the subject hereof, and no amendment or modification will be valid and effective unless such modification or amendment is agreed to in writing by the Parties. All prior written or oral understandings, offers or other communications of every kind pertaining to this Agreement are abrogated and withdrawn. For the avoidance of doubt, the Parties hereto agree that any obligations of the Concessionaire arising from the RFP will be deemed to form part of this Agreement.

20.7 Severability

Should any provision of this Agreement be held by a court of competent jurisdiction to be illegal, invalid or unenforceable, such provision may be modified by such court in compliance with the law giving effect to the intent of the Parties and enforced as modified. All other terms and conditions of this Client Agreement remain in full force and effect and will be construed in accordance with the modified provision.

20.8 Relationship of Parties

This Agreement will not be interpreted or construed to create an association, joint venture or partnership agreement between the Parties, or to impose any partnership obligation or liability upon either Party, and neither Party shall have any right, power or authority to enter into any agreement or undertaking for, or act on behalf of, or to act as or be an agent or representative of, or to otherwise bind, the other Party.

20.9 Third Parties

This Agreement is intended solely for the benefit of the Parties, and their respective successors and permitted assigns, and nothing in this Agreement shall be construed to create any duty to, standard of care with reference to, or any liability to, any person not a Party to this Agreement.

20.10 Notices

Notice to the Parties shall be in writing and shall be sent at the addresses first hereinabove mentioned (email accepted). In case, there is any change in the addresses of a Party, the same shall be communicated immediately to the other Party, failing which any notice sent to the earlier address of the said Party shall be deemed to be valid service of such notice.

Authority
Address:
Email:
Phone:
Kind Attention:

Concessionaire
Address:
Email:
Phone:
Kind Attention:

IN WITNESS WHEREOF, and intending to be legally bound, the Parties have duly executed this Agreement as of the date first written above.

Signed for and on behalf of
[*insert name of the Authority*]

Signed for and on behalf of
[*insert name of the Concessionaire*]

_____

By:
Name:
Title:

_____

By:
Name:
Title:

SCHEDULE 1 – SERVICES

[Please incorporate the standard services which are provided by UPHC including services related to operation and maintenance of the UPHC (cleanliness, operation hours, etc), who will maintain the security of UPHC, with a note that the Services may be modify in accordance with the requirement of the project.

Further, the Authority to identify the norms which will be followed by the Concessionaire in providing the Services (for example any norms listed by NUHM).]

SCHEDULE 2 – HEALTH CENTER

[Details of the health center and the assets to be handed over to the Concessionaire to be inserted in this schedule.]

SCHEDULE 3 – AUTHORITY SERVICES

[Any services that the Authority will provide should be included here, for example, if the Authority will provide medical supplies, ambulance, etc.]

SCHEDULE 4 – SERVICE FEES AND DOCUMENTS FOR PAYMENT

Part A: Fees
Health Center Procurement Fees: [_____]

Service Fees:
[_____]

Part B: Documents for Payment

[Government to include in this schedule the list of documents (including formats) to be provided by the Concessionaire for claiming payment.]

SCHEDULE 5 – KEY PERFORMANCE INDICATORS

[Please incorporate standard KPIs that are required for UPHCs in accordance with the project.]

SCHEDULE 6 – SALIENT FEATURES OF GRIEVANCE REDRESSAL POLICY

1.1. The Health Center will have a provision of complaint drop box at suitable and visible location where any aggrieved patient can register his/her complaint. Patient can also raise the concern/ complaint orally.

1.2. The process of grievance handling will be displayed at reception in local language and English for patient information. It will also mention the concerned authorized person name and phone number.

1.3. The Concessionaire will act promptly on receiving any complaint and the same should be addressed within 48 hours.

1.4. The Concessionaire will ensure that preventive mechanisms are in place so that complaints are not repeated again.

1.5. All patient complaints should be captured in digitised way and feed into the Health Management Information System (HMIS). The Concessionaire will produce quarterly reports on patient feedback received from the patients and share with the Authority.

SCHEDULE 7 – MONTHLY REPORT

[The information for monthly report to be identified here.]

Sample Concession Agreement (Bio-Medical Waste Management)

CONCESSION AGREEMENT

FOR

BIO-MEDICAL WASTE MANAGEMENT FACILITY PUBLIC–PRIVATE PARTNERSHIP PROJECTS

Between

Department of [_____]

And

[_____]

Concessionaire

For

Public–Private Partnership for Bio-Medical Waste Management Facility in

[_____]

BIO-MEDICAL WASTE MANAGEMENT FACILITY
PUBLIC–PRIVATE PARTNERSHIP CONCESSION AGREEMENT

This agreement is entered into on this [__] day of [__], 2020 at [_____] ("**Agreement**"):

BETWEEN

1.   [_____], represented by [_____] and having its principal office at [_____] (hereinafter referred to as the "**Authority**" which expression shall, unless repugnant to the context or meaning thereof, include its administrators, successors and assigns);

AND

2.   [*], a [*] incorporated under the provisions of Companies Act, 2013 and having its registered office at [*] (hereinafter referred to as the "**Concessionaire**" which expression shall, unless repugnant to the context or meaning thereof, include its successors and permitted assigns and substitutes).

"**Authority**" and "**Concessionaire**" will be referred to individually as the "**Party**" and collectively as the "**Parties**."

WHEREAS:

A.   The Government of [____] wishes to outsource the collection, transportation and management of the bio-medical waste produced from its urban primary health centers ("**Bio-Medical Waste**") located at [____] to private sector.

B.   The Authority had accordingly invited bids through its Request for Proposal No. [____] dated [____] ("**RFP**") for the selection of an entity for the collection, transportation, storage, treatment and disposal of the Bio-Medical Waste as more specifically provided in Schedule 1 (**Services**) in accordance with applicable laws and the terms and conditions of this Agreement.

C.   After evaluation of the bids received, the Authority accepted the bid of the Concessionaire in accordance with the terms of the RFP and issued the Letter of Acceptance No. [_____] dated [____] ("**LOA**") requiring, *inter alia*, the execution of this Agreement within 30 (thirty) days of the date of the issue of LOA.

D.   The Authority is accordingly entering into this Agreement with the Concessionaire for availing the Services of the Concessionaire in accordance with the terms and conditions of this Agreement.

NOW, THEREFORE, in consideration of the foregoing and the respective covenants and agreements set forth in this Agreement, the receipt and sufficiency of which is hereby acknowledged, and intending to be legally bound hereby, the Parties agree as follows:

1. Definitions and Interpretation

1.1. Definitions

The following words and expressions shall, unless the context otherwise requires, have the following meanings:

1.1.1. "**Authority Inspection Report**" will have the meaning as provided in Clause 10.3.

1.1.2. "**Award**" will have the meaning as provided in Clause 17.3.3.

1.1.3. "**Concessionaire Service Report**" will have the meaning as provided in Clause 10.1.

1.1.4. "**Concession Period**" will have the meaning as provided in Clause 2.2.

1.1.5. "**Confidential Information**" will have the meaning as provided in Clause 11.1.1.

1.1.6. "**Containers**" will have the meaning as provided in Clause 4.5.

1.1.7. "**Dispute**" will have the meaning as provided in Clause 17.1.1.

1.1.8. "**Effective Date**" will mean [_____].

1.1.9. "**Government Instrumentality**" means any department, division or sub-division of the Government of India or the State Government and includes any commission, board, authority, agency or municipal and other local authority or statutory body including Panchayat under the control of the Government of India or the State Government, as the case may be, and having jurisdiction over all or any part of the Project or the performance of all or any of the Services or obligations of the Concessionaire under or pursuant to this Agreement.

1.1.10. "**Identified Health Centers**" will have the meaning as provided in Schedule 2.

1.1.11. "**Indemnified Party**" will have the meaning as provided in Clause 16.2.

1.1.12. "**Indemnifying Party**" will have the meaning as provided in Clause 16.2.

1.1.13. "**Invoice**" will have the meaning as provided in Clause 6.2.

1.1.14. "**KPIs**" will have the meaning as provided in Clause 7 and Schedule 3.

1.1.15. "**LOA**" will have the meaning as provided in Recital C.

1.1.16. "**RFP**" will have the meaning as provided in Recital B.

1.1.17. "**Rules**" will have the meaning as provided in Clause 17.3.1.

1.1.18. "**Services**" will have the meaning as provided in Schedule 1.

1.1.19. "**Service Fees**" will have the meaning as provided in Clause 6.1.

1.2. Interpretation

In this Agreement, unless the context specifies otherwise:

1.2.1. headings are used for convenience only and shall not affect the interpretation of this Agreement;

1.2.2. reference to the singular includes a reference to the plural and vice versa, and reference to any gender includes a reference to all other genders;

1.2.3. references to the Recitals, Clauses and Schedules shall deemed to be a reference to the recitals, clauses and schedules of this Agreement;

1.2.4. the expression "this Clause" shall, unless followed by reference to a specific provision, be deemed to refer respectively to the whole Clause, not merely the sub-clause, paragraph or other provision in which the expression occurs;

1.2.5. references to any enactment are to be construed as referring also to any amendment or re-enactment (whether before or after the date of this Agreement), any previous enactment, which such enactment has replaced (with or without amendment) and to any regulation or order made under it;

1.2.6. references to "include" and "including" shall be construed without limitation.

2. Scope of the Project

2.1. Subject to the terms and conditions of this Agreement, the Authority grants to the Concessionaire the exclusive right during the Concession Period to (i) provide the Services for the health centers as identified in Schedule 2 (Identified Health Centers); and (ii) receive the Service Fees from the Authority for the Services, all in accordance with the terms and conditions of this Agreement.

2.2. This Agreement will become effective on the Signing Date and will continue for a period of [_____] months or years from the Effective Date ("Concession Period"), unless otherwise extended or terminated in accordance with this Agreement.

2.3. The Concessionaire will commence providing the Services from the Effective Date.

2.4. This Agreement may be extended by the Authority for a further period of [____] months or years if the Concessionaire achieves an average minimum KPI score of [_____] during the initial Concession Period.

2.5. For the purpose of this Agreement, the Authority and/or the Identified Health Centers will be considered as "**occupier**" and the Concessionaire will be considered as "**operator of a bio-medical waste facility**" under the Bio-Medical Waste (Management and Handling) Rules, 1998.

3. Roles and Responsibilities of the Concessionaire

3.1 The Concessionaire will collect the Bio-Medical Waste from the Containers maintained by the Identified Health Centers, twice every day at [7.00 AM and 8:00 PM] or any other times as many be mutually agreed by the Parties.

3.2 The Concessionaire will maintain a valid authorization from the State Pollution Control Board and other approvals as required under law to carry out the Services during the Concession Period.

3.3 The Concessionaire will be required to collect, transport, store and process and/or dispose the Bio-Medical Waste in accordance with the Bio-Medical Waste (Management and Handling) Rules, 1998, and any other applicable laws.

3.4 The Concessionaire will provide, operate and manage all the equipment for collection, transportation, storage, and processing or disposal of the Bio-Medical Waste.

3.5 The Concessionaire will recycle the Bio-Medical Waste within 48 hours of generation as required under the Bio-Medical Waste (Management and Handling) Rules, 1998.

3.6 The Concessionaire will maintain all the records and perform all obligations as required as an "**operator of a bio-medical waste facility**" related to the Bio-Medical Waste in accordance with applicable law and as required under this Agreement.

3.7 The Concessionaire will employ adequate number of skilled and trained human resources and will comply with the laws applicable to the recruitment, wages, minimum working hours, safety, cleanliness, insurance, gratuity, medical benefit, compensation, retrenchment benefit, etc.

3.8 The Concessionaire to ensure occupational safety of all its workers and others involved in handling of Bio-Medical Waste by providing appropriate tools for providing the Services and adequate health check-ups at the time of induction at least once in a year and maintaining the records for the same.

3.9 The Concessionaire to bear all costs and expenses in relation to the Services including expenses incurred towards salaries of its employees and any other related expenses.

4. Role and Responsibilities of the Authority

4.1 The Authority will take all steps to ensure that the Bio-Medical Waste is handled without any adverse effect to human health and the environment.

4.2 The Authority will maintain a valid authorization from the respective State Pollution Control Board for generation and handling of the Bio-Medical Waste.

4.3 The Authority will maintain all the records as required as an "**occupier**" related to the Bio-Medical Waste in accordance with applicable law and as required under this Agreement.

4.4 The Authority should not mix the Bio-Medical Waste with other waste. Further, the Authority is required to segregate the the Bio-Medical Waste into containers or bags at the point of generation in accordance with applicable laws (i.e., Bio-Medical Waste (Management and Handling) Rules, 1998) and provide it to the Concessionaire for collection within 12 hours of generation of the Bio-Medical Waste.

4.5 The Authority will be responsible for placing, holding and labelling the Bio-Medical Waste in containers in accordance with the applicable laws ("**Containers**") before they are collected by the Concessionaire.

4.6 The Authority will make all payments to the Concessionaire in the manner and within the time period specified in this Agreement.

5. Taxes and Duties

The Concessionaire will be liable to pay all taxes and duties applicable to the Concessionaire for the Services.

6. Payments

6.1 For the Services to be performed by the Concessionaire under this Agreement, the Authority will pay to the Concessionaire Rs. [___] ("Service Fees"), which is payable in monthly instalments of Rs. [_____].

6.2 The Concessionaire will, within first 7 days of each month, raise invoice for the previous month's Services on the Authority ("**Invoice**").

6.3 Save and except the disputed part of the Invoice (if any), the Authority will, within 15 days of receipt of the Invoice, make the payment for the undisputed part of the Invoice to the Concessionaire. The disputed part of the Invoice will be settled between the Parties in accordance with the dispute resolution mechanism provided in Clause 17.

7. Key Performance Indicator

7.1 Without prejudice to the obligations specified in this Agreement, the Concessionaire will provide the Services such that it meets the key performance indicators provide in Schedule 3 ("**KPIs**").

7.2 The Concessionaire will during the Concession Period, furnish to the Authority, a report, setting out the details provided in Clause 7.3, no later than 7 (seven) days after the close of each quarter of operation.

7.3 The report specified in Clause 7.2 will state in reasonable detail the compliance with all the KPIs specified in Schedule 3 (**KPIs**) along with an analysis of the reasons for failures, if any, and the strategies for addressing the same and for otherwise improving the performance of the Services.

7.4   The Concessionaire will ensure compliance of each of the KPIs specified in Schedule 3 (**KPIs**) and for any shortfall in performance, it will pay damages within 30 (thirty) days of every quarter in which the shortfall occurred. The damages due and payable under this Clause 7.4 will be determined in accordance with Schedule 3 (**KPIs**).

7.5   If the Concessionaire fails to achieve KPI score of [_____] for two consecutive quarters, then the Authority will be entitled to terminate this Agreement.

8. Right of Way

8.1   The Authority grants to the Concessionaire access to the Bio-Medical Waste at the designated location of the Identified Health Centers during the Concession Period.

8.2   The Concessionaire will ensure that during the performance of its obligations at the Identified Health Centers it (i) does not disturb the operation of the Identified Health Centers; (ii) obeys the rules and regulations of the Identified Health Centers; (iii) maintains cordial relationship with the employees, services providers, and management of the Identified Health Centers; and (iv) ensure safety of all personnel including patients at the Identified Health Centers.

9. Subcontract

The Concessionaire will not assign or sub-contract any of its rights or obligations under this Agreement without the prior written consent of the Authority.

10. Information Obligation

10.1. The Concessionaire is required to maintain and update on day to day basis the bio-medical waste management register and display the monthly record of categories and quantities of Bio-Medical Waste handled each day on its website according to the bio-medical waste generated in terms of category and colour coding in accordance with law (i.e., Bio-Medical Waste (Management and Handling) Rules, 1998), and also provide a copy of the daily register to the Authority on a weekly basis ("**Concessionaire Service Report**").

10.2. The Concessionaire is required to report all accidents, as soon as possible, that occur at the Identified Health Centers or any other site where Bio-Medical Waste is handled or during transportation of such waste.

10.3. In addition to inspection and verification to be conducted by the appropriate government body under applicable laws, the Authority will also have right to inspect and verify periodically, the Services that is being provided by the Concessionaire. The Authority will make a report of such inspection ("**Authority Inspection Report**") stating in reasonable detail the defects or deficiencies, if any, with particular reference to the maintenance and safety requirements, and send a copy thereof to the Concessionaire.

10.4. The Concessionaire will rectify the defects or deficiencies, if any, set forth in the Authority Inspection Report and furnish a report to the Authority within 15 days of the aforesaid reports; provided that where the remedy of such defects or deficiencies is likely to take more than 15 days, the Concessionaire will submit progress reports of the repair works once every week until such work is completed in conformity with this Agreement.

11. Confidentiality and Data Protection

11.1. Confidentiality

11.1.1. Each Party will maintain in strict confidence and protect the confidentiality of all information, reports, data, software or other material, whether written or oral, in electronic or magnetic format, and the contents thereof and any reports, digests or summaries created or derived from any of the foregoing that is provided by one Party to the other Party in relation to this Agreement ("**Confidential Information**"), and will not disclose any such Confidential Information to any third party without the prior written consent of the other Party; provided that each Party will be entitled to use Confidential Information for any and all lawful purposes.

11.1.2. Notwithstanding Clause 11.1.1, each Party may disclose Confidential Information to the extent that such Confidential Information:

(a) was properly in the possession of the receiving Party prior to disclosure thereof by the other Party;

(b) was in the public domain prior to its delivery to such Party or after such delivery if it becomes part of the public domain without breach of any confidentiality obligations by the receiving Party under this Agreement;

(c) was obtained from a third party with no known duty to maintain its confidentiality;

(d) is required to be disclosed by applicable law or judicial or administrative or arbitral process, provided that for any such disclosure, the disclosing Party will give the other Party prompt written notice, where possible, and use reasonable efforts to ensure that such disclosure is accorded confidential treatment and also to enable such other Party to seek a protective order or other appropriate remedy at such other Party's sole costs; and

(e) lawfully becomes available without any limitation as to its disclosure.

11.1.3. The Parties agree that upon termination of this Agreement, the receiving Party will promptly deliver to the disclosing Party the Confidential Information and copies thereof in its possession or under its direct or indirect control, and will destroy all memoranda, notes and other writings prepared by the receiving Party or directors, officers, employees or advisors, based on Confidential Information.

11.2. Data Protection

11.2.1. The Concessionaire represents that it will abide by and observes all laws, rules, regulations including but not limited to the data protection laws of India while performing its obligations under this Agreement.

11.2.2. The Concessionaire will indemnify the Authority against all actions, claims, demands, losses, damages, statutory penalties, expenses and cost in respect of breach of obligation under this Clauses 11.2.

12. Insurance

The Concessionaire will Maintain the Following Insurance:

12.1 comprehensive professional indemnity insurance;

12.2 the Concessionaire's general liability arising out of the Concession;

12.3 liability to third parties for goods or property damage;

12.4 workmen's compensation insurance; and

12.5 any other insurance that may be necessary to protect the Concessionaire and its employees, including all Force Majeure Events that are insurable at commercially reasonable premiums and not otherwise covered in Clauses 12.1 to 12.4 above.

13. Representations and Warranties

Each Party Hereby Represents and Warrants to the Other Party That:

13.1. it is duly organized and validly existing under the laws of the jurisdiction of its establishment or incorporation;

13.2. it has all necessary approvals, powers, licenses and authorities to enter into and perform its obligations under this Agreement;

13.3. its representative whose signature is affixed below hereto is fully authorized to sign this Agreement and to bind it pursuant to a valid power of attorney or resolution passed by its board of directors;

13.4. this Agreement constitutes legal, valid and binding obligations of such Party, enforceable against it in accordance with its terms;

13.5. it is not insolvent, and no receiver, liquidator, trustee, administrator, custodian or similar official has been appointed in respect of the whole or any substantial part of the business or assets of such Party;

13.6. the execution, delivery and performance of this Agreement by such Party will not (i) violate any provision of the constitutional documents of such Party; or (ii) require such Party to obtain any approvals or action of, or make any filing with or give any notice to, any governmental authority or any other person pursuant to any instrument, contract or other agreement to which such Party is a party or by which such Party is bound; (iii) conflict with or result in any material breach or violation of any of the terms and conditions of, or constitute a default under, any instrument, contract or other agreement to which such Party is a party or by which such Party is bound; (iv) to its knowledge, violate any order, judgment or decree against, or binding upon, such Party or upon its respective securities, properties or businesses; or (v) to its knowledge, violate any applicable laws; and

13.7. there is no lawsuit, arbitration, or legal, administrative or other proceedings or governmental investigation pending or, to the best of the knowledge of such Party, threatened, against it with respect to the subject matter of this Agreement or that would affect in any way its ability to enter into or perform its obligations under this Agreement.

14. Force Majeure

14.1. Definition of Force Majeure and Legislative and Political Event

14.1.1. In this Clause, "**Force Majeure**" means an exceptional event or circumstance:
   (a) which is beyond a Party's control,
   (b) which such Party could not reasonably have foreseen before entering into the Agreement,
   (c) which, having arisen, such Party could not reasonably have avoided or overcome, and
   (d) which is not substantially attributable to the other Party, which has a material adverse effect.

14.1.2. "**Change in Law**" means any of the following events occurring as a result of any action by any Government Instrumentality:
   (a) change, amendment, modification of, addition to, or deletion from a law; or
   (b) an enactment or making of a new law; or
   (c) repeal of existing law; or
   (d) change in the manner in which a law is applied, enforced or interpreted, which increases cost or makes it difficult for the Concessionaire to perform its obligations under this Agreement.

14.2. Notice of Force Majeure

14.2.1. If a Party is or will be prevented from performing any of its obligations under the Agreement by Force Majeure, then it will give notice to the other Party of the event or circumstances constituting the Force Majeure and will specify the obligations, the performance of which is or will be affected. The notice will be given within 14 days after the Party became aware, or should have become aware, of the relevant event or circumstance constituting Force Majeure.

14.2.2. The Party will, having given notice, be excused from performance of such obligations for so long as such Force Majeure prevents it from performing them.

14.2.3. Notwithstanding any other provision of this Clause, Force Majeure will not apply to obligations of either Party to make payments to the other Party under the Agreement.

14.3. Duty to Minimize Delay

14.3.1. Each Party will at all times use all reasonable endeavors to minimize any delay in the performance of the Agreement as a result of Force Majeure.

14.3.2. A Party will give notice to the other Party when it ceases to be affected by the Force Majeure.

14.4. Consequences of Force Majeure

The Parties will be responsible for its own losses related to Force Majeure.

14.5. Optional Termination and Payment

If the Service is prevented for a continuous period of 90 days by reason of Force Majeure of which notice has been given under Clause 14.2, or for multiple periods which totals more than 140 days, then either Party may give to the other Party a notice of termination of the Agreement. In this event, the termination will take effect 7 days after the notice is given.

14.6. Notice of Change in Law

14.6.1. If the Concessionaire incurs (or will incur) additional cost for providing the Services as a result of Change in Law occurring after the bid submission date (as provided in the RFP), then the Concessionaire will give notice to the Authority and will be entitled to compensation for the addition cost related to the Services due to Change in Law.

14.6.2. After receiving this notice, the Parties will proceed to agree on the addition cost failing which the cost will be determined by the Parties in accordance with the dispute resolution mechanism provided in Clause 17.

14.6.3. The Concessionaire will use all reasonable efforts to mitigate the impact of Change in Law.

15. Default and Termination

15.1. Termination Events

15.1.1. Without limiting any other rights or remedies, the Authority reserves the right to terminate this Agreement, if the Concessionaire:
   (a) fails to achieve KPI scores in accordance with Clause 7.4;
   (b) is in default under any material obligation hereunder and the default has not been cured within 15 days after receipt of notice of such breach or default, unless the Parties otherwise mutually agree; or
   (c) becomes insolvent, makes a general assignment for the benefit of creditors, files a voluntary petition in bankruptcy, or suffers or permits the appointment of a receiver for its business or assets.

15.1.2. Without limiting any other rights or remedies, the Concessionaire reserves the right to terminate this Agreement, if the Authority:
   (a) fails to make any payment in accordance with this Agreement;
   (b) is in default under any material obligation hereunder that has not been cured within 15 days after receipt of notice of such breach or default, unless the Parties otherwise mutually agree.

15.2. Consequence of Termination

15.2.1. The termination of this Agreement in whole or in part for any reason under this Clause 15 will not affect (i) any liabilities or obligations of either Party arising before such termination or out of the events causing such termination; or (ii) any damages or other remedies to which a Party may be entitled under this Agreement, by law or in equity, arising from any breaches of such liabilities or obligations.

15.2.2. Upon termination, if required by the Authority, the Concessionaire will continue to provide the Services for a further period of 3 months after termination in accordance with the terms and conditions of this Agreement.

16. Indemnity

16.1. General Indemnity

16.1.1. The Concessionaire will indemnify, defend and hold the Authority harmless against any and all proceedings, actions, and third-party claims for any loss, damage, cost, and expense of whatever kind and nature arising out of any act of the Concessionaire including failure of the Concessionaire to comply with applicable laws.

16.1.2. The Authority will indemnify, defend and hold the Concessionaire harmless against any and all proceedings, actions, and third-party claims for any loss, damage, cost, and expense of whatever kind and nature arising out of any act of the Authority including failure of the Authority to comply with applicable laws.

16.2. Notice and Contest of Claims

If any Party receives a claim from a third-party in respect of which it is entitled to the benefit of an indemnity under Clause 16.1 above ("**Indemnified Party**"), then such Party will notify the other Party responsible for indemnifying such claim hereunder ("**Indemnifying Party**") within 15 (fifteen) days of receipt of the claim and will not settle or pay the claim without the prior approval of the Indemnifying Party, which approval not to be unreasonably withheld or delayed. If the Indemnifying Party wishes to contest or dispute the claim, it may conduct the proceedings in the name of the Indemnified Party and will bear all costs involved in contesting the same. The Indemnified Party will provide all cooperation and assistance in contesting any claim and will sign all such writings and documents as the Indemnifying Party may reasonably require.

17. Dispute Resolution

17.1. Dispute

17.1.1. Any dispute, difference or controversy of whatever nature howsoever arising under or out of or in relation to this Agreement between the Parties, and so notified in writing by either Party to the other Party ("**Dispute**") will, in the first instance, be attempted to be resolved amicably in accordance with the conciliation procedure set forth in Clause 17.1.2.

17.1.2. The Parties agree to use their best efforts for resolving all Disputes arising under or in respect of this Agreement promptly, equitably and in good faith, and further agree to provide each other with reasonable access during normal business hours to all non-privileged records, information and data pertaining to any Dispute.

17.2. Conciliation

If any Dispute between the Parties cannot be amicably settled, then such Dispute may be referred to the [Chairman of the District or State Health Care Department] and the [CEO] of the Concessionaire for amicable settlement, and upon such reference, the said persons will meet no later than 14 days from the date of reference to discuss and attempt to amicably resolve the Dispute. If such meeting does not take place within the 14 days period or the Dispute is not amicably settled within 30 days of the meeting or such longer period as may be mutually agreed by the Parties, either Party may refer the Dispute to arbitration in accordance with the provisions of Clause 17.3.

17.3. Arbitration

17.3.1. Any Dispute which is not resolved amicably by conciliation, as provided in Clause 17.2, will be finally decided by reference to arbitration by a board of arbitrators appointed in accordance with Clause 17.3.2 below. Such arbitration will be held in accordance with the Rules of Arbitration of the International Center for Alternative Dispute Resolution, New Delhi ("**Rules**"), or such other rules as may be mutually agreed by the Parties, and shall be subject to the provisions of the Arbitration and Conciliation Act, 1996. The venue of such arbitration will be [_____], and the language of arbitration proceedings will be English.

17.3.2. There will be a board of 3 arbitrators, of whom each Party will select 1, and the 3rd arbitrator will be appointed by the 2 arbitrators so selected and in the event of disagreement between the 2 arbitrators, the appointment will be made in accordance with the Rules.

17.3.3. The arbitrators will make a reasoned award ("**Award**"). Any Award made in any arbitration will be final and binding on the Parties as from the date it is made, and the Concessionaire and the Authority agree and undertake to carry out such Award without delay.

17.3.4. This Agreement and the rights and obligations of the Parties shall remain in full force and effect, pending the Award in any arbitration proceedings hereunder.

17.4. Adjudication by Regulatory Authority or Commission

If any Dispute between the Parties is to be adjudicated under a statutory Regulatory Authority or Commission enacted under the Bio-Medical Waste (Management and Handling) Rules, 1998 or similar enactment, then such Dispute will be adjudicated upon by such Regulatory Authority or Commission in accordance with the applicable laws and all references to Dispute Resolution Procedure will be construed accordingly.

18. Miscellaneous

18.1. Governing Law and Jurisdiction

This Agreement will be construed and interpreted in accordance with and governed by the laws of India, and the courts at [___] will have exclusive jurisdiction over matters arising out of or relating to this Agreement.

18.2. Waiver of Immunity

Each Party unconditionally and irrevocably:
(a) agrees that the execution, delivery and performance by it of this Agreement constitute commercial acts done and performed for commercial purpose;

(b) agrees that, should any proceedings be brought against it or its assets, property or revenues in any jurisdiction in relation to this Agreement or any transaction contemplated by this Agreement, no immunity (whether by reason of sovereignty or otherwise) from such proceedings shall be claimed by or on behalf of the Party with respect to its assets;

(c) waives any right of immunity which it or its assets, property or revenues now has, may acquire in the future or which may be attributed to it in any jurisdiction; and

(d) consents generally in respect of the enforcement of any judgment or award against it in any such proceedings to the giving of any relief or the issue of any process in any jurisdiction in connection with such proceedings (including the making, enforcement or execution against it or in respect of any assets, property or revenues whatsoever irrespective of their use or intended use of any order or judgment that may be made or given in connection therewith).

18.3. Delayed Payments

The Parties hereto agree that payments due from one Party to the other Party under the provisions of this Agreement shall be made within the period set forth therein, and if no such period is specified, within 30 (thirty) days of receiving a demand along with the necessary particulars. In the event of delay beyond such period, the defaulting Party will pay interest for the period of delay calculated at a rate equal to 10% per annum, and recovery thereof will be without prejudice to the rights of the Parties under this Agreement including termination thereof.

18.4. Waiver

No waiver of any provision of this Agreement will constitute a waiver of any other provision(s) or of the same provision on another occasion. Failure of either Party to enforce any provision of this Agreement will not constitute a waiver of such provision or any other provision(s) of this Agreement.

18.5. Survival

Termination will not relieve the Concessionaire or the Authority, as the case may be, of any obligations hereunder which expressly or by implication survive termination hereof.

18.6. Entire Agreement

This Agreement together constitute the entire agreement between the Parties on the subject hereof, and no amendment or modification will be valid and effective unless such modification or amendment is agreed to in writing by the Parties. All prior written or oral understandings, offers or other communications of every kind pertaining to this Agreement are abrogated and withdrawn. For the avoidance of doubt, the Parties hereto agree that any obligations of the Concessionaire arising from the RFP will be deemed to form part of this Agreement.

18.7. Severability

Should any provision of this Agreement be held by a court of competent jurisdiction to be illegal, invalid or unenforceable, such provision may be modified by such court in compliance with the law giving effect to the intent of the Parties and enforced as modified. All other terms and conditions of this Client Agreement remain in full force and effect and will be construed in accordance with the modified provision.

18.8. Relationship of Parties

This Agreement will not be interpreted or construed to create an association, joint venture or partnership agreement between the Parties, or to impose any partnership obligation or liability upon either Party, and neither Party shall have any right, power or authority to enter into any agreement or undertaking for, or act on behalf of, or to act as or be an agent or representative of, or to otherwise bind, the other Party.

18.9. Third Parties

This Agreement is intended solely for the benefit of the Parties, and their respective successors and permitted assigns, and nothing in this Agreement shall be construed to create any duty to, standard of care with reference to, or any liability to, any person not a Party to this Agreement.

18.10. Notices

Notice to the Parties shall be in writing and shall be sent at the addresses first hereinabove mentioned (email accepted). In case, there is any change in the addresses of a Party, the same shall be communicated immediately to the other Party, failing which any notice sent to the earlier address of the said Party shall be deemed to be valid service of such notice.

Authority
Address:
Email:
Phone:
Kind Attention:

Concessionaire
Address:
Email:
Phone:
Kind Attention:

IN WITNESS WHEREOF, and intending to be legally bound, the Parties have duly executed this Agreement as of the date first written above.

Signed for and on behalf of
[*insert name of the Authority*]

Signed for and on behalf of
[*insert name of the Concessionaire*]

_____

By:
Name:
Title:

_____

By:
Name:
Title:

SCHEDULE 1 – SERVICES

The Concessionaire will collect, transport, store and process/dispose the waste as identified in the Bio-Medical Waste in accordance with the Bio-Medical Waste (Management and Handling) Rules, 1998, or as may be modified from time to time.

SCHEDULE 2 – IDENTIFIED HEALTH CARE CENTERS

[Name of districts and Identified Health Centers requiring services of BMWMF to be inserted in this schedule.]

S.No.	District	Identified Health Centers Requiring Services of BMWMF

SCHEDULE 3 – KEY PERFORMANCE INDICATORS

*[Please incorporate standard KPIs that are required for UPHCs.
The usually KPIs for this should be collecting on time, coming every day, providing regular information, record keeping, interface issue with employees, service providers, doctors, patients, at the time of collection of the waste. Please add anything else that you think is relevant.]*

Sample Concession Agreement (Diagnostic and Pathological Services)

CONCESSION AGREEMENT

FOR

DIAGNOSTIC AND PATHOLOGICAL SERVICES THROUGH PUBLIC–PRIVATE PARTNERSHIP

Between

Department of [_____]

And

[_____]

Concessionaire

For

Public–Private Partnership for Diagnostic and Pathological Services in

[_____]

DIAGNOSTIC AND PATHOLOGICAL SERVICES CONCESSION AGREEMENT

This agreement is entered into on this [__] day of [__], 2020 at [_____] ("**Agreement**"):

BETWEEN

1.   [_____], represented by [_____] and having its principal office at [_____] (hereinafter referred to as the "**Authority**" which expression shall, unless repugnant to the context or meaning thereof, include its administrators, successors and assigns);

AND

2.   [*], a [*] incorporated under the provisions of Companies Act, 2013 and having its registered office at [*] (hereinafter referred to as the "**Concessionaire**" which expression shall, unless repugnant to the context or meaning thereof, include its successors and permitted assigns and substitutes).

"**Authority**" and "**Concessionaire**" will be referred to individually as the "**Party**" and collectively as the "**Parties**".

WHEREAS:

A.   The Government of India has launched National Urban Health Mission ("**NUHM**") for providing primary health care services to the urban population with special focus on slum and other vulnerable sections of the society. As a part of NUHM, the Government of [_____] ("**State Government**") has decided to outsource diagnostic and pathological services as identified in Schedule 1 (**Diagnostic and Pathological Services**) of the Urban Primary Health Centers (UPHCs) as identified in Schedule 2 (**Identified Health Centers**) to private sector.

B.   The Authority had accordingly invited bids through its Request for Proposal No. [_____] dated [_____] ("**RFP**") for the selection of an entity for providing the Diagnostic and Pathological Services in the Identified Health Centers in accordance with the terms and conditions of this Agreement.

C.   After evaluation of the bids received, the Authority accepted the bid of the Concessionaire in accordance with the terms of the RFP and issued the Letter of Acceptance No. [_____] dated [_____] ("**LOA**") requiring, inter alia, the execution of this Agreement within 30 (thirty) days of the date of the issue of LOA.

D.   The Authority is accordingly entering into this Agreement with the Concessionaire for availing the Diagnostic and Pathological Services, subject to and on the terms and conditions as set forth hereinafter.

NOW, THEREFORE, in consideration of the foregoing and the respective covenants and agreements set forth in this Agreement, the receipt and sufficiency of which is hereby acknowledged, and intending to be legally bound hereby, the Parties agree as follows:

1. Definitions and Interpretation

1.1. Definitions

The following words and expressions shall, unless the context otherwise requires, have the following meanings:

1.1.1. **Authority Inspection Report**" will have the meaning as provided in Clause 12.3.

1.1.2. "**Award**" will have the meaning as provided in Clause 19.3.3.

1.1.3. "**Confidential Information**" will have the meaning as provided in Clause 13.1.1.

1.1.4. "**Concession Period**" will have the meaning as provided in Clause 2.2.

1.1.5. "**Diagnostic and Pathology Services**" will have the meaning as provided in Recital A and Schedule 1.

1.1.6. "**Dispute**" will have the meaning as provided in Clause 19.1.1.

1.1.7. "**Effective Date**" will mean [_____].

1.1.8. "**Good Industry Practice**" means the practices, methods, techniques, designs, standards, skills, diligence, efficiency, reliability and prudence which are generally and reasonably expected from a reasonably skilled and experienced operator engaged In the same type of services as envisaged under this Agreement and which would be expected to result in the performance of its obligations by the Concessionaire in accordance with this Agreement and applicable laws in reliable, safe, economical and efficient manner.

1.1.9. "**Government Instrumentality**" means any department, division or sub-division of the Government of India or the State Government and includes any commission, board, authority, agency or municipal and other local authority or statutory body including Panchayat under the control of the Government of India or the State Government, as the case may be, and having jurisdiction over all or any part of the services or obligations of the Concessionaire under or pursuant to this Agreement.

1.1.10. "**Indemnified Party**" will have the meaning as provided in Clause 18.2.

1.1.11. "**Indemnifying Party**" will have the meaning as provided in Clause 18.2.

1.1.12. "**Identified Health Centers**" will have the meaning as provided in Recital A and Schedule 2.

1.1.13. "**Invoice**" will have the meaning as provided in Clause 6.1.

1.1.14. "**KPIs**" will have the meaning as provided in Clause 7 and Schedule 5.

1.1.15. "**LOA**" will have the meaning as provided in Recital C.

1.1.16. "**Monthly Reports**" will have the meaning as provided in Clause 12.1.

1.1.17. "**Patient and Doctor Satisfaction Survey**" will have the meaning as provided in Clause 8.1 and Schedule 6.

1.1.18. "**Personal Data**" will have the meaning as provided in Clause 13.2.2.

1.1.19. "**RFP**" will have the meaning as provided in Recital B.

1.1.20. "**Rules**" will have the meaning as provided in Clause 19.3.1.

1.1.21. "**Signing Date**" will mean the date of execution of this Agreement.

1.1.22. "**Service Rooms**" will have the meaning as provided in Clause 3.3.

1.1.23. "**State Government**" will have the meaning as provided in Recital A.

1.2. Interpretation

In this Agreement, unless the context specifies otherwise:

1.2.1. headings are used for convenience only and shall not affect the interpretation of this Agreement;

1.2.2. reference to the singular includes a reference to the plural and vice versa, and reference to any gender includes a reference to all other genders;

1.2.3. references to the Recitals, Clauses and Schedules shall deemed to be a reference to the recitals, clauses and schedules of this Agreement;

1.2.4. the expression "this Clause" shall, unless followed by reference to a specific provision, be deemed to refer respectively to the whole Clause, not merely the sub-clause, paragraph or other provision in which the expression occurs;

1.2.5. references to any enactment are to be construed as referring also to any amendment or re-enactment (whether before or after the date of this Agreement), any previous enactment, which such enactment has replaced (with or without amendment) and to any regulation or order made under it;

1.2.6. references to "include" and "including" shall be construed without limitation.

2. Scope of the Agreement

2.1. Subject to the terms and conditions of this Concession Agreement, the Authority grants to the Concessionaire the exclusive right during the Concession Period to (i) provide the Diagnostic and Pathological Services for the Identified Health Centers; and (ii) receive the service fees from the Authority, all in accordance with the terms and conditions of this Agreement.

2.2. This Agreement will become effective on the Signing Date and will continue for a period of [____] months or years from the Effective Date ("**Concession Period**"), unless otherwise extended or terminated in accordance with this Agreement.

2.3. The Concessionaire will commence providing the Diagnostic and Pathological Services from the Effective Date.

2.4. This Agreement may be extended by the Authority for a further period of [___] months or years if the Concessionaire achieves an average minimum KPI score of [___] during the initial Concession Period.

3. Roles and Responsibilities of the Concessionaire

3.1 The Concessionaire is required to obtain and maintain all consents and approvals required for providing the Diagnostic and Pathological Services under the applicable laws.

3.2 The Concessionaire will comply with all the applicable laws including the Clinical Establishment (Central Government) Rules, 2012 and other laws for providing the Diagnostic and Pathological Services.

3.3 The Authority will provide space or rooms to the Concessionaire at the Identified Health Centers for providing the Diagnostic and Pathological Services ("**Service Rooms**"). The Concessionaire, during the term of the Concession Agreement, will ensure that the Diagnostic and Pathological Services are available on the days and time specified in Schedule 3 (**Time Schedule for Services**).

3.4 The Concessionaire will maintain the Service Rooms clean and hygienic in accordance with the applicable laws and Good Industry Practices.

3.5 The Concessionaire will employ adequate number of skilled and trained human resources and will comply with the laws applicable to the recruitment, wages, minimum working hours, safety, cleanliness, insurance, gratuity, medical benefit, compensation, retrenchment benefit, etc.

3.6 The Concessionaire will ensure that during the performance of its Diagnostic and Pathological Services at the Identified Health Centers the employees and agents of the Concessionaire (i) will not disturb the operation of the Identified Health Centers, (ii) obeys the rules and regulations of the Identified Health Centers, (iii) maintains cordial relationship with the employees, services providers and management of the Identified Health Centers, and (iv) ensure safety of all personnel including patients at the Identified Health Centers.

3.7   The Concessionaire to bear all costs and expenses in relation to the Diagnostic and Pathological Services including expenses incurred towards salaries of its employees, consultants, agents and any other cost related to Diagnostic and Pathological Services.

3.8   The Concessionaire will display each type of Diagnostic and Pathological Services provided and facilities available, for the benefit of patients at a conspicuous place in the local as well as in English language.

3.9   A no-fee receipt will be provided by the Concessionaire to every patient. A copy of all such receipts will be submitted on a monthly basis by the Concessionaire to the Authority.

4.   Discontinuity of the Services

In case of discontinuity of the Diagnostic and Pathological Services by the Concessionaire for more than [24] hours, it is the liability of the Concessionaire to get the tests done through any other service provider at no cost to the Authority. If the Concessionaire fails to do this, then the Authority may get the tests done at market rate from any other service provider and the total amount paid to the other service provider will be deducted from the Invoices of the Concessionaire.

5.   Role and Responsibilities of the Authority

5.1.   The Authority will, upon written request from the Concessionaire, and subject to the Concessionaire complying with applicable laws, provide reasonable assistance to the Concessionaire for procuring the applicable permits required from any Government Instrumentality for providing the Diagnostic and Pathological Services.

5.2.   The Authority will provide to the Concessionaire all reasonable facilities and utilities required at the Identified Health Centers, including water and electricity for providing the Diagnostic and Pathological Services.

5.3.   The Authority will pay the fees for the services to the Concessionaire in accordance with this Agreement.

5.4.   The Authority will ensure peaceful access and use of the Identified Health Centers by the Concessionaire in accordance with the provisions of this Agreement.

6.   Price and Payments

6.1   The Concessionaire will raise its invoice within [7] days of the beginning of each month for the Diagnostic and Pathological Services provided in the previous month ("Invoice").

6.2   Along with the Invoice, the Concessionaire will furnish to the Authority a report in a form acceptable to the Authority, stating in reasonable detail the Diagnostic and Pathological Services provided by the Concessionaire in the previous month.

6.3. The Invoice will be calculated based on the Diagnostic and Pathological Services provided in a month at the rate identified in Schedule 4 (**Rates of Diagnostic and Pathological Services**).

6.4. Save and except the disputed party of the Invoice (if any), the Authority will, within 15 days of receipt of the Invoice, make the payment for the undisputed part of the Invoice to the Concessionaire. The disputed part of the Invoice will be settled between the Parties in accordance with the dispute resolution mechanism provided in Clause 19.

7. Key Performance Indicator

7.1 Without prejudice to the obligations specified in this Agreement, the Concessionaire will provide the Diagnostic and Pathological Services such that it meets the key performance indicators provide in Schedule 5 ("**KPIs**").

7.2. The Concessionaire will during the Concession Period, furnish to the Authority, a report, setting out the details provided in Clause 7.3, no later than 7 days after the close of each quarter of operation.

7.3. The report specified in Clause 7.2 will state in reasonable detail the compliance with all the KPIs specified in Schedule 5 (**KPIs**) along with an analysis of the reasons for failures, if any, and the strategies for addressing the same and for otherwise improving the Diagnostic and Pathological Services.

7.4. The Concessionaire will ensure compliance of each of the KPIs specified in Schedule 5 (**KPIs**) and for any shortfall in performance, it will pay damages within 30 (thirty) days of every quarter in which the shortfall occurred. The damages due and payable under this Clause 6.4 will be determined in accordance with Schedule 5 (**KPIs**).

7.5. If the Concessionaire fails to achieve KPI score of [____] for two consecutive quarters, then the Authority will be entitled to terminate this Agreement.

8. Patient and Doctor Satisfaction Survey, Grievance Redressal Policy

8.1. Patient and Doctor Satisfaction Survey

8.1.1. The Concessionaire will conduct Patient and Doctor Satisfaction Survey of the Diagnostic and Pathological Services at each of the Identified Health Center once in each quarter. The survey will be conducted by handing out a Patient and a Doctor Satisfaction Form as provided in Schedule 6 (**Patient and Doctor Satisfaction Survey**) to randomly selected patients and doctors at Identified Health Centers. The Concessionaire will submit a report of the findings of such survey to the Authority in every quarter and will ensure that the Diagnostic and Pathological Services achieves and maintains an overall score of least [80%] in such survey. Each survey will include responses from at least [100] patients and [5] doctors at the Identified Health Centers.

8.1.2. In addition, the Authority may at its discretion, cost and expense, conduct Patient and Doctor Satisfaction Survey not more than once in every quarter to determine the compliance of the provisions of this Clause 8.1 by the Concessionaire.

8.1.3. If the Patient and Doctor Satisfaction Survey reveals that more than 20% of the patients and doctors surveyed by the Concessionaire or the Authority, as the case may be, ranked the Diagnostic and Pathological Services below [80%] rating, then the Authority may levy and collect from the Concessionaire damages in an amount equal to [20]% of the Invoice of that quarter.

8.2. Grievance Redressal Policy

8.2.1. The Authority may develop a Grievance Redressal Policy to monitor and address any issues or complaints regarding the Diagnostic and Pathological Services.

8.2.2. If any patient or doctor complains of the Concessionaire, then the Concessionaire will, upon receiving the complaint, act promptly (not exceeding 48 hours) to address the complaint.

8.2.3. The Concessionaire will ensure that preventive mechanisms are in place so that complaints are not repeated again.

9. Right of Way

9.1. The Authority will provide to the Concessionaire, one-time assets and/or consumable assets, from time to time, if any, as identified in Schedule 7 (**Assets**).

9.2. The Authority grants to the Concessionaire access and license to the Service Rooms and common facilities such as toilets and other facilities at Identified Health Centers as may be required to provide the Diagnostic and Pathological Services.

9.3. It is expressly agreed that the license granted to the Concessionaire will terminate automatically without the need for any action to be taken by the Authority to terminate the license, upon the termination or expiry of this Agreement for any reason whatsoever.

9.4. After the Signing Date and before the Effective Date, the Parties will, on a mutually agreed date and time, inspect the Identified Health Centers and prepare a memorandum containing an inventory of the assets, equipment and machinery. Such memorandum will specify in reasonable details the Service Room(s) and assets, equipment and machinery for which license is granted to the Concessionaire. Signing of the memorandum by the Authority will be deemed to constitute a valid license to the Concessionaire for the use of the Service Rooms and the assets, equipment and machinery during the Concession Period in accordance with the provisions of this Agreement.

10. Management of Assets

10.1. Save and except any asset identified in Schedule 7 (**Assets**), all other assets, equipment and consumables required for providing the Diagnostic and Pathological Services will be provided by the Concessionaire.

10.2. Any equipment provided by the Authority will be operated and maintained by the Concessionaire is accordance with the Good Industry Practice.

11. Subcontract

The Concessionaire will not assign or sub-contract any of its rights or obligations under this Agreement without the prior written consent of the Authority.

12. Information Obligation

12.1. The Concessionaire will maintain and provide to the Authority on a monthly basis (i) the records in relation to the Diagnostic and Pathological Services provided by the Concessionaire in a given month, and (ii) all information and statistics required to be maintained under applicable laws ("**Monthly Reports**").

12.2. The Authority will have right to inspect the Service Rooms and the Diagnostic and Pathological Services being provided by the Concessionaire from time to time. The Authority will make a report of such inspection ("**Authority Inspection Report**") stating in reasonable details of the defects or deficiencies, if any, with particular reference to the maintenance and safety requirements, and send a copy thereof to the Concessionaire. The Concessionaire will rectify the defects or deficiencies, if any, set forth in the Authority Inspection Report and furnish a report to the Authority within 15 days of the aforesaid reports.

13. Confidentiality and Data Protection

13.1. Confidentiality

13.1.1. Each Party will maintain in strict confidence and protect the confidentiality of all information, reports, data, software or other material, whether written or oral, in electronic or magnetic format, and the contents thereof and any reports, digests or summaries created or derived from any of the foregoing that is provided by one Party to the other Party in relation to this Agreement ("**Confidential Information**"), and will not disclose any such Confidential Information to any third party without the prior written consent of the other Party; provided that each Party will be entitled to use Confidential Information for any and all lawful purposes.

13.1.2. Notwithstanding Clause 13.1.1, each Party may disclose Confidential Information to the extent that such Confidential Information:

(a) was properly in the possession of the receiving Party prior to disclosure thereof by the other Party;

(b) was in the public domain prior to its delivery to such Party or after such delivery if it becomes part of the public domain without breach of any confidentiality obligations by the receiving Party under this Agreement;

(c) was obtained from a third party with no known duty to maintain its confidentiality;

(d) is required to be disclosed by applicable law or judicial or administrative or arbitral process, provided that for any such disclosure, the disclosing Party will give the other Party prompt written notice, where possible, and use reasonable efforts to ensure that such disclosure is accorded confidential treatment and also to enable such other Party to seek a protective order or other appropriate remedy at such other Party's sole costs; and

(e) lawfully becomes available without any limitation as to its disclosure.

13.1.3. The Parties agree that upon termination of this Agreement, the receiving Party will promptly deliver to the disclosing Party the Confidential Information and copies thereof in its possession or under its direct or indirect control, and will destroy all memoranda, notes and other writings prepared by the receiving Party or directors, officers, employees or advisors, based on Confidential Information.

13.2. Data Protection

13.2.1. The Concessionaire represents that it will abide by and observes all laws, rules, regulations including but not limited to the data protection laws of India while performing its obligations under this Agreement.

13.2.2. The Concessionaire will protect the personal data which it receives in connection with the provision of the Diagnostic and Pathological Services ("**Personal Data**") by making security arrangements (as required under law) to prevent unauthorized or accidental access, collection, use, disclosure, copying, modification, disposal or destruction of Personal Data, or other similar risks.

13.2.3. The Concessionaire will only permit the authorized personnel to access Personal Data on a need to know basis.

13.2.4. The Concessionaire will not retain Personal Data (or any documents or records containing Personal Data, electronic or otherwise) for any period of time longer than that is necessary to serve the purposes of this Agreement or as may be provided under law.

13.2.5. The Concessionaire will immediately notify the Authority when the Concessionaire becomes aware of any breach of Personal Data.

13.2.6. The Concessionaire will indemnify the Authority against all actions, claims, demands, losses, damages, statutory penalties, expenses and cost in respect of breach of obligation under this Clause 13.2.

14. Insurance

14.1. The Concessionaire will Maintain the Following Insurance:

14.1.1. professional indemnity insurance;

14.1.2. the Concessionaire's general liability arising out of the Concession;

14.1.3. liability to third parties for goods or property damage;

14.1.4. workmen's compensation insurance; and

14.1.5. any other insurance that may be necessary to protect the Concessionaire and its employees.

15. Representations and Warranties

Each Party Hereby Represents and Warrants to the Other Party That:

15.1   it is duly organized and validly existing under the laws of the jurisdiction of its establishment or incorporation;

15.2.   it has all necessary approvals, powers, licenses and authorities to enter into and perform its obligations under this Agreement;

15.3.   its representative whose signature is affixed below hereto is fully authorized to sign this Agreement and to bind it pursuant to a valid power of attorney or resolution passed by its board of directors;

15.4.   this Agreement constitutes legal, valid and binding obligations of such Party, enforceable against it in accordance with its terms;

15.5.   it is not insolvent, and no receiver, liquidator, trustee, administrator, custodian or similar official has been appointed in respect of the whole or any substantial part of the business or assets of such Party;

15.6.   the execution, delivery and performance of this Agreement by such Party will not (i) violate any provision of the constitutional documents of such Party; or (ii) require such Party to obtain any approvals or action of, or make any filing with or give any notice to, any governmental authority or any other person pursuant to any instrument, contract or other agreement to which such Party is a party or by which such Party is bound; (iii) conflict with or result in any material breach or violation of any of the terms and conditions of, or constitute a default under, any instrument, contract or other agreement to which such Party is a party or by which such Party is bound; (iv) to its knowledge, violate any order, judgment or decree against, or binding upon, such Party or upon its respective securities, properties or businesses; or (v) to its knowledge, violate any applicable laws; and

15.7.   there is no lawsuit, arbitration, or legal, administrative or other proceedings or governmental investigation pending or, to the best of the knowledge of such Party, threatened, against it with respect to the subject matter of this Agreement or that would affect in any way its ability to enter into or perform its obligations under this Agreement.

16. Force Majeure

16.1. Definition of Force Majeure

16.1.1.   In this Clause, "**Force Majeure**" means an exceptional event or circumstance:
   (a)   which is beyond a Party's control,
   (b)   which such Party could not reasonably have provided against before entering into the Agreement,
   (c)   which, having arisen, such Party could not reasonably have avoided or overcome,
   (d)   which is not substantially attributable to the other Party, and
   (e)   which has a material adverse effect.

16.1.2.   Force Majeure event will include (i) change in law and (ii) political events, which increases cost or makes it difficult for the Concessionaire to perform its obligations under this Agreement.

16.2. Notice of Force Majeure

16.2.1.   If a Party is or will be prevented from performing any of its obligations under the Agreement by Force Majeure, then it will give notice to the other Party of the event or circumstances constituting the Force Majeure and will specify the obligations, the performance of which is or will be affected. The notice will be given within 14 days after the Party became aware, or should have become aware, of the relevant event or circumstance constituting Force Majeure.

16.2.2.   The Party will, having given notice, be excused from performance of such obligations for so long as such Force Majeure prevents it from performing them.

16.2.3.   Notwithstanding any other provision of this Clause, Force Majeure will not apply to obligations of either Party to make payments to the other Party under the Agreement.

16.3. Duty to Minimize Delay

16.3.1.   Each Party will at all times use all reasonable endeavours to minimize any delay in the performance of the Agreement as a result of Force Majeure.

16.3.2.   A Party will give notice to the other Party when it ceases to be affected by the Force Majeure.

16.4. Consequences of Force Majeure

If the Concessionaire is prevented from performing any of his obligations under the Agreement by Force Majeure of which notice has been given under Clause 16.2, and suffers delay and/or incurs cost by reason of such Force Majeure, then the Concessionaire will be entitled to payment of increased cost, which needs to be mutually agreed by the Parties. If the Parties are unable to mutually agree on the increased cost, then the dispute will be settled between the Parties in accordance with the dispute resolution mechanism provided in Clause 19.

16.5. Optional Termination and Payment

16.5.1. If the Diagnostic and Pathological Services is prevented for a continuous period of 30 days by reason of Force Majeure of which notice has been given under Clause 16.2, or for multiple periods which totals more than 90 days, then either Party may give to the other Party a notice of termination of the Agreement. In this event, the termination will take effect 7 days after the notice is given.

16.5.2. Upon such termination, the Concessionaire will determine the value of the Diagnostic and Pathological Services provided and issue an Invoice.

17. Default and Termination

17.1. Termination Events

17.1.1. Without limiting any other rights or remedies, the Authority reserves the right to terminate this Agreement, if the Concessionaire:
   (a) fails to achieve KPI scores in accordance with Clause 7.4;
   (b) is in default under any material obligation hereunder and the default has not been cured within 15 days after receipt of notice of such breach or default, unless the Parties otherwise mutually agree; or
   (c) becomes insolvent, makes a general assignment for the benefit of creditors, files a voluntary petition in bankruptcy, or suffers or permits the appointment of a receiver for its business or assets.

17.1.2. Without limiting any other rights or remedies, the Concessionaire reserves the right to terminate this Agreement, if the Authority:
   (a) fails to pay any invoice in accordance with Clause 6.1;
   (b) is in default under any material obligation hereunder that has not been cured within 15 days after receipt of notice of such breach or default, unless the Parties otherwise mutually agree.

17.2. Consequence of Termination

17.2.1. The termination of this Agreement in whole or in part for any reason under this Clause 17 will not affect (i) any liabilities or obligations of either Party arising before such termination or out of the events causing such termination; or (ii) any damages or other remedies to which a Party may be entitled under this Agreement, at law or in equity, arising from any breaches of such liabilities or obligations.

17.2.2. Upon termination, the Concessionaire will vacate the Service Rooms. If required by the Authority, the Concessionaire will continue to provide the Diagnostic and Pathological Services for a further maximum period of 3 months after termination in accordance with the terms and conditions of this Agreement.

18. Indemnity

18.1. General Indemnity

18.1.1. The Concessionaire will indemnify, defend and hold the Authority harmless against any and all proceedings, actions and third-party claims for any loss, damage, cost and expense of whatever kind and nature arising out of any act of the Concessionaire including failure of the Concessionaire to comply with applicable laws.

18.1.2. The Authority will indemnify, defend and hold the Concessionaire harmless against any and all proceedings, actions and third-party claims for any loss, damage, cost and expense of whatever kind and nature arising out of any act of the Authority.

18.2. Notice and Contest of Claims

If any Party receives a claim from a third-party in respect of which it is entitled to the benefit of an indemnity under Clause 18.1 above ("**Indemnified Party**"), then such Party will notify the other Party responsible for indemnifying such claim hereunder ("**Indemnifying Party**") within 15 (fifteen) days of receipt of the claim and will not settle or pay the claim without the prior approval of the Indemnifying Party, which approval not to be unreasonably withheld or delayed. If the Indemnifying Party wishes to contest or dispute the claim, it may conduct the proceedings in the name of the Indemnified Party and will bear all costs involved in contesting the same. The Indemnified Party will provide all cooperation and assistance in contesting any claim and will sign all such writings and documents as the Indemnifying Party may reasonably require.

19. Dispute Resolution

19.1. Dispute

19.1.1. Any dispute, difference or controversy of whatever nature howsoever arising under or out of or in relation to this Agreement between the Parties, and so notified in writing by either Party to the other Party ("Dispute") will, in the first instance, be attempted to be resolved amicably in accordance with the conciliation procedure set forth in Clause 19.1.2.

19.1.2. The Parties agree to use their best efforts for resolving all Disputes arising under or in respect of this Agreement promptly, equitably and in good faith, and further agree to provide each other with reasonable access during normal business hours to all non-privileged records, information and data pertaining to any Dispute.

19.2. Conciliation

If any Dispute between the Parties cannot be amicably settled, then such Dispute may be referred to the [Chairman of the District/State Health Care Department] and the [CEO] of the Concessionaire for amicable settlement, and upon such reference, the said persons will meet no later than 14 days from the date of reference to discuss and attempt to amicably resolve the Dispute. If such meeting does not take place within the 14 day period or the Dispute is not amicably settled within 30 days of the meeting or such longer period as may be mutually agreed by the Parties, either Party may refer the Dispute to arbitration in accordance with the provisions of Clause 19.3.

19.3. Arbitration

19.3.1. Any Dispute which is not resolved amicably by conciliation, as provided in Clause 19.2, will be finally decided by reference to arbitration by a board of arbitrators appointed in accordance with Clause 19.3.2 below. Such arbitration will be held in accordance with the Rules of Arbitration of the International Center for Alternative Dispute Resolution, New Delhi ("**Rules**"), or such other rules as may be mutually agreed by the Parties, and shall be subject to the provisions of the Arbitration and Conciliation Act, 1996. The venue of such arbitration will be [_____], and the language of arbitration proceedings will be English.

19.3.2. There will be a board of 3 arbitrators, of whom each Party will select 1, and the 3rd arbitrator will be appointed by the 2 arbitrators so selected and in the event of disagreement between the 2 arbitrators, the appointment will be made in accordance with the Rules.

19.3.3. The arbitrators will make a reasoned award ("**Award**"). Any Award made in any arbitration will be final and binding on the Parties as from the date it is made, and the Concessionaire and the Authority agree and undertake to carry out such Award without delay.

19.3.4. This Agreement and the rights and obligations of the Parties shall remain in full force and effect, pending the Award in any arbitration proceedings hereunder.

19.4. Adjudication by Regulatory Authority or Commission

In the event of constitution of a statutory Regulatory Authority or Commission with powers to adjudicate upon disputes between the Concessionaire and the Authority, all Disputes arising after such constitution shall, instead of reference to arbitration under Clause 19.3, be adjudicated upon by such Regulatory Authority or Commission in accordance with the applicable law and all references to Dispute Resolution Procedure will be construed accordingly.

20. Miscellaneous

20.1. Governing Law and Jurisdiction

This Agreement will be construed and interpreted in accordance with and governed by the laws of India, and the courts at [___] will have exclusive jurisdiction over matters arising out of or relating to this Agreement.

20.2. Waiver of Immunity

Each Party unconditionally and irrevocably:
  (a) agrees that the execution, delivery and performance by it of this Agreement constitute commercial acts done and performed for commercial purpose;
  (b) agrees that, should any proceedings be brought against it or its assets, property or revenues in any jurisdiction in relation to this Agreement or any transaction contemplated by this Agreement, no immunity (whether by reason of sovereignty or otherwise) from such proceedings shall be claimed by or on behalf of the Party with respect to its assets;
  (c) waives any right of immunity that it or its assets, property or revenues now has, may acquire in the future or which may be attributed to it in any jurisdiction; and
  (d) consents generally in respect of the enforcement of any judgment or award against it in any such proceedings to the giving of any relief or the issue of any process in any jurisdiction in connection with such proceedings (including the making, enforcement or execution against it or in respect of any assets, property or revenues whatsoever irrespective of their use or intended use of any order or judgment that may be made or given in connection therewith).

20.3. Delayed Payments

The Parties hereto agree that payments due from one Party to the other Party under the provisions of this Agreement shall be made within the period set forth therein, and if no such period is specified, within 30 (thirty) days of receiving a demand along with the necessary particulars. In the event of delay beyond such period, the defaulting Party will pay interest for the period of delay calculated at a rate equal to 10% per annum, and recovery thereof will be without prejudice to the rights of the Parties under this Agreement including termination thereof.

20.4. Waiver

No waiver of any provision of this Agreement will constitute a waiver of any other provision(s) or of the same provision on another occasion. Failure of either Party to enforce any provision of this Agreement will not constitute a waiver of such provision or any other provision(s) of this Agreement.

20.5. Survival

Termination will not relieve the Concessionaire or the Authority, as the case may be, of any obligations hereunder which expressly or by implication survive termination hereof.

20.6. Entire Agreement

This Agreement together constitute the entire agreement between the Parties on the subject hereof, and no amendment or modification will be valid and effective unless such modification or amendment is agreed to in writing by the Parties. All prior written or oral understandings, offers or other communications of every kind pertaining to this Agreement are abrogated and withdrawn. For the avoidance of doubt, the Parties hereto agree that any obligations of the Concessionaire arising from the RFP will be deemed to form part of this Agreement.

20.7. Severability

Should any provision of this Agreement be held by a court of competent jurisdiction to be illegal, invalid or unenforceable, such provision may be modified by such court in compliance with the law giving effect to the intent of the Parties and enforced as modified. All other terms and conditions of this Client Agreement remain in full force and effect and will be construed in accordance with the modified provision.

20.8. No Partnership

This Agreement will not be interpreted or construed to create an association, joint venture or partnership between the Parties, or to impose any partnership obligation or liability upon either Party, and neither Party shall have any right, power or authority to enter into any agreement or undertaking for, or act on behalf of, or to act as or be an agent or representative of, or to otherwise bind, the other Party.

20.9. Third Parties

This Agreement is intended solely for the benefit of the Parties, and their respective successors and permitted assigns, and nothing in this Agreement shall be construed to create any duty to, standard of care with reference to, or any liability to, any person not a Party to this Agreement.

20.10. Notices

Notice to the Parties shall be in writing and shall be sent at the addresses first hereinabove mentioned (email accepted). In case, there is any change in the addresses of a Party, the same shall be communicated immediately to the other Party, failing which any notice sent to the earlier address of the said Party shall be deemed to be valid service of such notice.

Authority
Address:
Email:
Phone:
Kind Attention:

Concessionaire
Address:
Email:
Phone:
Kind Attention:

IN WITNESS WHEREOF, and intending to be legally bound, the Parties have duly executed this Agreement as of the date first written above.

Signed for and on behalf of   Signed for and on behalf of
[*insert name of the Authority*]   [*insert name of the Concessionaire*]

_____   _____

By: By:
Name: Name:
Title: Title:

SCHEDULE 1 – DIAGNOSTIC AND PATHOLOGICAL SERVICES

(Please identify the services to be provided in Identified Health Centers such as clinical services, clinical laboratory services, medical imaging services, support clinical services, facility management services, etc.)

SCHEDULE 2 – IDENTIFIED HEALTH CARE CENTERS

[Name of districts and Identified Health Centers requiring services of BMWMF to be inserted in this schedule.]

S.No.	District	Identified Health Centers Requiring Diagnostic and Pathological Services

SCHEDULE 3 – TIME SCHEDULE FOR SERVICES

[Please insert the days, time schedule, number of hours in a day the services are to be provided.]

SCHEDULE 4 – RATES OF DIAGNOSTIC AND PATHOLOGICAL SERVICES

[Please insert the rates proposed by the bidder]

SCHEDULE 5 – KEY PERFORMANCE INDICATORS

[Please insert the KPIs]

SCHEDULE 6 – PATIENT AND DOCTOR SATISFACTION SURVEY

[Please insert the survey form]

SCHEDULE 7 – ASSETS

[Please insert the list of assets to be provided by the Government to the Concessionaire including equipment, medicines, consumables.]

CONCESSION AGREEMENT

FOR

APPOINTMENT OF SPECIALISTS DOCTORS THROUGH PUBLIC–PRIVATE PARTNERSHIP STRUCTURE

Between

Department of [_____]

And

[_____]

Concessionaire

For

Public–Private Partnership for Appointment of Specialists in

[_____]

APPOINTMENT OF SPECIALISTS CONCESSION AGREEMENT

This agreement is entered into on this [__] day of [__], 2020 at [_____] ("**Agreement**"):

BETWEEN

1. [_____], represented by [_____] and having its principal office at [_____] (hereinafter referred to as the "**Authority**" which expression shall, unless repugnant to the context or meaning thereof, include its administrators, successors and assigns);

AND

2. [*], a [*] incorporated under the provisions of Companies Act, 2013 and having its registered office at [*] (hereinafter referred to as the "**Concessionaire**" which expression shall, unless repugnant to the context or meaning thereof, include its successors and permitted assigns and substitutes).

"**Authority**" and "**Concessionaire**" will be referred to individually as the "Party" and collectively as the "**Parties**".

WHEREAS:

A. The Government of India has launched National Urban Health Mission ("NUHM") for providing primary health care services to the urban population with special focus on slum and other vulnerable sections of the society. As a part of NUHM, the Government of [_____] ("State Government") has decided to outsource diagnostic and pathological services as identified in Schedule 1 (Diagnostic and Pathological Services) of the Urban Primary Health Centers (UPHCs) as identified in Schedule 2 (Identified Health Centers) to private sector.

B. The Authority had accordingly invited bids through its Request for Proposal No. [_____] dated [_____] ("**RFP**") for the selection of an entity for providing the Diagnostic and Pathological Services in the Identified Health Centers in accordance with the terms and conditions of this Agreement.

C. After evaluation of the bids received, the Authority accepted the bid of the Concessionaire in accordance with the terms of the RFP and issued the Letter of Acceptance No. [_____] dated [_____] ("**LOA**") requiring, *inter alia*, the execution of this Agreement within 30 (thirty) days of the date of the issue of LOA.

D. The Authority is accordingly entering into this Agreement with the Concessionaire for availing the Diagnostic and Pathological Services, subject to and on the terms and conditions as set forth hereinafter.

NOW, THEREFORE, in consideration of the foregoing and the respective covenants and agreements set forth in this Agreement, the receipt and sufficiency of which is hereby acknowledged, and intending to be legally bound hereby, the Parties agree as follows:

1. Definitions and Interpretation

1.1. Definitions

1.1.1. **"Award"** will have the meaning as provided in Clause 17.3.3.

1.1.2. **"Confidential Information"** will have the meaning as provided in Clause 11.1.1.

1.1.3. **"Concession Period"** will have the meaning as provided in Clause 2.3.

1.1.4. **"Dispute"** will have the meaning as provided in Clause 17.1.1.

1.1.5. **"Effective Date"** will be [_____].

1.1.6. **"Equipment"** will have the meaning as provided in Clause 8 and Schedule 7.

1.1.7. **"Force Majeure"** will have the meaning as provided in Clause 14.1.1.

1.1.8. **"Good Industry Practice"** means the practices, methods, techniques, designs, standards, skills, diligence, efficiency, reliability and prudence which are generally and reasonably expected from a reasonably skilled and experienced operator engaged in the same type of undertaking as envisaged under this Agreement and which would be expected to result in the performance of its obligations by the Concessionaire in accordance with this Agreement and applicable laws in reliable, safe, economical and efficient manner.

1.1.9. **"Government Instrumentality"** means any department, division or sub-division of the Government of India or the State Government and includes any commission, board, authority, agency or municipal and other local authority or statutory body including Panchayat under the control of the Government of India or the State Government, as the case may be, and having jurisdiction over all or any part of the Project or the performance of all or any of the services or obligations of the Concessionaire under or pursuant to this Agreement.

1.1.10. **"Identified Health Centers"** will have the meaning as provided in Schedule 2.

1.1.11. **"Indemnified Party"** will have the meaning as provided in Clause 16.2.

1.1.12. **"Indemnifying Party"** will have the meaning as provided in Clause 16.2.

1.1.13. **"KPIs"** will have the meaning as provided in Clause 6 and Schedule 6.

1.1.14. **"LOA"** will have the meaning as provided in Recital C.

1.1.15. **"Personal Data"** will have the meaning as provided in Clause 11.2.2.

1.1.16. **"RFP"** will have the meaning as provided in Recital B.

1.1.17. "**Rules**" will have the meaning as provided in Clause 17.3.1.

1.1.18. "**Signing Date**" will mean the date of execution of this Agreement.

1.1.19. "**Specialist Doctors**" will mean the specialist doctors to be provided by the Concessionaire for the Specialist Services, all in accordance with Schedule 1.

1.1.20. "**Specialist Services**" will mean the specialist services to be provided by the Specialist Doctors, all in accordance with Schedule 1.

1.1.21. "**Specialist Doctors and Services**" will have the meaning as provided in Schedule 1.

1.1.22. "**State Government**" will have the meaning as provided in Recital A.

1.2. Interpretation

In this Agreement, unless the context specifies otherwise:

1.2.1. headings are used for convenience only and shall not affect the interpretation of this Agreement;

1.2.2. reference to the singular includes a reference to the plural and vice versa, and reference to any gender includes a reference to all other genders;

1.2.3. references to the Recitals, Clauses and Schedules shall deemed to be a reference to the recitals, clauses and schedules of this Agreement;

1.2.4. the expression "this Clause" shall, unless followed by reference to a specific provision, be deemed to refer respectively to the whole Clause, not merely the sub-clause, paragraph or other provision in which the expression occurs;

1.2.5. references to any enactment are to be construed as referring also to any amendment or re-enactment (whether before or after the date of this Agreement), any previous enactment, which such enactment has replaced (with or without amendment) and to any regulation or order made under it;

1.2.6. references to "include" and "including" shall be construed without limitation.

2. Scope of the Service

2.1. Subject to the terms and conditions of this Agreement, the Authority grants to the Concessionaire the exclusive right during the Concession Period to (i) provide the Specialists Doctors and Services for the Identified Health Centers; and (ii) receive the fees from the Authority, all in accordance with the terms and conditions of this Agreement.

2.2. The Concessionaire will ensure that the Specialist Doctors will be available at the Identified Health Centers on the days and time provided in Schedule 3 (**Time Schedule for Services**).

2.3. This Agreement will become effective on the Signing Date and will continue for a period of [_____] months or years from the Effective Date ("**Concession Period**"), unless otherwise extended or terminated in accordance with this Agreement.

2.4. The Concessionaire will provide the Specialist Doctors and Services from the Effective Date.

3. Roles and Responsibilities of the Concessionaire

3.1. The Concessionaire is required to obtain and maintain all consents and approvals required for providing the Specialist Doctors and Services, if any, under the applicable laws.

3.2. The Concessionaire will provide the Specialist Doctors in accordance with the requirements provided in Schedule 1 (**Specialist Doctors and Services**). The Specialist Doctors should have the minimum qualification as provided in Schedule 4 (**Minimum Qualification of the Specialist Doctors**).

3.3. The Concessionaire will ensure that during the performance of its obligations at the Identified Health Centers the Specialist Doctors (i) do not disturb the operation of the Identified Health Centers; (ii) obeys the rules and regulations of the Identified Health Centers; (iii) maintains cordial relationship with the employees, services providers and management of the Identified Health Centers; and (iv) ensure safety of all personnel including patients at the Identified Health Centers.

3.4. The Concessionaire will comply with the provisions of this Agreement, applicable laws and conform to Good Industry Practice for securing the safety of the patients, visitors and staff.

4. Role and Responsibilities of the Authority

4.1. The Authority will provide access, rooms, utilities and other reasonable assistance to the Concessionaire and its Specialist Doctors for providing the Specialist Services at the Identified Health Centers.

4.2. The Authority will, upon written request from the Concessionaire, and subject to the Concessionaire complying with applicable laws, provide reasonable assistance to the Concessionaire for procuring the applicable permits required from any Government Instrumentality for providing the Specialist Doctors and Services.

4.3. The Authority will make all payments to the Concessionaire in the manner and within the time period specified in this Agreement.

4.4. The Authority will ensure safety of the Specialist Doctors while providing the Specialist Services at the Identified Health Centers.

5. Payments

5.1.   The Concessionaire will raise its invoice within [7] days of the beginning of each month for the Specialist Doctors and Services provided in the previous month ("**Invoice**").

5.2.   Along with the Invoice, the Concessionaire will furnish to the Authority a report in a form acceptable to the Authority, stating in reasonable details of the Specialist Doctors and Services provided by the Concessionaire in the previous month.

5.3.   The Invoice will be calculated based on the Specialist Doctors attending the Identified Health Centers for providing the Specialist Services in a month at the rate identified in Schedule 5 (**Rates of Specialist Doctors**).

5.4.   Save and except the disputed part of the Invoice (if any), the Authority will, within 15 days of receipt of the Invoice, make the payment for the undisputed part of the Invoice to the Concessionaire. The disputed part of the Invoice will be settled between the Parties in accordance with the dispute resolution mechanism provided in Clause 17.

6. Key Performance Indicators

6.1.   Without prejudice to the obligations specified in this Agreement, the Concessionaire will provide the Specialist Doctors and Services such that it meets the key performance indicators provide in Schedule 6 ("**KPIs**").

6.2.   The Concessionaire will during the Concession Period, furnish to the Authority, a report, setting out the details provided in Clause 6.2, no later than 7 days after the close of each quarter of operation.

6.3.   The report specified in Clause 6.2 will state in reasonable detail the compliance with all the KPIs specified in Schedule 6 (KPIs) along with an analysis of the reasons for failures, if any, and the strategies for addressing the same and for otherwise improving the Specialists' Services.

6.4.   The Concessionaire will ensure compliance of each of the KPIs specified in Schedule 6 (**KPIs**) and for any shortfall in performance, it will pay damages within 30 (thirty) days of every quarter in which the shortfall occurred. The damages due and payable under this Clause 6.4 will be determined in accordance with Schedule 6 (**KPIs**).

6.5.   If the Concessionaire fails to achieve KPI score of [____] for two consecutive quarters, then the Authority will be entitled to terminate this Agreement.

7. Grievance Redressal Policy

7.1. The Authority may develop a Grievance Redressal Policy to monitor and address any issues or complaints regarding quality of services, denial of services, behaviour of Specialist Doctors and Services, etc.

7.2. If any patient receiving the Specialist Services complain of any Specialist Doctor appointment by the Concessionaire, then the Concessionaire will, upon receiving the complaint, act promptly (not exceeding 48 hours) to address the complaint.

7.3. The Concessionaire will ensure that preventive mechanisms are in place so that complaints are not repeated again.

8. Equipment and Medicines

8.1. The Authority will provide to the Concessionaire equipment, medicine and other assistance, if any, as identified in Schedule 7 (**Equipment**).

8.2. Save and except any movable assets identified in Schedule 7 (**Equipment**), all the assets, equipment and consumables required for providing the Specialist Services will be provided by the Concessionaire.

9. Subcontract

The Concessionaire will not assign or sub-contract any of its rights or obligations under this Agreement without the prior written consent of the Authority.

10. Information Obligation

During Concession Period, the Concessionaire will, no later than 7 (seven) days after the close of each month, furnish to the Authority, a monthly report in a form acceptable to the Authority, stating in reasonable detail the information identified in Schedule 8 ("**Monthly Report**").

11. Confidentiality and Data Protection

11.1. Confidentiality

11.1.1. Each Party will maintain in strict confidence and protect the confidentiality of all information, reports, data, software or other material, whether written or oral, in electronic or magnetic format, and the contents thereof and any reports, digests or summaries created or derived from any of the foregoing that is provided by one Party to the other Party in relation to this Agreement ("**Confidential Information**"), and will not disclose any such Confidential Information to any third party without the prior written consent of the other Party; provided that each Party will be entitled to use Confidential Information for any and all lawful purposes.

11.1.2. Notwithstanding Clause 11.1.1, each Party may disclose Confidential Information to the extent that such Confidential Information:

(a) was properly in the possession of the receiving Party prior to disclosure thereof by the other Party;

(b) was in the public domain prior to its delivery to such Party or after such delivery if it becomes part of the public domain without breach of any confidentiality obligations by the receiving Party under this Agreement;

(c) was obtained from a third party with no known duty to maintain its confidentiality;

(d) is required to be disclosed by applicable law or judicial or administrative or arbitral process, provided that for any such disclosure, the disclosing Party will give the other Party prompt written notice, where possible, and use reasonable efforts to ensure that such disclosure is accorded confidential treatment and also to enable such other Party to seek a protective order or other appropriate remedy at such other Party's sole costs; and

(e) lawfully becomes available without any limitation as to its disclosure.

11.1.3. The Parties agree that upon termination of this Agreement, the receiving Party will promptly deliver to the disclosing Party the Confidential Information and copies thereof in its possession or under its direct or indirect control, and will destroy all memoranda, notes and other writings prepared by the receiving Party or directors, officers, employees or advisors, based on Confidential Information.

11.2. Data Protection

11.2.1. The Concessionaire represents that it and the Specialist Doctors appointed by the Concessionaire will abide by and observes all laws, rules, regulations including but not limited to the data protection laws of India while performing its obligations under this Agreement.

11.2.2. The Concessionaire (and will ensure that the Specialist Doctors) will protect the personal data which it receives in connection with the provision of the Specialist Doctors and Services ("Personal Data") by making security arrangements (as required under law) to prevent unauthorized or accidental access, collection, use, disclosure, copying, modification, disposal or destruction of Personal Data, or other similar risks.

11.2.3. The Concessionaire will only permit the authorized personnel to access Personal Data on a need to know basis.

11.2.4. The Concessionaire (and will ensure that the Specialist Doctors) will not retain Personal Data (or any documents or records containing Personal Data, electronic or otherwise) for any period of time longer than that is necessary to serve the purposes of this Agreement or as may be provided under law.

11.2.5. The Concessionaire will immediately notify the Authority when the Concessionaire becomes aware of any breach of Personal Data.

11.2.6. The Concessionaire will indemnify the Authority against all actions, claims, demands, losses, damages, statutory penalties, expenses and cost in respect of breach of obligation under this Clauses 11.2.

12. Insurance

12.1 The Concessionaire will Maintain the Following Insurance:

12.1.1. professional liability insurance;

12.1.2. the Concessionaire's general liability arising out of the Concession;

12.1.3. liability to third parties for goods or property damage;

12.1.4. workmen's compensation insurance; and

12.1.5. any other insurance that may be necessary to protect the Concessionaire and its employees, consultants.

13. Representations and Warranties

Each Party Hereby Represents and Warrants to the Other Party That:

13.1. it is duly organized and validly existing under the laws of the jurisdiction of its establishment or incorporation;

13.2. it has all necessary approvals, powers, licenses and authorities to enter into and perform its obligations under this Agreement;

13.3. its representative whose signature is affixed below hereto is fully authorized to sign this Agreement and to bind it pursuant to a valid power of attorney or resolution passed by its board of directors;

13.4. this Agreement constitutes legal, valid and binding obligations of such Party, enforceable against it in accordance with its terms;

13.5. it is not insolvent, and no receiver, liquidator, trustee, administrator, custodian or similar official has been appointed in respect of the whole or any substantial part of the business or assets of such Party;

13.6. the execution, delivery and performance of this Agreement by such Party will not (i) violate any provision of the constitutional documents of such Party; or (ii) require such Party to obtain any approvals or action of, or make any filing with or give any notice to, any governmental authority or any other person pursuant to any instrument, contract or other agreement to which such Party is a party or by which such Party is bound; (iii) conflict with or result in any material breach or violation of any of the terms and conditions of, or constitute a default under, any instrument, contract or other agreement to which such Party is a party or by which such Party is bound; (iv) to its knowledge, violate any order, judgment or decree against, or binding upon, such Party or upon its respective securities, properties or businesses; or (v) to its knowledge, violate any applicable laws; and

13.7. there is no lawsuit, arbitration, or legal, administrative or other proceedings or governmental investigation pending or, to the best of the knowledge of such Party, threatened, against it with respect to the subject matter of this Agreement or that would affect in any way its ability to enter into or perform its obligations under this Agreement.

14. Force Majeure

14.1. Definition of Force Majeure

14.1.1. In this Clause, "**Force Majeure**" means an exceptional event or circumstance:
(a) which is beyond a Party's control,
(b) which such Party could not reasonably have provided against before entering into the Agreement,
(c) which, having arisen, such Party could not reasonably have avoided or overcome,
(d) which is not substantially attributable to the other Party, and
(e) which has a material adverse effect.

14.1.2. Force Majeure event will include (i) change in law and (ii) political events, which increases cost or makes it difficult for the Concessionaire to perform its obligations under this Agreement.

14.2. Notice of Force Majeure

14.2.1. If a Party is or will be prevented from performing any of its obligations under the Agreement by Force Majeure, then it will give notice to the other Party of the event or circumstances constituting the Force Majeure and will specify the obligations, the performance of which is or will be affected. The notice will be given within 14 days after the Party became aware, or should have become aware, of the relevant event or circumstance constituting Force Majeure.

14.2.2. The Party will, having given notice, be excused from performance of such obligations for so long as such Force Majeure prevents it from performing them.

14.2.3. Notwithstanding any other provision of this Clause, Force Majeure will not apply to obligations of either Party to make payments to the other Party under the Agreement.

14.3. Duty to Minimize Delay

14.3.1. Each Party will at all times use all reasonable endeavours to minimize any delay in the performance of the Agreement as a result of Force Majeure.

14.3.2. A Party will give notice to the other Party when it ceases to be affected by the Force Majeure.

14.4. Consequences of Force Majeure

If the Concessionaire is prevented from performing any of his obligations under the Agreement by Force Majeure of which notice has been given under Clause 14.2, and suffers incurs cost by reason of such Force Majeure, then the Concessionaire will be entitled to payment of increased cost, which needs to be mutually agreed by the Parties. If the Parties are unable to mutually agree on the increased cost, then the dispute will be settled between the Parties in accordance with the dispute resolution mechanism provided in Clause 17.

14.5. Optional Termination and Payment

14.5.1. If the Specialist Service is prevented for a continuous period of 30 days by reason of Force Majeure of which notice has been given under Clause 14.2, or for multiple periods which totals more than 60 days, then either Party may give to the other Party a notice of termination of the Agreement. In this event, the termination will take effect 7 days after the notice is given.

14.5.2. Upon such termination, the Concessionaire will determine the value of the unpaid Specialist Doctors and Services provided and issue an Invoice to the Authority.

15. Default and Termination

15.1. Termination Events

15.1.1. Without limiting any other rights or remedies, the Authority reserves the right to terminate this Agreement, if the Concessionaire:
   (a) fails to achieve KPI scores in accordance with Clause 6.4;
   (b) is in default under any material obligation hereunder and the default has not been cured within 15 days after receipt of notice of such breach or default, unless the Parties otherwise mutually agree; or
   (c) becomes insolvent, makes a general assignment for the benefit of creditors, files a voluntary petition in bankruptcy, or suffers or permits the appointment of a receiver for its business or assets.

15.1.2. Without limiting any other rights or remedies, the Concessionaire reserves the right to terminate this Agreement, if the Authority:
   (a) fails to pay any invoice in accordance with Clause 5.1;
   (b) is in default under any material obligation hereunder that has not been cured within 15 days after receipt of notice of such breach or default, unless the Parties otherwise mutually agree.

15.2. Consequence of Termination

15.2.1. The termination of this Agreement in whole or in part for any reason under this Clause 15 will not affect (i) any liabilities or obligations of either Party arising before such termination or out of the events causing such termination; or (ii) any damages or other remedies to which a Party may be entitled under this Agreement, at law or in equity, arising from any breaches of such liabilities or obligations.

15.2.2. If required by the Authority, the Concessionaire will continue to provide the Specialist Doctors and Services for a further period of 3 months after termination in accordance with the terms and conditions of this Agreement.

16. Indemnity

16.1. General Indemnity

16.1.1. The Concessionaire will indemnify, defend and hold the Authority harmless against any and all proceedings, actions and third-party claims for any loss, damage, cost and expense of whatever kind and nature arising out of any act of the Concessionaire and the Specialist Doctors and Services including failure of the Concessionaire to comply with applicable laws.

16.1.2. The Authority will indemnify, defend and hold the Concessionaire harmless against any and all proceedings, actions and third-party claims for any loss, damage, cost and expense of whatever kind and nature arising out of any act of the Authority.

16.2. Notice and contest of claims

If any Party receives a claim from a third-party in respect of which it is entitled to the benefit of an indemnity under Clause 16.1 above ("**Indemnified Party**"), then such Party will notify the other Party responsible for indemnifying such claim hereunder ("**Indemnifying Party**") within 15 (fifteen) days of receipt of the claim and will not settle or pay the claim without the prior approval of the Indemnifying Party, which approval not to be unreasonably withheld or delayed. If the Indemnifying Party wishes to contest or dispute the claim, it may conduct the proceedings in the name of the Indemnified Party and will bear all costs involved in contesting the same. The Indemnified Party will provide all cooperation and assistance in contesting any claim and will sign all such writings and documents as the Indemnifying Party may reasonably require.

17. Dispute Resolution

17.1. Dispute

17.1.1. Any dispute, difference or controversy of whatever nature howsoever arising under or out of or in relation to this Agreement between the Parties, and so notified in writing by either Party to the other Party ("**Dispute**") will, in the first instance, be attempted to be resolved amicably in accordance with the conciliation procedure set forth in Clause 17.1.2.

17.1.2. The Parties agree to use their best efforts for resolving all Disputes arising under or in respect of this Agreement promptly, equitably and in good faith, and further agree to provide each other with reasonable access during normal business hours to all non-privileged records, information and data pertaining to any Dispute.

17.2. Conciliation

If any Dispute between the Parties cannot be amicably settled, then such Dispute may be referred to the [Chairman of the District/State Health Care Department] and the [CEO] of the Concessionaire for amicable settlement, and upon such reference, the said persons will meet no later than 14 days from the date of reference to discuss and attempt to amicably resolve the Dispute. If such meeting does not take place within the 14 day period or the Dispute is not amicably settled within 30 days of the meeting or such longer period as may be mutually agreed by the Parties, either Party may refer the Dispute to arbitration in accordance with the provisions of Clause 17.3.

17.3. Arbitration

17.3.1. Any Dispute which is not resolved amicably by conciliation, as provided in Clause 17.2, will be finally decided by reference to arbitration by a board of arbitrators appointed in accordance with Clause 17.3.2 below. Such arbitration will be held in accordance with the Rules of Arbitration of the International Center for Alternative Dispute Resolution, New Delhi ("**Rules**"), or such other rules as may be mutually agreed by the Parties, and shall be subject to the provisions of the Arbitration and Conciliation Act, 1996. The venue of such arbitration will be [_____], and the language of arbitration proceedings will be English.

17.3.2. There will be a board of 3 arbitrators, of whom each Party will select 1, and the 3rd arbitrator will be appointed by the 2 arbitrators so selected and in the event of disagreement between the 2 arbitrators, the appointment will be made in accordance with the Rules.

17.3.3. The arbitrators will make a reasoned award ("**Award**"). Any Award made in any arbitration will be final and binding on the Parties as from the date it is made, and the Concessionaire and the Authority agree and undertake to carry out such Award without delay.

17.3.4. This Agreement and the rights and obligations of the Parties shall remain in full force and effect, pending the Award in any arbitration proceedings hereunder.

17.4. Adjudication by Regulatory Authority or Commission

In the event of constitution of a statutory Regulatory Authority or Commission with powers to adjudicate upon disputes between the Concessionaire and the Authority, all Disputes arising after such constitution shall, instead of reference to arbitration under Clause 17.3, be adjudicated upon by such Regulatory Authority or Commission in accordance with the applicable law and all references to Dispute Resolution Procedure will be construed accordingly.

18. Miscellaneous

18.1. Governing Law and Jurisdiction

This Agreement will be construed and interpreted in accordance with and governed by the laws of India, and the courts at [___] will have exclusive jurisdiction over matters arising out of or relating to this Agreement.

18.2. Waiver of immunity

Each Party unconditionally and irrevocably:
   (a)   agrees that the execution, delivery and performance by it of this Agreement constitute commercial acts done and performed for commercial purpose;
   (b)   agrees that, should any proceedings be brought against it or its assets, property or revenues in any jurisdiction in relation to this Agreement or any transaction contemplated by this Agreement, no immunity (whether by reason of sovereignty or otherwise) from such proceedings shall be claimed by or on behalf of the Party with respect to its assets;
   (c)   waives any right of immunity which it or its assets, property or revenues now has, may acquire in the future or which may be attributed to it in any jurisdiction; and
   (d)   consents generally in respect of the enforcement of any judgment or award against it in any such proceedings to the giving of any relief or the issue of any process in any jurisdiction in connection with such proceedings (including the making, enforcement or execution against it or in respect of any assets, property or revenues whatsoever irrespective of their use or intended use of any order or judgment that may be made or given in connection therewith).

18.3. Delayed Payments

The Parties hereto agree that payments due from one Party to the other Party under the provisions of this Agreement shall be made within the period set forth therein, and if no such period is specified, within 30 (thirty) days of receiving a demand along with the necessary particulars. In the event of delay beyond such period, the defaulting Party will pay interest for the period of delay calculated at a rate equal to 10% per annum, and recovery thereof will be without prejudice to the rights of the Parties under this Agreement including termination thereof.

18.4. Waiver

No waiver of any provision of this Agreement will constitute a waiver of any other provision(s) or of the same provision on another occasion. Failure of either Party to enforce any provision of this Agreement will not constitute a waiver of such provision or any other provision(s) of this Agreement.

18.5. Survival

Termination will not relieve the Concessionaire or the Authority, as the case may be, of any obligations hereunder which expressly or by implication survive termination hereof.

18.6. Entire Agreement

This Agreement together constitute the entire agreement between the Parties on the subject hereof, and no amendment or modification will be valid and effective unless such modification or amendment is agreed to in writing by the Parties. All prior written or oral understandings, offers or other communications of every kind pertaining to this Agreement are abrogated and withdrawn. For the avoidance of doubt, the Parties hereto agree that any obligations of the Concessionaire arising from the RFP will be deemed to form part of this Agreement.

18.7. Severability

Should any provision of this Agreement be held by a court of competent jurisdiction to be illegal, invalid or unenforceable, such provision may be modified by such court in compliance with the law giving effect to the intent of the Parties and enforced as modified. All other terms and conditions of this Client Agreement remain in full force and effect and will be construed in accordance with the modified provision.

18.8. No partnership

This Agreement will not be interpreted or construed to create an association, joint venture or partnership between the Parties, or to impose any partnership obligation or liability upon either Party, and neither Party shall have any right, power or authority to enter into any agreement or undertaking for, or act on behalf of, or to act as or be an agent or representative of, or to otherwise bind, the other Party.

18.9. Third parties

This Agreement is intended solely for the benefit of the Parties, and their respective successors and permitted assigns, and nothing in this Agreement shall be construed to create any duty to, standard of care with reference to, or any liability to, any person not a Party to this Agreement.

18.10. Notices

Notice to the Parties shall be in writing and shall be sent at the addresses first hereinabove mentioned (email accepted). In case, there is any change in the addresses of a Party, the same shall be communicated immediately to the other Party, failing which any notice sent to the earlier address of the said Party shall be deemed to be valid service of such notice.

Authority
Address:
Email:
Phone:
Kind Attention:

Concessionaire
Address:
Email:
Phone:
Kind Attention:

IN WITNESS WHEREOF, and intending to be legally bound, the Parties have duly executed this Agreement as of the date first written above.

Signed for and on behalf of
[*insert name of the Authority*]

Signed for and on behalf of
[*insert name of the Concessionaire*]

_____

By:
Name:
Title:

_____

By:
Name:
Title:

SCHEDULE 1 – SPECIALIST DOCTORS AND SERVICES

[Please insert the list of (i) Specialist Doctors and (ii) Specialist Services needed at the Identified Health Centers.]

SCHEDULE 2 – IDENTIFIED HEALTH CARE CENTERS

[Please insert the name of districts and Health Centers requiring Specialist Doctors and Services.]

S.No.	District	Health Centers Requiring Specialists' Services

SCHEDULE 3 – TIME SCHEDULE FOR SERVICES

[Please insert the time, date and number of hours of Specialist Doctors and Services required at the Identified Health Centers.]

SCHEDULE 4 – MINIMUM QUALIFICATION OF THE SPECIALIST DOCTORS

[Please insert the minimum qualification requirement of each Specialist Doctor.]

SCHEDULE 5 – RATES AND/OR BUDGET OF SPECIALIST DOCTORS AND SERVICES

[Please insert the tentative rates and/or budget for Specialist Doctors and Services in this schedule.]

SCHEDULE 6 – KEY PERFORMANCE INDICATORS

[Please insert the Key Performance Indicators.]

SCHEDULE 7 – EQUIPMENT

[Please insert the lists of the equipment and other utilities to be provided by the Authority to the Specialist Doctors and/or Concessionaire.]

SCHEDULE 8 – MONTHLY REPORT

[The information for monthly report to be identified here.]

Sample Concession Agreement (Appointment of Training Provider)

CONCESSION AGREEMENT

FOR

APPOINTMENT OF TRAINING PROVIDER

Between

Department of [_____]

And

[_____]

Concessionaire

For

Public–Private Partnership for Appointment of Training Provider

[_____]

DIAGNOSTIC AND PATHOLOGICAL SERVICES CONCESSION AGREEMENT

This agreement is entered into on this [__] day of [__], 2020 at [_____] ("**Agreement**"):

BETWEEN

1.	[_____], represented by [_____] and having its principal office at [_____] (hereinafter referred to as the "**Authority**" which expression shall, unless repugnant to the context or meaning thereof, include its administrators, successors and assigns);

AND

2.	[*], a [*] incorporated under the provisions of Companies Act, 2013 and having its registered office at [*] (hereinafter referred to as the "**Concessionaire**" which expression shall, unless repugnant to the context or meaning thereof, include its successors and permitted assigns and substitutes).

"**Authority**" and "**Concessionaire**" will be referred to individually as the "**Party**" and collectively as the "**Parties**".

WHEREAS:

A.	The Government of [___] wishes to appoint training providers for the training of [*auxiliary nurse midwife (ANMs)/ employees/____*], who will improve the health care services provided by the Government in the State.

B.	The Authority had accordingly invited bids through its Request for Proposal No. [____] dated [____] ("**RFP**") for the selection of a training provider for providing the Training Services (as defined below) in accordance with applicable laws and the terms and conditions of this Agreement.

C.	After evaluation of the bids received, the Authority accepted the bid of the Concessionaire in accordance with the terms of the RFP and issued the Letter of Acceptance No. [_____] dated [____] ("**LOA**") requiring, inter alia, the execution of this Agreement within 30 (thirty) days of the date of the issue of LOA.

D.	The Authority is accordingly entering into this Agreement with the Concessionaire for availing the Training Services in accordance with the terms and conditions of this Agreement.

NOW, THEREFORE, in consideration of the foregoing and the respective covenants and agreements set forth in this Agreement, the receipt and sufficiency of which is hereby acknowledged, and intending to be legally bound hereby, the Parties agree as follows:

1. Definitions and Interpretation

1.1. Definitions

1.1.1. **"Award"** will have the meaning as provided in Clause 17.3.3.

1.1.2. **"Change in Law"** will have the meaning as provided in Clause 14.1.2.

1.1.3. **"Concessionaire Service Report"** will have the meaning as provided in Clause 10.1.

1.1.4. **"Concession Period"** will have the meaning as provided in Clause 2.6.

1.1.5. **"Confidential Information"** will have the meaning as provided in Clause 11.1.1.

1.1.6. **"Dispute"** will have the meaning as provided in Clause 17.1.1.

1.1.7. **"Force Majeure"** will have the meaning as provided in Clause 14.1.1.

1.1.8. **"Government Instrumentality"** means any department, division or sub-division of the Government of India or the State Government and includes any commission, board, authority, agency or municipal and other local authority or statutory body including Panchayat under the control of the Government of India or the State Government, as the case may be, and having jurisdiction over all or any part of the Project or the performance of all or any of the Services or obligations of the Concessionaire under or pursuant to this Agreement.

1.1.9. **"Indemnified Party"** will have the meaning as provided in Clause 16.2.

1.1.10. **"Indemnifying Party"** will have the meaning as provided in Clause 16.2.

1.1.11. **"Invoice"** will have the meaning as provided in Clause 6.2.

1.1.12. **"KPIs"** will have the meaning as provided in Clause 7 and Schedule 6.

1.1.13. **"LOA"** will have the meaning as provided in Recital C.

1.1.14. **"Participants"** will have the meaning as provided in Clause 2.2.

1.1.15. **"Participants Details"** will have the meaning as provided in Schedule 2.

1.1.16. **"Participants Satisfaction Survey"** will have the meaning as provided in Schedule 7.

1.1.17. **"Qualification of the Trainer"** will have the meaning as provided in Schedule 3.

1.1.18. **"RFP"** will have the meaning as provided in Recital B.

1.1.19. **"Rules"** will have the meaning as provided in Clause 17.3.1.

1.1.20. **"Training Cycle"** will mean one round of training (which part of the Training Services to be provided for a particular cycle will be decided by the Authority) provided by the Concessionaire to the Participants in accordance with this Agreement.

1.1.21. **"Training Fees Structure"** will have the meaning as provided in Schedule 5.

1.1.22. **"Training Localities"** will have the meaning as provided in Schedule 4.

1.1.23. **"Training Services"** will have the meaning as provided in Schedule 1.

1.2. Interpretation

In this Agreement, unless the context specifies otherwise:

1.1.1. headings are used for convenience only and shall not affect the interpretation of this Agreement;

1.1.2. reference to the singular includes a reference to the plural and vice versa, and reference to any gender includes a reference to all other genders;

1.1.3. references to the Recitals, Clauses and Schedules shall deemed to be a reference to the recitals, clauses and schedules of this Agreement;

1.1.4. the expression "this Clause" shall, unless followed by reference to a specific provision, be deemed to refer respectively to the whole Clause, not merely the sub-clause, paragraph or other provision in which the expression occurs;

1.1.5. references to any enactment are to be construed as referring also to any amendment or re-enactment (whether before or after the date of this Agreement), any previous enactment, which such enactment has replaced (with or without amendment) and to any regulation or order made under it;

1.1.6. references to "include" and "including" shall be construed without limitation.

2. Scope of the Project

2.1 Subject to the terms and conditions of this Agreement, the Authority appoints the Concessionaire, during the Concession Period, to (i) provide the training services as identified in Schedule 1 (**Training Services**) to the individuals identified by the Authority from time to time; and (ii) receive the fees for the Training Services from the Authority, all in accordance with the terms and conditions of this Agreement.

2.2 At the beginning of each Training Cycle, the Authority will (i) identify the individuals who will be trained ("**Participants**"), and (ii) the training that is to be provided to the Participants by the Concessionaire. The Authority, from the Training Services, will decide which training(s) to be provided by the Concessionaire to the Participants in a particular Training Cycle.

2.3   The Authority will provide to the Concessionaire, at the beginning of each Training Cycle, details of the Participants as identified in Schedule 2 (**Participants Details**).

2.4   The Concessionaire will not discriminate any Participants on the basis of sex, religion, caste, region, or on any other basis whatsoever.

2.5   This Agreement will become effective on the Signing Date and will continue for a period of [_____] months or years ("**Concession Period**"), unless otherwise extended or terminated in accordance with this Agreement.

2.6   During the Concession Period, the Concessionaire will be required to provide training to multiple groups of Participants and conduct multiple Training Cycle as identified by the Authority from time to time.

2.7   This Agreement may be extended by the Authority for a further period of [____] months or years if the Concessionaire achieves an average minimum KPI score of [_____] during the initial Concession Period.

3.   Roles and Responsibilities of the Concessionaire

3.1   The Concessionaire will maintain all the licenses, consent and approvals required for providing the Training Services.

3.2   The Training Services will be provided by the Concessionaire on such days as may be identified by the Authority at the beginning of each Training Cycle.

3.3   The Concessionaire will provide trainers or teachers who has the minimum qualifications identified in Schedule 3 (**Qualification of Trainers**).

3.4   The Concessionaire will provide classrooms for the trainings. The classrooms will be provided within the areas identified in Schedule 4 (**Training Localities**).

3.5   The Concessionaire will maintain the classrooms (i) net and clean, and (ii) big enough to accommodate the Participants comfortably; if the Participants cannot be comfortable accommodated in 1 classroom, then the Concessionaire will divide the Participants in sections and have multiple class or multiple sessions, as many be required.

3.6   The training centers should have clean toilets for the Participants.

3.7   The training will be divided into multiple sessions such that each training session does not continue for more than [1] hours, and each day does not have more than [4] hours of training sessions. There should be at least [15] minutes of break between 2 training session.

3.8   The Concessionaire will provide reading materials to the Participants in relation to the training.

3.9   The Concessionaire will provide light refreshment (for example water, tea, coffee, biscuits, cakes) to the Participants in between classes.

3.10 [At the end of the Training Cycle, the Concessionaire will conduct exams to ascertain the knowledge gained by the Participants and only those Participants who achieves a minimum score in line with the best practice in the industry will be issued pass certificate.]

3.11 The Concessionaire to bear all costs and expenses in relation to its obligation under this Agreement.

4. Role and Responsibilities of the Authority

4.1 The Authority will provide to the Concessionaire in timely manner the details of the Participants.

4.2 The Authority will make all payments to the Concessionaire in the manner and within the time period specified in this Agreement.

5. Taxes and Duties

The Concessionaire will be liable to pay all taxes and duties applicable to the Concessionaire for the Training Services.

6. Payments

6.1 The Concessionaire will be paid for training the Participants in accordance with the fees identified for various trainings in Schedule 5 (**Training Fees Structure**).

6.2 The Concessionaire will, within first 7 days of completion of each Training Cycle, raise an invoice for the training conducted in accordance with fees identified in Schedule 5 (**Training Fees Structure**) ("**Invoice**").

6.3 Save and except the disputed part of the Invoice (if any), the Authority will, within 15 days of receipt of the Invoice, make the payment for the undisputed part of the Invoice to the Concessionaire. The disputed part of the Invoice will be settled between the Parties in accordance with the dispute resolution mechanism provided in Clause 17.

7. Key Performance Indicator

7.1 Without prejudice to the obligations specified in this Agreement, the Concessionaire will provide the Training Services such that it meets the key performance indicators provide in Schedule 6 ("KPIs").

7.2 The Concessionaire during the Concession Period, at the end of each Training Cycle, furnish to the Authority, a report, setting out the details provided in Clause 7.3, no later than 7 (seven) days after the close of each quarter of operation.

7.3 The report specified in Clause 7.2 will state in reasonable detail the compliance with all the KPIs specified in Schedule 6 (**KPIs**) along with an analysis of the reasons for failures, if any, and the strategies for addressing the same and for otherwise improving the performance of the Training Services.

7.4 The Concessionaire will ensure compliance of each of the KPIs specified in Schedule 6 (KPIs) and for any shortfall in performance, it will pay damages within 30 (thirty) days of end of each Training Cycle in which the shortfall occurred. The damages due and payable under this Clause 7.4 will be determined in accordance with Schedule 6 (**KPIs**).

7.5 If the Concessionaire fails to achieve KPI score of [____] for two consecutive Training Cycles, then the Authority will be entitled to terminate this Agreement.

8. Patient and Doctor Satisfaction Survey, Grievance Redressal Policy

8.1 Participants Satisfaction Survey

8.1.1 The Concessionaire will at the end of each Training Cycle conduct a Participants Satisfaction Survey. The survey will be conducted by handing out a Participants Satisfaction Form, as provided in Schedule 7 (**Participants Satisfaction Survey**), to all the Participants. The Concessionaire will submit a report of the findings of such survey to the Authority after each Training Cycle and will ensure that the Concessionaire achieves and maintains an overall score of at least [____] in such survey.

8.1.2 In addition, the Authority may, at its discretion, cost and expense conduct Participants Satisfaction Survey not more than once in each Training Cycle to determine the quality of the training provided by the Concessionaire.

8.1.3 If the Participants Satisfaction Survey reveals that more than 20% (twenty percent) of the Participants surveyed by the Concessionaire or the Authority, as the case may be, ranked the Training Services of the Concessionaire during a particular Training Cycle below [80%] rating, then the Authority may levy and collect from the Concessionaire, damages in an amount equal to [20]% of the Training Fees for that Training Cycle.

8.2 Grievance Redressal Policy

Unless a Grievance Redressal Policy is provided by the Authority, the Concessionaire will monitor and address any issues or complaints by the Participants in accordance with the principles related to Grievance Redressal Policy provided in Schedule 8 (**Salient Feature of Grievance Redressal Policy**).

9. Subcontract

The Concessionaire will not assign or sub-contract any of its rights or obligations under this Agreement without the prior written consent of the Authority.

10. Information Obligation

10.1. The Concessionaire is required to maintain and update on day to day basis (i) the attendance report of the Participants, (ii) details of the training conducted, (iii) details of the trainers, (iv) time of the training, and (v) any other relevant information in relation to the Training Services ("**Concessionaire Service Report**"). The Concessionaire is required to provide this report on monthly basis to the Authority.

10.2. The Concessionaire is required to report all incidents, as soon as possible, that occur at the training centers or the classroom or any other place during the training.

11. Confidentiality and Data Protection

11.1. Confidentiality

11.1.1. Each Party will maintain in strict confidence and protect the confidentiality of all information, reports, data, software or other material, whether written or oral, in electronic or magnetic format, and the contents thereof and any reports, digests or summaries created or derived from any of the foregoing that is provided by one Party to the other Party in relation to this Agreement ("**Confidential Information**"), and will not disclose any such Confidential Information to any third party without the prior written consent of the other Party; provided that each Party will be entitled to use Confidential Information for any and all lawful purposes.

11.1.2. Notwithstanding Clause 11.1.1, each Party may disclose Confidential Information to the extent that such Confidential Information:
   (a) was properly in the possession of the receiving Party prior to disclosure thereof by the other Party;
   (b) was in the public domain prior to its delivery to such Party or after such delivery if it becomes part of the public domain without breach of any confidentiality obligations by the receiving Party under this Agreement;
   (c) was obtained from a third party with no known duty to maintain its confidentiality;
   (d) is required to be disclosed by applicable law or judicial or administrative or arbitral process, provided that for any such disclosure, the disclosing Party will give the other Party prompt written notice, where possible, and use reasonable efforts to ensure that such disclosure is accorded confidential treatment and also to enable such other Party to seek a protective order or other appropriate remedy at such other Party's sole costs; and
   (e) lawfully becomes available without any limitation as to its disclosure.

11.1.3. The Parties agree that upon termination of this Agreement, the receiving Party will promptly deliver to the disclosing Party the Confidential Information and copies thereof in its possession or under its direct or indirect control, and will destroy all memoranda, notes and other writings prepared by the receiving Party or directors, officers, employees or advisors, based on Confidential Information.

11.2. Data Protection

11.2.1. The Concessionaire represents that it will abide by and observes all laws, rules, regulations including but not limited to the data protection laws of India while performing its obligations under this Agreement.

11.2.2. The Concessionaire will indemnify the Authority against all actions, claims, demands, losses, damages, statutory penalties, expenses and cost in respect of breach of obligation under this Clause 11.2.

12. Insurance

The Concessionaire will Maintain the Following Insurance:

12.1   comprehensive professional indemnity insurance;

12.2   the Concessionaire's general liability arising out of the Concession;

12.3   liability to third parties for goods or property damage;

12.4   workmen's compensation insurance; and

12.5   any other insurance that may be necessary to protect the Concessionaire and its employees, including all Force Majeure Events that are insurable at commercially reasonable premiums and not otherwise covered in Clauses 12.1 to 12.4 above.

13. Representations and Warranties

Each Party Hereby Represents and Warrants to the Other Party That:

13.1.   it is duly organized and validly existing under the laws of the jurisdiction of its establishment or incorporation;

13.2.   it has all necessary approvals, powers, licenses and authorities to enter into and perform its obligations under this Agreement;

13.3.   its representative whose signature is affixed below hereto is fully authorized to sign this Agreement and to bind it pursuant to a valid power of attorney or resolution passed by its board of directors;

13.4.   this Agreement constitutes legal, valid and binding obligations of such Party, enforceable against it in accordance with its terms;

13.5.   it is not insolvent, and no receiver, liquidator, trustee, administrator, custodian or similar official has been appointed in respect of the whole or any substantial part of the business or assets of such Party;

13.6.   the execution, delivery and performance of this Agreement by such Party will not (i) violate any provision of the constitutional documents of such Party; or (ii) require such Party to obtain any approvals or action of, or make any filing with or give any notice to, any governmental authority or any other person pursuant to any instrument, contract or other agreement to which such Party is a party or by which such Party is bound; (iii) conflict with or result in any material breach or violation of any of the terms and conditions of, or constitute a default under, any instrument, contract or other agreement to which such Party is a party or by which such Party is bound; (iv) to its knowledge, violate any order, judgment or decree against, or binding upon, such Party or upon its respective securities, properties or businesses; or (v) to its knowledge, violate any applicable laws; and

13.7.   there is no lawsuit, arbitration, or legal, administrative or other proceedings or governmental investigation pending or, to the best of the knowledge of such Party, threatened, against it with respect to the subject matter of this Agreement or that would affect in any way its ability to enter into or perform its obligations under this Agreement.

14. Force Majeure

14.1. Definition of Force Majeure and Legislative and Political Event

14.1.1.   In this Clause, "**Force Majeure**" means an exceptional event or circumstance:
   (a)   which is beyond a Party's control,
   (b)   which such Party could not reasonably have foreseen before entering into the Agreement,
   (c)   which, having arisen, such Party could not reasonably have avoided or overcome, and
   (d)   which is not substantially attributable to the other Party,
   which has a material adverse effect.

14.1.2.   "**Change in Law**" means any of the following events occurring as a result of any action by any Government Instrumentality:
   (a)   change, amendment, modification of, addition to, or deletion from a law; or
   (b)   an enactment or making of a new law; or
   (c)   repeal of existing law; or
   (d)   change in the manner in which a law is applied, enforced or interpreted, which increases cost or makes it difficult for the Concessionaire to perform its obligations under this Agreement.

14.2. Notice of Force Majeure

14.2.1. If a Party is or will be prevented from performing any of its obligations under the Agreement by Force Majeure, then it will give notice to the other Party of the event or circumstances constituting the Force Majeure and will specify the obligations, the performance of which is or will be affected. The notice will be given within 14 days after the Party became aware, or should have become aware, of the relevant event or circumstance constituting Force Majeure.

14.2.2. The Party will, having given notice, be excused from performance of such obligations for so long as such Force Majeure prevents it from performing them.

14.2.3. Notwithstanding any other provision of this Clause, Force Majeure will not apply to obligations of either Party to make payments to the other Party under the Agreement.

14.3. Duty to Minimize Delay

14.3.1. Each Party will at all times use all reasonable endeavours to minimize any delay in the performance of the Agreement as a result of Force Majeure.

14.3.2. A Party will give notice to the other Party when it ceases to be affected by the Force Majeure.

14.4. Consequences of Force Majeure

The Parties will be responsible for its own losses related to Force Majeure.

14.5. Optional Termination and Payment

If the Training Service is prevented for a continuous period of 90 days by reason of Force Majeure of which notice has been given under Clause 14.2, or for multiple periods which totals more than 140 days, then either Party may give to the other Party a notice of termination of the Agreement. In this event, the termination will take effect 7 days after the notice is given.

14.6. Notice of Change in Law

14.6.1. If the Concessionaire incurs (or will incur) additional cost for providing the Training Services as a result of Change in Law occurring after the bid submission date (as provided in the RFP), then the Concessionaire will give notice to the Authority and will be entitled to compensation for the addition cost related to the Training Services due to Change in Law.

14.6.2. After receiving this notice, the Parties will proceed to agree on the addition cost, failing which, the cost will be determined by the Parties in accordance with the dispute resolution mechanism provided in Clause 17.

14.6.3. The Concessionaire will use all reasonable efforts to mitigate the impact of Change in Law.

15. Default and Termination

15.1. Termination Events

15.1.1. Without limiting any other rights or remedies, the Authority reserves the right to terminate this Agreement, if the Concessionaire:
(a) fails to achieve KPI scores in accordance with Clause 7.5;
(b) is in default under any material obligation hereunder and the default has not been cured within 15 days after receipt of notice of such breach or default, unless the Parties otherwise mutually agree; or
(c) becomes insolvent, makes a general assignment for the benefit of creditors, files a voluntary petition in bankruptcy, or suffers or permits the appointment of a receiver for its business or assets.

15.1.2. Without limiting any other rights or remedies, the Concessionaire reserves the right to terminate this Agreement, if the Authority:
(a) fails to make any payment in accordance with this Agreement;
(b) is in default under any material obligation hereunder that has not been cured within 15 days after receipt of notice of such breach or default, unless the Parties otherwise mutually agree.

15.2. Consequence of Termination

15.2.1. The termination of this Agreement in whole or in part for any reason under this Clause 15 will not affect (i) any liabilities or obligations of either Party arising before such termination or out of the events causing such termination; or (ii) any damages or other remedies to which a Party may be entitled under this Agreement, by law or in equity, arising from any breaches of such liabilities or obligations.

15.2.2. Upon termination, if required by the Authority, the Concessionaire will continue to provide the Training Services for the ongoing Training Cycle(s) in accordance with the terms and conditions of this Agreement.

16. Indemnity

16.1. General Indemnity

16.1.1. The Concessionaire will indemnify, defend and hold the Authority harmless against any and all proceedings, actions and third-party claims for any loss, damage, cost and expense of whatever kind and nature arising out of any act of the Concessionaire including failure of the Concessionaire to comply with applicable laws.

16.1.2. The Authority will indemnify, defend and hold the Concessionaire harmless against any and all proceedings, actions and third-party claims for any loss, damage, cost and expense of whatever kind and nature arising out of any act of the Authority including failure of the Authority to comply with applicable laws.

16.2. Notice and Contest of Claims

If any Party receives a claim from a third-party in respect of which it is entitled to the benefit of an indemnity under Clause 16.1 above ("**Indemnified Party**"), then such Party will notify the other Party responsible for indemnifying such claim hereunder ("**Indemnifying Party**") within 15 (fifteen) days of receipt of the claim and will not settle or pay the claim without the prior approval of the Indemnifying Party, which approval not to be unreasonably withheld or delayed. If the Indemnifying Party wishes to contest or dispute the claim, it may conduct the proceedings in the name of the Indemnified Party and will bear all costs involved in contesting the same. The Indemnified Party will provide all cooperation and assistance in contesting any claim and will sign all such writings and documents as the Indemnifying Party may reasonably require.

17. Dispute Resolution

17.1. Dispute

17.1.1. Any dispute, difference or controversy of whatever nature howsoever arising under or out of or in relation to this Agreement between the Parties, and so notified in writing by either Party to the other Party ("Dispute") will, in the first instance, be attempted to be resolved amicably in accordance with the conciliation procedure set forth in Clause 17.1.2.

17.1.2. The Parties agree to use their best efforts for resolving all Disputes arising under or in respect of this Agreement promptly, equitably and in good faith, and further agree to provide each other with reasonable access during normal business hours to all non-privileged records, information and data pertaining to any Dispute.

17.2. Conciliation

If any Dispute between the Parties cannot be amicably settled, then such Dispute may be referred to the [Chairman of the District/State Health Care Department] and the [CEO] of the Concessionaire for amicable settlement, and upon such reference, the said persons will meet no later than 14 days from the date of reference to discuss and attempt to amicably resolve the Dispute. If such meeting does not take place within the 14 days period or the Dispute is not amicably settled within 30 days of the meeting or such longer period as may be mutually agreed by the Parties, either Party may refer the Dispute to arbitration in accordance with the provisions of Clause 17.3.

17.3. Arbitration

17.3.1. Any Dispute which is not resolved amicably by conciliation, as provided in Clause 17.2, will be finally decided by reference to arbitration by a board of arbitrators appointed in accordance with Clause 17.3.2 below. Such arbitration will be held in accordance with the Rules of Arbitration of the International Centre for Alternative Dispute Resolution, New Delhi ("Rules"), or such other rules as may be mutually agreed by the Parties, and shall be subject to the provisions of the Arbitration and Conciliation Act, 1996. The venue of such arbitration will be [_____], and the language of arbitration proceedings will be English.

17.3.2. There will be a board of 3 arbitrators, of whom each Party will select 1, and the 3rd arbitrator will be appointed by the 2 arbitrators so selected and in the event of disagreement between the 2 arbitrators, the appointment will be made in accordance with the Rules.

17.3.3. The arbitrators will make a reasoned award ("**Award**"). Any Award made in any arbitration will be final and binding on the Parties as from the date it is made, and the Concessionaire and the Authority agree and undertake to carry out such Award without delay.

17.3.4. This Agreement and the rights and obligations of the Parties shall remain in full force and effect, pending the Award in any arbitration proceedings hereunder.

17.4. Adjudication by Regulatory Authority or Commission

In the event of constitution of a statutory Regulatory Authority or Commission with powers to adjudicate upon disputes between the Concessionaire and the Authority, all Disputes arising after such constitution shall, instead of reference to arbitration under Clause 17.3, be adjudicated upon by such Regulatory Authority or Commission in accordance with the applicable law and all references to Dispute Resolution Procedure will be construed accordingly.

18. Miscellaneous

18.1. Governing Law and Jurisdiction

This Agreement will be construed and interpreted in accordance with and governed by the laws of India, and the courts at [___] will have exclusive jurisdiction over matters arising out of or relating to this Agreement.

18.2. Waiver of Immunity

Each Party unconditionally and irrevocably:

    (a)   agrees that the execution, delivery and performance by it of this Agreement constitute commercial acts done and performed for commercial purpose;

    (b)   agrees that, should any proceedings be brought against it or its assets, property or revenues in any jurisdiction in relation to this Agreement or any transaction contemplated by this Agreement, no immunity (whether by reason of sovereignty or otherwise) from such proceedings shall be claimed by or on behalf of the Party with respect to its assets;

    (c)   waives any right of immunity which it or its assets, property or revenues now has, may acquire in the future or which may be attributed to it in any jurisdiction; and

    (d)   consents generally in respect of the enforcement of any judgment or award against it in any such proceedings to the giving of any relief or the issue of any process in any jurisdiction in connection with such proceedings (including the making, enforcement or execution against it or in respect of any assets, property or revenues whatsoever irrespective of their use or intended use of any order or judgment that may be made or given in connection therewith).

18.3. Delayed Payments

The Parties hereto agree that payments due from one Party to the other Party under the provisions of this Agreement shall be made within the period set forth therein, and if no such period is specified, within 30 (thirty) days of receiving a demand along with the necessary particulars. In the event of delay beyond such period, the defaulting Party will pay interest for the period of delay calculated at a rate equal to 10% per annum, and recovery thereof will be without prejudice to the rights of the Parties under this Agreement including termination thereof.

18.4. Waiver

No waiver of any provision of this Agreement will constitute a waiver of any other provision(s) or of the same provision on another occasion. Failure of either Party to enforce any provision of this Agreement will not constitute a waiver of such provision or any other provision(s) of this Agreement.

18.5. Survival

Termination will not relieve the Concessionaire or the Authority, as the case may be, of any obligations hereunder which expressly or by implication survive termination hereof.

18.6. Entire Agreement

This Agreement together constitute the entire agreement between the Parties on the subject hereof, and no amendment or modification will be valid and effective unless such modification or amendment is agreed to in writing by the Parties. All prior written or oral understandings, offers or other communications of every kind pertaining to this Agreement are abrogated and withdrawn. For the avoidance of doubt, the Parties hereto agree that any obligations of the Concessionaire arising from the RFP will be deemed to form part of this Agreement.

18.7. Severability

Should any provision of this Agreement be held by a court of competent jurisdiction to be illegal, invalid or unenforceable, such provision may be modified by such court in compliance with the law giving effect to the intent of the Parties and enforced as modified. All other terms and conditions of this Client Agreement remain in full force and effect and will be construed in accordance with the modified provision.

18.8. Relationship of Parties

This Agreement will not be interpreted or construed to create an association, joint venture or partnership agreement between the Parties, or to impose any partnership obligation or liability upon either Party, and neither Party shall have any right, power or authority to enter into any agreement or undertaking for, or act on behalf of, or to act as or be an agent or representative of, or to otherwise bind, the other Party.

18.9. Third Parties

This Agreement is intended solely for the benefit of the Parties, and their respective successors and permitted assigns, and nothing in this Agreement shall be construed to create any duty to, standard of care with reference to, or any liability to, any person not a Party to this Agreement.

18.10. Notices

Notice to the Parties shall be in writing and shall be sent at the addresses first hereinabove mentioned (email accepted). In case, there is any change in the addresses of a Party, the same shall be communicated immediately to the other Party, failing which any notice sent to the earlier address of the said Party shall be deemed to be valid service of such notice.

Authority
Address:
Email:
Phone:
Kind Attention:

Concessionaire
Address:
Email:
Phone:
Kind Attention:

IN WITNESS WHEREOF, and intending to be legally bound, the Parties have duly executed this Agreement as of the date first written above.

Signed for and on behalf of
[*insert name of the Authority*]

Signed for and on behalf of
[*insert name of the Concessionaire*]

_____

By.
Name:
Title:

_____

By:
Name:
Title:

SCHEDULE 1 – TRAINING SERVICES

[Please identify and insert the training services to be provided by the Concessionaire.]

SCHEDULE 2 – PARTICIPANTS DETAILS

[Please insert the details of the participants that will be provided to the Concessionaire.]

SCHEDULE 3 – MINIMUM QUALIFICATION OF TRAINERS

[Please insert the minimum qualification requirements of the Trainers.]

SCHEDULE 4 – TRAINING LOCALITIES

[Please provide the areas where the Concessionaire is required to procure classes for the training.]

SCHEDULE 5 – TRAINING FEES STRUCTURE

[Please insert the training fees for different trainings.]

SCHEDULE 6 – KPIs

[Please insert the KPIs to be achieved by the Concessionaire.]

SCHEDULE 7 – PARTICIPANTS SATISFACTION SURVEY

[Please insert the format of the survey form.]

SCHEDULE 8 – SALIENT FEATURES OF GRIEVANCE REDRESSAL POLICY

1.1. The Health Care Centre will have a provision of complaint drop box at suitable and visible location where any aggrieved patient can register his/her complaint. Patient can also raise the concern/ complaint orally.

1.2. The process of grievance handling will be displayed at reception in local language and English for patient information. It will also mention the concerned authorized person name and phone number.

1.3. The Concessionaire will act promptly on receiving any complaint and the same should be addressed within 48 hours.

1.4. The Concessionaire will ensure that preventive mechanisms are in place so that complaints are not repeated again.

1.5. All patient complaints should be captured in digitised way and feed into the Health Management Information System (HMIS). The Concessionaire will produce quarterly reports on patient feedback received from the patients and share with the Authority.

Sample Key Performance Indicators for Urban Primary Health Centers under Public–Private Partnership

Guiding Principles

- Should be aligned with similar key performance indicators (KPIs) in urban primary health centers (UPHCs) operated by the Government of India or urban local bodies to ensure uniformity across UPHCs irrespective of operating agencies

- Should be aligned with KPIs in the Sustainable Development Goals, national programs, and other initiatives to avoid conflict and duplication of efforts

- Disease program-specific KPIs should align with the indicators set by the national program

- The number should not be unwieldy, and information must lead to productive action

- Must be SMART, or specific, measurable, assignable, realistic, and time-related

- Must be appropriate and flexible to suit local needs and aligned with the frequency and source of collection of data as per local health management information system

- KPI matching performance standards should be established on the basis of local baseline studies and with inputs from domain specialists

No.	Service	Estimated Number of Beneficiaries[a]	Key Performance Indicator	Expected Performance Standard[b]	Source of Information	Frequency of Data Collection[c]
1	General OPD Services	50,000 (exact population of the catchment area)	Rate of OPD attending patients per 100,000 population per day[1]	TBD[d]	UPHC records	Monthly
2	Care in Pregnancy (Maternal Health)	2% of population	Percentage of pregnant women receiving at least four antenatal care visits[2]	90%	UPHC records	Quarterly
			Percentage of deliveries conducted by trained birth attendants[3]	90%	UPHC records	Quarterly
3	Neonatal and Infant Health	2% of population	Percentage of infants receiving three doses of DPT (diphtheria, pertussis, [whooping cough], and tetanus) vaccine[4]	90%	UPHC records	Quarterly
			Infant mortality rate /1,000 live births/year[5]	National target	UPHC records	Annually
4	Child Health, Adolescent Health (1–19)	30% of population	Under 5 mortality/1,000 live births[6]	National target	UPHC records	Monthly
			Proportion of adolescents who correctly identify the two major ways of preventing sexual transmission of HIV[7]	TBD	UPHC records	Monthly
5	Reproductive Health and Contraceptive Services	60% of population	Maternal mortality ratio: The number of maternal deaths per 100,000 live births[8]	National target	UPHC records	Monthly
			Proportion of women of reproductive age (aged 15–49 years) who have their need for family planning satisfied with modern methods[9]	TBD	UPHC records	Quarterly
6	Management of Endemic Communicable Diseases	50,000 (exact population of the catchment area)	Hepatitis B incidence per 100,000 population[10]	TBD	UPHC records	Quarterly

continued on next page

Appendix 10 *continued*

No.	Service	Estimated Number of Beneficiaries[a]	Key Performance Indicator	Expected Performance Standard[b]	Source of Information	Frequency of Data Collection[c]
7	Management of Common Noncommunicable Diseases	50,000 (exact population of the catchment area)	Percentage of people aged 30+ screened for diabetes mellitus[11]	National target	UPHC records	Monthly
			Percentage of people aged 30+ screened for hypertension[12]	National target	UPHC records	Monthly
8	Management of National Health Programs	50,000 (exact population of the catchment area)	Tuberculosis incidence per 1,000 population[13]	National target	UPHC records	Monthly
9	Management of Mental Illnesses	50,000 (exact population of the catchment area)	Suicide mortality rate[14]	TBD	UPHC records	Monthly
10	Dental Care	50,000 (exact population of the catchment area)	Children and adult (1–17 years) who were visited by a health care worker and provided information on prevention of dental diseases and dental hygiene[15]	TBD	UPHC records	Monthly
11	Eye Care and/or Eye, Ear, Nose, and Throat Care	50,000 (exact population of the catchment area)	Proportion of people with cataract referred for surgery[16]	TBD	UPHC records	Monthly
12	Geriatric Care (65+)	Around 5% of population	Number of weekly geriatric clinics run by a trained medical officer[17]	TBD	UPHC records	Monthly
13	Emergency Medicine	50,000 (exact population of the catchment area)	Availability of appropriate and prompt referral services including stabilization of patient[18]	TBD	UPHC records	Monthly
14	General Laboratory Services	50,000 (exact population of the catchment area)	Proportion of laboratory procedures that are undertaken using validated standard operating procedures[19]	TBD	UPHC records	Monthly
15	Human Resource Availability	50,000 (exact population of the catchment area)	Average absenteeism rate as a percentage of the total working days among all employees[20]	TBD	UPHC records	Monthly

continued on next page

Appendix 10 *continued*

No.	Service	Estimated Number of Beneficiaries[a]	Key Performance Indicator	Expected Performance Standard[b]	Source of Information	Frequency of Data Collection[c]
16	Immunization Sessions	50,000 (exact population of the catchment area)	Percentage of planned immunization sessions that were conducted during the month[21]	National target	UPHC records	Monthly
17	Operationalization of Services	50,000 (exact population of the catchment area)	Number of days in a month that the facility was nonoperational	TBD	UPHC records	Monthly
18	Availability of Medicines as per Essential Drug List	50,000 (exact population of the catchment area)	Number of stock-outs of 1 week or more of essential drugs, vaccines, and supplies for the selected programs during the last year[22]	TBD	UPHC records	Monthly

KPI = key performance indicator, OPD = outpatient department, TBD = to be determined, UPHC = urban primary health center.

[a] Exact populations and percentages of populations to be calculated by local officials. The estimated numbers are as per Census of India (2011).
[b] KPI matching performance standards should be established on the basis of local baseline studies and with inputs from domain specialists.
[c] Should be aligned with the frequency of data collection under the health management information system.
[d] To be determined at the state or municipal level.

[1] World Health Organization. The Global Health Observatory: Outpatient Visits (per 100,000).
https://www.who.int/data/gho/data/indicators/indicator-details/GHO/outpatient-visits-(per-100-000) (accessed 27 June 2020).
[2] UNICEF. 2019. Antenatal Care. https://data.unicef.org/topic/maternal-health/antenatal-care/ (accessed 27 June 2020).
[3] Medium.com. SDG 3 Indicators. https://medium.com/sdgs-resources/sdg-3-indicators-43806cbf63e9 (accessed 27 June 2020).
[4] World Health Organization. The Global Health Observatory: DTP3 Immunization Coverage among One-Year-Olds (%).
https://www.who.int/data/gho/data/indicators/indicator-details/GHO/dtp3-immunization-coverage-among-one-year-olds-(-) (accessed 27 June 2020).
[5] Footnote 3.
[6] Footnote 3.
[7] World Health Organization. 2015. Global Reference List of Health Indicators for Adolescents (aged 10–19 years).
https://apps.who.int/iris/bitstream/handle/10665/204625/WHO_MCA_15.3_eng.pdf;jsessionid=FA50BECEC8A34E01DEFB3D46259E86EC?sequence=1 (accessed 27 June 2020).
[8] Footnote 3.
[9] Footnote 3.
[10] Footnote 3.
[11] DocMode. 2019. Screening for Hypertension and Diabetes. https://docmode.org/screening-for-hypertension-and-diabetes/ (accessed 27 June 2020).
[12] Footnote 11.
[13] Footnote 3.
[14] Footnote 3.
[15] Centers for Disease Control and Prevention. Indicator Definitions—Oral Health. https://www.cdc.gov/cdi/definitions/oral-health.html#ORH2_1 (accessed 27 June 2020).
[16] Australian Government, Australian Institute of Health and Welfare. Cataract Clinical Care Standard Indicators: 4 – Proportion of Patients Referred for Cataract Surgery Who Progress to Cataract Surgery. https://meteor.aihw.gov.au/content/index.phtml/itemId/711429 (accessed 27 June 2020).

continued on next page

Appendix 10 *continued*

17   Government of India, Directorate General of Health Services. 2011. Operational Guidelines—National Programme for Health Care of the Elderly (NPHCE). https://main.mohfw.gov.in/sites/default/files/8324324521Operational_Guidelines_NPHCE_final.pdf. New Delhi: Ministry of Health and Family Welfare.

18   Government of India, Directorate General of Health Services. 2006. Indian Public Health Standards (IPHS) For Primary Health Centres. http://iapsmgc.org/userfiles/4IPHS_for_PHC.pdf. New Delhi: Ministry of Health and Family Welfare.

19   World Health Organization. 2012. Quality Assurance in Bacteriology and Immunology. 3rd ed. SEARO Regional Publication. No. 47. https://apps.who.int/iris/bitstream/handle/10665/205730/B4855.pdf?sequence=1&isAllowed=y. New Delhi: WHO Regional Office for South-East Asia.

20   DataPine. Absenteeism Rate: How Engaged are Your Employees? https://www.datapine.com/kpi-examples-and-templates/human-resources#absenteeism-rate (accessed 27 June 2020).

21   World Health Organization. Indicators for Monitoring District and National Performance. https://www.who.int/immunization/monitoring_surveillance/routine/indicators/core_set_national_district.pdf?ua=1 (accessed 27 June 2020).

22   World Health Organization. 2001. The Use of Indicators for Communicable Disease Control at District Level. https://apps.who.int/iris/bitstream/handle/10665/68467/WHO_CDS_TB_2001.289.pdf?sequence=1 (accessed 27 June 2020).

Source: Asian Development Bank.

www.ingramcontent.com/pod-product-compliance
Lightning Source LLC
Chambersburg PA
CBHW050042220326
41599CB00045B/7252